Lio's drawing of his leaving hospital.

Martin Spinelli is a senior lecturer in the School of Media, Film and Music at the University of Sussex. He has authored dozens of essays in anthologies and journals such as *Postmodern Culture*, *Convergence* and *The International Journal of Cultural Studies*. His radio pieces have been heard on BBC Radio 3 and Radio 4, and his innovative series *LINEbreak* and *Radio Radio* have been broadcast on stations and networks around the world.

After the Crash

Martin Spinelli

MAINSTREAM
PUBLISHING

EDINBURGH AND LONDON

First published in Great Britain in 2012 by
MAINSTREAM PUBLISHING COMPANY
(EDINBURGH) LTD
7 Albany Street
Edinburgh EH1 3UG

ISBN 9781780575223

This book is a work of non-fiction based on the life, experiences and recollections of the author. In some cases, names of people, places, dates, sequences or the detail of events have been changed to protect the privacy of others. The author has stated to the publishers that, except in such cases, not affecting the substantial accuracy of the work, the contents of this book are true

A catalogue record for this book is available
from the British Library

Printed in Great Britain by
CPI Group (UK) Ltd, Croydon, CR0 4YY

1 3 5 7 9 10 8 6 4 2

for Sasha

Acknowledgements & Note

The paediatric intensive care staff and the paediatric neurological team at King's College Hospital – the people largely responsible for Lio's astonishing recovery after the motorway accident of 7 September 2006 that killed his mother and should have killed him – also share in the credit for this book. In particular, I wish to thank Dr David McCormick, Lio's neurologist, whose praise for Lio's website encouraged me to transform it into *After the Crash*.

Lio's grandparents – Nigel, Penny and Trudy – were all indispensable in helping me find time to write this book, as were Lio's four au pairs: Graziella, Serena, Alice and (most of all) Sara Zenone, who also took the photo on the front cover.

My friends and acquaintances Lucia Cirillo, Kenneth Sherwood, Susannah Waters, Sarah Clowes, Nicole Dryburgh, Rhidian Brook, Gus Cristie, Louise Flind, Ed Shapiro, Gilly Smith, Kate Gardner and Umi Sinha were all generous with insights into the story or into routes to publication.

My counsellor James Clifton helped significantly to navigate the myriad decisions that cropped up during the process and had some very useful ideas that found their way into the book.

In New York, Laura Nolan and (especially) Pat Willard were extremely gracious with their suggestions and utterly unselfish with their time on the phone, helping me to refine and clarify the story midway through the book's development.

Val Hudson was one of the last, and most cogent, readers. The thoughtfulness of her comments about structure and the patient way she shared her considerable experience helped this book reach the widest possible audience.

The astute and very professional eye of Deborah Warner, my editor at Mainstream, also helped make this a better book.

Thanks as well to Jonathan Holmes, Sasha's friend and foil for her last writing about beauty.

Finally I am grateful to my agent, Charlie Viney, who completely understood my vision for *After the Crash* and worked extremely hard to realise it.

All the events described in *After the Crash* are faithful to my memory. Other people may have other memories that are equally valid. In several cases, names and some identifying details have been changed.

Contents

Part 1

As a friend of mine once wrote: How is a flower beautiful? It's beautiful because it says: I am going to die. Is this transience a key to understanding beauty? As Whitman said: 'What indeed is finally beautiful except death and love?'

I have just returned from bright red poppies; random, and beautiful. But even the poppy, the flower of slaughtered lives, did not call me to death. Instead it called me to colour: vibrant and bold. The flower is not conscious of death; it cannot speak death. Consciousness of death is no part of the flower, but of ourselves. And you may say the piquancy of colour comes in the knowledge of its fading, of its mortality – but still, this was not what I thought in the moment, in the warm sun.

– Sasha Roberts

In the Mountains

That was it. That was the moment – the moment for both of us. It was love at first throw. I couldn't have imagined what a couple of ridiculous hours in a field with bats and balls might set in motion. No one ever told me precisely how that match came about, but I'm sure lots of alcohol was involved. Apparently a professor in the English department at the University of Sussex, where I was studying, had challenged one of his mates at the University of Essex. When the prof from Sussex sobered up, he realised that there was no way he could find a team that had the slightest chance of doing well. So instead of trying to win, he decided to seize the moral high ground and field a team of women and foreigners who had never played the game before. He asked me to be his bowler and Sasha to be his wicketkeeper.

It was a sunny and warm afternoon when our cars parked along the edge of a green quad on the Essex campus. Before our captain sent us out to the field, he passed out small wax-paper cups and poured us all a good measure of not-bad whisky. We cheered and toasted our impending defeat.

'I hope you're not as clueless as I am about all this,' I said to Sasha.

She smiled shyly, tucked a lock of long, blonde hair behind her ear, then threw herself in. 'Oh, come on. I'm sure you've seen cricket on the telly once or twice.'

'I'm afraid it's mostly American football where I come

from.' I stepped closer to tune out the noise of everyone else.

'That's the trouble with you Yanks. No sense of the big wide world over the sea,' she teased, now grinning fully.

'And you Brits are so much better, are you?' I tried to give like I was getting. 'Can you tell me the difference between tight end and a wide receiver?'

'Are you being rude?' she said, with a quizzical look.

'Not at all,' I replied, my own smile now uncontainable. 'Maybe one day I'll draw you a diagram.' I had made her laugh for the first time. 'No, really,' I continued. 'At least give me some idea of what I'm supposed to be doing so I don't look like a total fool.'

'Just keep your arm straight when you throw me the ball and remember to bounce it in front of the wicket and you won't embarrass yourself,' she said and headed off to the pitch. Then she turned with a smirk and added, 'And if you throw it straight, I won't embarrass myself either.'

We got trounced, of course, but I'm proud to say we out-drank the other side by a huge margin. The silliness of this first proper encounter was something Sasha and I would dine out on for the rest of our lives.

Fifteen years later, at around 8.30 on the morning of 7 September 2006, Sasha drove me to the train station near our home in Lewes, a town with medieval cobbled streets, a castle and a Georgian brewery. Our quick-witted son Lio (pronounced like 'Leo' in English but just spelled an Italian way) was in the back seat. As his sun-bleached hair bobbed and his eyes (the same sky-blue as his mother's) darted from flint houses to chalky cliffs, he was happily naming everything he saw. I had a conference to go to at the University of Sunderland in the north of England and Sasha was going to work at the University of Kent in Canterbury to unpack her office after it had been redecorated over the summer. She was full of excitement at the thought of new shelves and desks and cabinets and paint.

We had just got back a few days earlier from a fabulous summer holiday in Italy and France. We were tanned, fit and happy. As we pulled out from the parking space in front of our house, Lio said, '*J'ai froid*' ('I'm cold'), in a very nice little French accent. He was extremely good with languages and would often introduce himself by saying, 'Hello, my name is Lio and I speak five languages.' This was a bit of an exaggeration, of course; however, he did speak excellent four-year-old English, excellent four-year-old Italian, a smattering of French phrases and just a few words of German and Spanish. But even considering that we had just come back from France, the earnestness and the seriousness in his voice as he was telling us he was chilly seemed odd. The morning was fresh, but not really cold. It didn't matter, though. Sasha and I smiled to each other, proud of our little boy's skills.

Sasha parked in front of the red-brick station and, as I was getting out of the car, I told Lio I loved him and that I would see him in a few days. I was about to close the door, but something made me turn around, get back in and put my hand on his cheek.

'Remember,' I said, 'I'll always be with you.' I wouldn't normally have done this, and as I retell it now it seems a touch over the top, but that's exactly what I said and did. We had been apart for longer periods before, but I had never felt the need to say anything like this. Lio smiled sweetly, leaned into my hand and blew me a noisy kiss. As I got out of the car a second time, I felt slightly light-headed.

As Sasha came round to give me a hug, I had an uncanny feeling about the scene. I wasn't just kissing her goodbye but also somehow watching our goodbye from ten metres in the air. I slid my hands down her back to stroke her through her second-hand embroidered cotton blouse, a bit wrinkled and threadbare but one of her favourites and she always wore it well. As I breathed in through her lemony-scented hair, I remember thinking how extremely cold her body felt, much colder than she should have been given the sunny late-summer morning.

'I love you,' I said.

She smiled and said something a bit much for our simple, commonplace parting, a parting that had happened dozens of times before. 'Don't let these pessimistic Brits get you down,' she said.

I didn't know what she was talking about. In fact, I often thought of myself as one of the slightly cynical ones, someone who was good at managing expectations and even better at criticising foolishness where I found it. I nodded absently and smiled a crooked smile.

She kissed me again, let me go and walked around the back of our car. She got in, put the key in the ignition, smiled one last time at me through the glass and headed off. I had a strange, slightly queasy feeling in the pit of my stomach as I watched them drive up Station Street and out of sight. Usually, I wouldn't have watched them drive off – I would have simply gone into the station, got out my ticket and gone to the platform. Yet on that morning I stood still, captured by an intense desire to stop them and to insist that they come with me, to convince Sasha to put off unpacking her office and for us to find another room in the hotel up in Sunderland. Thinking she'd never go for that, I even wondered about bribery. I thought about enticing her with a little more vacation up north or promising to treat her to a spending spree at her favourite cookware shop if she'd just stay home that day. Then I imagined just taking Lio with me up to the conference and having him play quietly in the front row of the lecture hall while I gave my talk.

That was what I thought as I stood in front of the station and watched our car disappear up the hill.

I wish I could say that it was love at first sight, but lust at first sight would be more honest. The first time I saw Sasha, some six months before our meeting on the cricket pitch, I was a twenty-two-year-old student in his first week of classes in a Masters programme. I was at the University of Sussex for a degree, but, as it was my first proper experience of living outside the US, I also wanted to taste something of the world and have a few adventures, if not simple conquests. Sasha was a PhD student and I wandered into a 'welcome to graduate school' event where she was speaking. With her waist-length blonde hair, John Lennon specs and slightly hippy clothes, I was the one who was conquered. I never really stood a chance. As she spoke, I sat in the back row and thought about sleeping with her. Over the next months, I kept my eyes open for any sign of her. I found notices for undergraduate lectures she was giving about seventeenth-century women reading Shakespeare's sonnets, about competing strands of feminism and about ornaments carved into Renaissance beds. Even though I didn't have much interest in sonnets or feminism or Renaissance beds per se, I went along.

I would sit in the back, grinning stupidly. Once or twice I even ventured a rambling question after her lecture, but it wasn't until that cricket match later that spring that I managed to have a conversation with her. And out of that alcohol-fuelled, flirty couple of hours in the sun flowed lots of other little encounters. She introduced me to her favourite pub in Brighton, the Basketmakers, and then to her favourite pub in Lewes, the Lewes Arms, where she just happened to be performing in a ludicrously bawdy charity pantomime. She was a Kate Adie-esque correspondent trying to make sense of the very bad behaviour in Never-Never-Land. She claimed she didn't get half of the jokes written for her and invited me along to see if I could understand any better. We walked in the gardens in Stanmer Park near campus on bright mornings, laughing like ten year olds as we sprayed each other with hosepipes that the staff had foolishly left unattended.

At the end of spring, Sasha's brother Jeff was coming home for a visit. He was a musician living in Padua who taught English on the side. Sasha had told me about her family's lifelong connection with Italy and I had invented the excuse of wanting to learn Italian for academic reasons in order to get closer to her. Taking my hints, Sasha invited me to meet Jeff up in London at their parents' home the weekend he was coming back. It was a gorgeous old end-of-terrace Victorian house in Wandsworth on a street almost too leafy to be London. Her father Nigel, a bookish and quiet man approaching 60, shook my hand and looked at me curiously. When I complimented him on the house, he warmed up fast and showed me some of the nineteenth-century ornaments that he had managed to save when he had refurbished it, a mantelpiece here, some tiles there. As he gave me the tour, he told me how they'd bought the house about 30 years earlier for a pittance when it was, he suspected, the neighbourhood 'knocking shop' and about how he had worked long and hard, fixing it up from the wee hours of the morning, doing most of the work himself.

Sasha's mother Penny, on hearing this, teased sweetly, 'That's why the kitchen light switches give us trouble to this day.' Penny had penetrating eyes and her long, greying hair was the only sign of her age. She had been an artist all her life. She'd sold big pieces, taught at art colleges and was then running her own business with a colleague installing art in public spaces like corporate headquarters and upper-class airline lounges.

The house was very much Penny's too, and her vibrant touches lit every corner. It was cluttered with paintings and silk-screened wall hangings and odd bits of broken sculpture from around the world. To my tidy, suburban-American eye, it was eclectic and shambolic. Its decor wasn't at all upmarket, like some of the others that dazzled out through neighbouring windows, and the whole family seemed proud of that.

I liked Jeff the moment I met him. He was quieter than his sister, but had the same eyes and chin. He was introspective, and even though he was a bit preoccupied with things happening back in Italy (he was having a relationship go bad) he had this sympathetic, slightly ethereal quality about him while we chatted about Padua. As he told me about the food, about the university, about the women and about one woman in particular, he spoke with the confidence of someone ten years older than me instead of three years younger. He was deeply committed to his own vision of music and followed his own star in the rest of his life – I admired him.

Jeff told me that he and Sasha had been going to the same little Italian valley for more than 20 years. When they'd first started visiting, they'd been the only English people seen since the war.

Jeff had enjoyed himself down in Padua, but now he wanted to make a fresh start of things back in London. Before he could leave Italy, though, he needed to tie up some loose ends and find someone to take over his teaching work. Without even thinking about it, I volunteered myself there and then. I did want to see a bit of Europe. I did want to learn Italian. But I also wanted to give Sasha the opportunity to show me *her* Italy; I wanted to get to know it with her and see her enthusiasm for it first hand. Two summers earlier I had spent a couple of weeks backpacking around Italy. It was fun and I hit all the major attractions in the usual big cities: Florence, Pisa, Perugia, Rome, Naples and Venice. But what was being offered now was an opportunity to see real Italian life, to experience something other than the crowds around the Leaning Tower and the Colosseum.

On my way into Venice during that backpacking trip, I had in fact stopped at Padua on special assignment from my mother. I remembered it as a sprawling, living city, past its prime but with the stunning Basilica di Sant'Antonio at its heart. My mother had asked me to go there and light a candle for her. St Anthony had become her patron over the decades of fertility struggles, big family stresses, illnesses and weekly lost-again-found-again car keys. While not appreciating the gesture in the same way as her, I obliged happily and called her from a phone box in front of the Basilica after I'd done it. As I weaved in and out of its shady porticoes to and from the train station, I thought that Padua was the kind of place I'd like to come back to and spend some time in properly, but that particular afternoon the Grand Canal beckoned and I was on my way.

The summer after meeting Jeff I travelled out to Padua, where I met him again, arranged to take over his teaching gig and had him help me find a place to live. Sasha drove out a few days later and met me in the apartment Jeff shared with two Italians on the outskirts of the city. As we wandered around the medieval streets, Sasha and I planned our first trip together up north into the Dolomite Mountains. Sasha had told me about the Dolomites: made of pink and orange marble, they created, she said, the most beautiful sunsets imaginable. She told me about tiny little villages that touched the clouds where they spoke impenetrably old dialects and borderless languages heard only in the mountains. And over a cool glass of prosecco at a shady table overlooking an ancient church, she told me about her family's place in the mountains, an old mill in an unfashionable valley in between the Dolomites and the Pre-Alpi, in between the cities of Belluno and Feltre.

After a few more days of sorting out details with Jeff, Sasha and I got our things together, packed up her clunky white Peugeot and headed north one moonless evening. It was a two-hour drive and we didn't get into the mountains until well after dark. When we came out of a tunnel into the valley, I saw stars directly up above me but not at the sides.

'Welcome to the mountains,' Sasha said, smiling in the dashboard light.

'Those can't be the mountains,' I said, not wanting to be taken in. 'They can't be that steep and high.'

'That's them,' Sasha said gently.

'Impossible. They must be clouds.' I genuinely didn't believe her and was getting a bit cross because I thought she was having me on.

'Fine,' she chuckled. 'You'll see in the morning.'

The car trundled along in the night over hills and through villages until we came to a stony forest road blocked by a steel bar. Sasha got out and raised it, and we headed up a very narrow track that twisted through maize fields and down a steep, bumpy hill. We pulled up under the roof of a barn, where at one time horse-drawn carts must have parked to unload grain and to load up polenta. We grabbed a few essentials from the boot and headed inside. Nigel and Penny were there on holiday, but they had gone to sleep already. Sasha lit an oil lamp and I lit some candles. Shadows danced across antique rough-hewn beams and the slightly dilapidated chairs and chests that had been salvaged from ruined houses nearby. It was very old and very solid, a bit cluttered and chaotic, but so perfectly Sasha and her family.

Prodded awake by curiosity, I slipped out of bed early the

next morning to have a look around. It was perfect. It was the kind of house I had dreamt about for years. It was rough. It needed some work and attention, but it was a house you could love. Thick stone walls, a small wood-burning stove, creosote-stained wooden shutters, a stone roof over the old mill room, running water but no central heating, electricity or phone. It was blissful isolation, tranquillity distilled. There were some nearby trees, but it had unblocked views of the mountains to the west, which included one of the most majestic of the Dolomites, Monte Pizzocco.

I bounced over every inch of it that morning, and when Sasha got up the first thing I said to her was, 'How on earth did you find this place?'

'For years and years we stayed on the other side of the valley,' she began after she had settled herself under a viny arbour for some breakfast. 'We had a little house that we rented every summer from when I was small. It wasn't much, a hay barn really, near San Gregorio. When Mum was in her 20s, she was the au pair for a well-off family in another part of Italy. She kept in contact with them over the years and that led to renting the barn. But a few years ago the owners decided that they wanted to take the place back for themselves.'

She broke off to pour her tea, but I was impatient. 'OK, but this place, how did you find this mill?'

'A few years ago, I was out here visiting some friends with my old boyfriend,' she went on. 'Every once in a while we'd go off and look for houses up for sale. I saw something in the window of a farm estate agent in Belluno,' she said while tearing off a large chunk of bread and slathering it with dark-purple jam. 'It was a sweet place nearby and it had a little stream, too, so I called up Dad and he flew right out.'

'But it was damp, and completely covered with trees, so

it would have been dark most of the time,' Nigel chimed in. 'And it wasn't as quiet.'

'So we asked the agent if he had anything else similar,' Sasha picked up. 'He said he had an old mill, but it was in pretty bad shape, and he didn't know if it was worth the trip to see it. But he'd made us curious and we convinced him to take us out to it.'

'I just had such a good feeling about the place when we first came down the hill. Even though we couldn't see anything around it because it was really misty on the day,' Nigel said. 'But the walls were all sound and the place was remarkably dry from the breeze that always comes off the river. I told the agent we wanted it on the spot and I flew back to England to convince Penny.'

'These two had told me what they were plotting over the phone,' Penny said with a bit of grin and a bit of a grimace at her daughter and husband. 'I had my heart set on finding some place in Tuscany – the colours of the land are much more intense there. But the mill is ours and it's beautiful. Don't you think?'

Over the next few summers Nigel, Penny, Jeff and Sasha, along with friends and a few builders they'd dragged out from England, set to work knocking down walls, mending the roof, installing windows, fitting a kitchen that Nigel had built back in England from spare pieces from other jobs, and putting in a basic bathroom. Penny boiled masses of pasta for them every night and made full English breakfasts for the builders every morning. In relatively short order, they had transformed it from an abandoned shell into a unique and quietly stunning little mountain retreat. Yet there was still lots of work to do on the place: repairing stone terracing outside, painting, plastering, putting in drains, guttering and landscaping.

From my American perspective, it was other-worldly – a 300-year-old mill surrounded by trees and wild flowers, peeking out at the most breathtaking mountains. I was completely enchanted and asked if there was anything that needed doing. So after breakfast, shovel in hand, I started work building an earthen ramp down from the top of a stone wall to the meadow below. I had done jobs like this before: hundreds of times with my father and three brothers I had sawn and hammered and dug and wired. And this work felt as positive and productive as all those projects back in the States, even more so – I felt lightened somehow, needed somehow, by this old mill. Sasha helped me that morning shift some of the bigger stones around and I knew as we heaved and sweated together that what she and I had was more than just good chemistry. I knew then and there that she and I had a future. And I think she knew it too.

That afternoon Sasha took me on our first real walk up beneath the mountains. We drove further north to the town of Agordo, passing a mix of farms and small industry on the way. Val Belluno had always been a working valley. It was where real Italians lived and grafted to make an honest living. Outside of the towns, with their narrow medieval streets and their ancient churches, we saw chisel plants, sawmills and eyeglass factories. Because of this hodge-podge of old and new, the valley had never been, thankfully, choked with tourists.

The cliff-faces on either side of us seemed somehow to grow taller the more the car climbed. When we reached the pass, we parked in front of Rifugio San Sebastiano (one of the small guest houses that dot the Dolomites where you can get a very good, simple meal and a bed for the night without spending too much money), strapped on our packs and headed for Rifugio Carestiato at the base of the mountain just above. The rich smell of cows in the fields near the pass gave way to the intoxicating scent of pines further up – it was like taking a bath in Christmas trees. Huge firs framed scenes of light and cloud and orangey mountainsides. The magnificence of it made me forget the exercise and the thinning air and before long I was giddy and breathless. Sasha, however, long used to the steep climbs with less oxygen, was bounding along like a native.

I was dripping with sweat and gasping for air as she sauntered along 20 paces ahead of me without a care. I put my hands on my knees to catch my breath and looked up at her backside swaying further and further away up the trail. I was so into this girl, I wanted her in every possible way – poor sap that I was. There was no way I was going to let her see me collapse. If she wanted to stuff a rucksack full of cheese and water and blankets and slide over scree, then I was going to do the same. If she wanted to scramble over boulders the size of houses, then I was going to do the same or break my neck trying. I would strain every muscle in my body just to wrap myself up in her whims. Hopeless.

'Are you all right?' her sweet voice interrupted my daydream. 'Maybe we should take a break?'

'No, no!' I said, lurching myself upright. 'I was just enjoying the view.' I smirked inside, while I heaved another breath. 'I'll be right there.' And with that, suppressing the fear of a heart attack, I leapt up the trail and caught her up.

About a half-hour later we'd found a bench out in front of the rifugio and it wasn't long before prosecco bubbles were tickling our noses. I sat recovering, silently transfixed by snowy peaks licking the midsummer sky. I turned and squinted at the jagged tower of a mountain above the rifugio and asked, 'Have you ever been up there?'

'Nope,' Sasha said brightly, 'but I've always wanted to. One day, maybe.' This pleased me and she gave my sweaty knee a light slap with the back of her hand. 'Before I can even think about doing something like that I've got to improve my climbing vocabulary,' she said and began rummaging around in her rucksack. Out she pulled a dog-eared, red-and-green translation dictionary, cracked it open and started looking for the word for 'harness'.

'I'd have to ask the rifugio keeper if you need any special gear for that trail. Some of them around here are kitted out with steel cables that you have to attach yourself to, but maybe this is something you can just climb. Either way I think we should save this one,' she said and turned her shimmering face to me. 'I've got something else in mind for our first proper overnight walk.'

'I really should start learning *some* Italian,' I lamented.

'Of course you will!' Sasha reassured. 'Living here, it'll be impossible not to.' Then she foraged around in her bag again and pulled out a sheet of paper in a yellow plastic sleeve. 'Here,' she offered. 'This ought to get you started.'

It was a page of idiomatic expressions. I laughed and started to read: '*fame da lupo* – very hungry, *al verde* – broke (no money), *chiaro e tondo* – absolutely'. I paused, inhaled deeply through my nostrils and just let it all sink in.

Over the next few days, we tinkered with bits around the old mill, swam in the stream that ran beside it, watched cheese being made in mountain pastures, ate exquisite salami and sunbathed beside pools of crystal-clear, icy water; yet we still hadn't slept together. Somehow the unstated assumption had just fallen into place that our first time would wait until we were alone and up high in the mountains. I just knew she wanted it this way, so I forced myself not to push things physically.

Maps consulted, rucksacks packed, car loaded, rifugio booked – finally, the moment had arrived. We drove above Feltre on the western side of the valley, among sheep with floppy ears, through tunnels where icicles hung in midsummer and past crumbling little villages with balconies cascading with flowers. We parked the car down below. She knew the way and I followed. We walked in silence, plucking fruit from banks of wild alpine strawberries as we passed. The trail was steep and her breath came hard and fast as her pace quickened; my heart pounded in my chest, and want coursed in my veins. Just on the cusp of the treeline we found a secluded little clearing well off the trail and spread out a red blanket under the dazzling mountain sun. Our lips exchanged kisses rather than words. She placed a sweet red berry on my tongue. Then we disappeared.

We giggled as we used what was left of the water in our bottle to wash our salty faces. With the sun sliding low, we picked up our bits and pieces, tied our bootlaces and rolled up our red blanket. Relaxed and completely at ease with each other, perhaps for the first time, we strode, pinky hooked in pinky, the last mile to our rifugio above the clouds.

That night, after we finished enormous plates of meat and cheese and polenta around a large hooded fire in the corner of rustic Rifugio Boz, she said dreamily that she was so lucky that she had found someone who liked the mountains as much as she did. I nodded and laughed a bit at what she hadn't said.

At the end of my year in Padua, we faced the first of too many separations. It was one thing living on the same continent, where liaisons were only a two-hour plane ride away, but I was about to move to Buffalo, New York, to start a PhD. I had always had my eye on a career as a lecturer and, given that Sasha was an academic, it now seemed more right than ever that I pursue it. If I could make it work, our time, our schedules, our glorious summer holidays, our lives would be wonderfully in sync.

But this future would come at a price. For Sasha, getting to me (now on the snowy eastern shore of Lake Erie) was much more taxing than it used to be: eight hours in the air, followed by seven hours on the road from New York City up to Buffalo. On her first visit, a couple of months after I'd started studying, I came down to New York to collect her at JFK. I met her down the ramp from Customs with a small bunch of flowers and a grin so big it hurt my cheeks. It was mid-afternoon, but she had already had a full day of travel; the car ride would be exhausting. She smiled when she spotted me in the crowd and our kiss had a nervous energy about it. I so desperately wanted her to enjoy her first experience of the States because, who could know, we might find ourselves living there at one point. While I was convinced we would have a life together, I wasn't sure what shape it would take. She was anxious for the same reasons.

We didn't speak much in the car on the way up. She had found the 'law enforcement' mentality of American Immigration Control irritating. As we drove, she gaped at the size of the shopping malls and the cars and the buildings. She marvelled at how quickly the city gave way to wide-open suburbs with large houses on ample plots, and at how the suburbs changed in a blink to snowy forests on rolling hills. She held my hand while she goggled out the window.

When we were approaching Buffalo, I roused her and asked her what she might like for breakfast the next morning.

'Anything, sweetheart, I'm not bothered. Maybe some fruit and yogurt,' she said. But then she added suddenly, as if she'd forgotten something crucial, 'As long as there's some tea.' I hadn't yet understood the ritual importance of the tea for Sasha. It wasn't about hydration or warmth; it was about greeting the day in a civilised fashion. Sasha was not at all formal, but she was extremely attached to the ceremonial way tea marked out her day.

'Do you have any Earl Grey?' she asked hopefully.

'No,' I apologised. 'But I can sort you out.'

'But it's 2 a.m.'

'This is America. We're always open for business,' I

grinned, as I pulled the car into Tops International Supermarket. I opened her door and told her to mind the ice. We slid through the entrance and were bathed in white fluorescent light. Sasha's red-rimmed eyes squinted and struggled to focus. 'How can they expect people to work at this hour?' she muttered. 'This place is massive, like an empty warehouse.'

I took her by the hand and skated us to the tea aisle. 'Here you are,' I said with a touch of pride. 'Find what you want while I go and grab some milk and fruit,' and I dashed off. In no more than three minutes, I turned the corner back again into the tea section. There she was, my dynamic, brilliantly clever, mountain-climbing Sasha, on her knees near the other end, sobbing faintly with a plastic-wrapped box dangling loosely from her fingers. I raced up to her, losing an apple on the way.

'I can't find it,' she mumbled between sighs. 'Look, there's Lipton and Nestlé and Brisk and Bromley.' She pulled herself up and started trailing slowly along the shelves. 'Tops Everyday Value Tea, Tops Premium Decaf, Red Rose Original, Barry's Naturally Decaffeinated, Celestial Seasonings Cinnamon Apple, Spiced Herb, Bigelow Cozy Camomile, Stash Premium Peppermint, Sweet Dreams, I Love Lemon—'

'Oh, don't worry, love,' I said, relieved, and now trying not to sound amused. 'I'll find it.'

She went on dreamily listing 'Teekane Herbal Wellness, Liquorice Spice, Tazo Herbal Infusion, Good Earth Original Sweet & Spicy' before I found her a purple box of Earl Grey, tucked a few strands of hair behind her ear and led her by the arm to the checkout.

As I got stuck into work on my PhD about writers experimenting with new technologies, I also returned to one of my old passions: radio. From when I was a young

29

child in New Jersey, I remember laughing myself silly to the ridiculous radio adventures of Chicken Man, the completely inept superhero, on our local AM station. At university in Virginia, I had become fascinated by the seriousness of National Public Radio. I was so captivated by it that, despite my lack of the necessary prerequisites, I managed to talk my way into an internship at the local NPR station. Before long I started to do news stories for them, which even led to a part-time paying gig for a few months.

After one semester at Buffalo, I got myself plugged into an NPR station there. Some work doing news reports led to anchoring the news on the weekends and to producing documentary series for them. After a few years, I lobbied to start producing programmes that connected to the writing I loved: the *Lannan Foundation Writers at Work* series, various literary lecture series and eventually a huge and nationally distributed literary interview series called *LINEbreak* that I produced with my mentor, the poet and professor Charles Bernstein. Out of *LINEbreak* flowed dozens of other literary interview programmes, as well as more surreal little radio projects about devils and breath and flat-packed furniture, each more ambitious than the last. These were weird, quirky things that lacked a clear storyline and that were broadcast mostly on small radio art stations in Europe and a couple of times on the BBC. I didn't care that they had small audiences, or that my father would tell me he didn't really understand them – I was having fun doing them. Over the years, I gradually built up an international reputation for creative radio and this led to commissions and conference invitations in equal measure. My career as half-academic/half-radio producer was up and running.

But whenever I could pull myself away from work, almost every chance we had and every time we could afford it, Sasha and I would return to Italy. I stayed in touch with the friends I had made in Padua and whenever we told them we had bought our plane tickets they would organise little outings for us. One quiet midweek evening just after Carnevale, our friend Stefano and his girlfriend Elisa took us to a secluded little trattoria off the tourist trail in Venice. As bells rang midnight, and after four bottles of Fragolino had been drained, we wandered through glittering little lanes and over narrow gilt bridges until we found ourselves on an almost deserted Piazza San Marco. Waiters at the tables of the posh cafes on the square chatted idly as they began making moves to clear up things for the night. A small trio of a piano, cello and violin, out in the night air, were still entertaining a tiny clutch of people at a bar near the bell tower. Sasha started bouncing lightly in the moonlight, then she took Elisa by the hand and spun her around. Stefano slid in between them and I was the only one left timidly under the porticoes.

Sasha glided over to me and trilled into my ear, 'Come on. You recognise this. We practised it a few times back in Buffalo.'

'Is it a waltz?' I giggled.

'Yes! It's a waltz.' She smiled a smile of pure delight, grabbed my hand with her right, slid her left strongly around my waist and began murmuring, 'One two three, one two three, one two three . . .' I started whirling around, taking huge, clumsy strides in a race to catch up with Stefano and Elisa, who were dancing away already halfway up the square. One or two cafe patrons looked on, slightly puzzled by our breach of piazza etiquette. But Sasha didn't care – she never cared about what other people thought; it never even entered her mind, especially when she was having fun. Another thing that made me want her more each passing day.

Where to Be

When I finished my PhD in early 1999, Sasha had been working as a lecturer in Renaissance literature at the University of Kent at Canterbury for a couple of years, and prior to that she had been a researcher at Roehampton University. I managed to get a good job in New York City on my first time on the job market: I landed a position to establish an academic radio specialisation at Brooklyn College of the City University of New York and would start that autumn.

But before the job there were one or two little things that needed doing. The first was to have our wedding. I had asked Sasha to marry me four years earlier while perched high up in the crown of the Dolomites, in a rifugio on the south of the Pale di San Martino. She said 'yes' without a second's hesitation. As we sprawled outside on our red blanket to bask in each other's company and enjoy the last orange light of the evening, a large group of large Austrian trekkers began yodelling into the cliff-face with its tremendous echo. It was a surreal, impromptu concert that seemed put on just for us. We had no idea there were people who took yodelling so seriously, or could do it so well, and we laughed and touched each other's faces and let ourselves get lost in the mystery of that moment above the clouds.

When I arrived in England a few weeks before the wedding, I burned with adrenalin and ricocheted with excitement, so much so that now my memories of these days lack any sense of time and order. Everything happened all at once, like a crescendo of fireworks, and when I think about these days now they seem as jumbled as our box of souvenirs: frilly envelopes containing cards of good wishes written in the very loopy handwriting of old Italian women; the programme for our wedding day, with drawings by Penny of the buildings of old Lewes and our wedding procession down Keere Street led by a Sussex fiddler; a heart, with our initials sharing the 'S' inside it. Postcards of Gauguin's barely clad natives that Sasha sent me in the days before our wedding (even though we were living together), saying, 'Wish I was on our honeymoon now!'

Not having a ton of money to spend but wanting to do something unique and special, Sasha and I organised and ordered everything for our wedding ourselves. We found sweet but modest B&Bs for family. We reserved tables in the gardens of local pubs for lunches on the days before. We picked bushels of strawberries with our friends. We took two empty backpacks on the ferry from Newhaven to the charming harbour town of Dieppe in France one morning and caught the midnight ferry back with a staggering load of cheese and pâté and *saucisson*. I built a wooden form in the shape of a heart and lined it with aluminium foil to serve as the tray for our tiramisu wedding cake.

When our wedding day arrived, Sasha had arranged for us both to have massages at a health centre off the high street in Lewes. Just as I was lying down on the table, *Pick of the Week* was starting on Radio 4. It's a programme that showcases what one of the BBC's senior editors or some other personality thinks are the best moments on radio from the past seven days, and that week's instalment featured a bit of me. A few days earlier I had appeared on Laurie Taylor's programme *Room for Improvement* and spoke about strange radio, challenging radio and radio in other languages with different ways of editing. I joked that I hoped I didn't get a black mark against my name in the

BBC guest book for encouraging people to turn off their radios every now and again to simply process and savour what they had just heard. I bristled with enthusiasm. I was electric. I was getting a massage, hours away from marrying the most splendid woman I could imagine, about to embark on the most glorious honeymoon, while my thoughts about radio were being singled out as particularly worthy. I glowed.

Our wedding packed St Pancras Church in Lewes. Friends and family from all over the world had come to share it with us, and Sasha missed a step in her walk up the aisle to hug our Italian friend Mirco, who had completely surprised her in the pews – we had thought he wasn't going to make it. We stood beneath Victorian stained glass and exchanged vows and rings and kisses, while Father Erik Flood, the cantankerous parish priest, delivered an uncharacteristically gentle sermon about love being the pathway to the divine. Then through clouds of confetti we floated down the twisting streets of Lewes, with passing cars hooting at us to wish us luck.

Our honeymoon seemed to stretch across the whole of the summer. My job in New York hadn't started yet, so I had no real responsibilities and I had a bit of money saved up from my radio work; Sasha was working full-time but had arranged things so that she didn't have any on-campus obligations. We left the wedding party clean-up in the hands of our friends and disappeared to a farmhouse B&B nearby. The next morning we caught a ferry to Calais, as we had done most summers, and drove through France on our way into Italy, discovering an amazing little cliff town high above a gorge on the French side of the Alps. Called Pont de Beauvoisin, it was our first stop and it boasted the winner of that year's prize for the best chocolate shop in all of France. We had saved the bride and groom from the top of our tiramisu wedding cake (a couple of four-inch plastic dolls we had bought at Woolworths) and I held them up in front of the town sign on the bridge as Sasha snapped a photo.

For my birthday later that year, Sasha made me a huge collage of photos that mostly featured our two wedding dolls. The bridge in the French mountains. Blue-and-yellow striped boats and barrels of white fishing nets beneath an old stone town on the Tremiti Islands. Sasha lying on her side on the top of a medieval wall, smiling and looking at our Michelin atlas. Her topless and reading on the pebbles of a secret beach on Paxos. Me smiling coyly, all dark hair and white shirt, showing off my beautiful silvery wedding ring. Sasha in a baby-blue bra and pants holding onto the white column of our sea-view rental. Me tanned and bare-chested scrambling around the ruins of a temple to Hades and Aphrodite. The view from a room above an ancient square where we struggled terribly to produce the Greek words for bread, cheese and petrol. Sasha, with plaits in her hair, on a trail surrounded by the most beautiful mountains in the world.

We came back to England that August with our tiny car scraping every speed bump, it was so full of loot. We unloaded dozens of bottles of wine and shoehorned them into a small cupboard, shook sand out of our dirty clothes in the back garden and set to work planning our next meeting. I had to leave for New York to start my new job at the end of the week. Sasha was going to come over to the States for Christmas and I had a break in November and could make it back over for a week then, but we were still looking at almost three months without seeing each other after the most blissful honeymoon conceivable.

While Sasha still loved her research, working apart became more of a grind. Like me, she had difficulty saying 'no' to things that interested her and she often had to produce 50,000 words a month for various books and articles. These were projects that meant a lot to her, but her sense of what was important and of how she wanted to spend her time was evolving. By the middle of autumn, she said the longing to be together combined with her daily word count was making her very restless to do something different.

'We can be together from June (or earlier if you can get over here),' she wrote, describing her plans to negotiate some leave for the next academic year so she could be in New York 'with the odd break while I come back to England and pretend to be an English academic'. This was how we made things work – a few months here, a few weeks there. That same letter continued: 'Sometimes I think an academic job is a wonderful way to earn a living and feel very reluctant to give up a tenured job where I have lots of control over the courses I teach and like my colleagues; other times I feel creatively frustrated, and daydream that *if* I was a successful children's writer that things might be even better.' Sasha was extremely good at drawing and illustrating, and had toyed for a while with the idea of trying to do it for a living. Yet with mortgages and plans for a family, it was hard to give up the stability of a career that she did so well.

Together again in mid-winter, we took a trip to Morocco, where we hired a car and wound our way through the High Atlas Mountains, bartering blue jeans and ibuprofen for rugs and dyed scarves. On the plane back to New York, I developed a horrendous flu that I must have picked up in Africa. My mother Trudy, who lived only an hour away in New Jersey, brought gallon upon gallon of chicken soup to me in Brooklyn. Most grown-up mother–son relationships are a bit fraught and ours was no exception. Since I had left for graduate school there had been a sort of uneasy truce between us. Our differences in politics, philosophies of life, education, ways of communicating, reading matter and choice of friends often got the better of me (even if she never seemed too troubled). My father had died of a heart attack a few months before. This had devastated me, and while she was certainly deeply shaken, she had remained remarkably composed at the loss of the only man she had ever loved. She was incredibly tough in nearly every way. Approaching 70, and with a pin in her hip, she rented jet-skis while on holiday and played tennis every week. She was a mother of four and deeply Catholic. While she never mentioned it, I could tell she was ever so slightly worried about losing me permanently to Europe. As a future and stable home for Sasha and me was an open question in everyone's mind, I decided in the coming months to try to do some things for her and with her in an effort to reconnect somehow. So, after I saw off the nasty Moroccan bug, I was true to my word. I shovelled snow off her driveway, fixed her doorbell, pruned her trees and invited her to dinner in the city every now and again.

As Sasha and I bounced from one side of the ocean to the other to be together, we were also, inevitably, putting down roots in our home countries. The more I worked in New York and did things for my mother on the weekends, the more I could imagine a future in New York; and the more Sasha developed programmes at Kent and established herself as a high-flying academic there, the more she began to think of England as a future, permanent home. Our families also pulled us in opposite directions, and too much of this anxious staring into the future led to our first major fight.

Sasha had got a grant to do some research at the Folger Shakespeare Library in Washington DC and was living with me in a small apartment in a Hasidic part of Brooklyn. She would take trips of two or three days at a time to go down to Washington and spend the rest of her time writing in our apartment. It was a difficult period for me: on top of the recent loss of my father, my cousin Gregory (someone I had grown up with and whom I was very close to) committed suicide over a lost love. Our neighbourhood, a place not quite right for our demographic, was starting to frustrate Sasha – there were few restaurants and no bars, and our local F train was not the best and often took more than half an hour to get into Manhattan. One day while I was giving a lecture in another part of the state, she called me and started complaining about being treated rudely by someone who hadn't understood her accent in the corner bagel shop. I snapped. I was frustrated at her frustration. I yelled at her and said that she wasn't trying, that she wasn't trying to appreciate what there was in New York, and then – stressed out and tired as I was from growing responsibilities at the university, sad as I was about the loss of my cousin, worried as I was about the money all our travelling was costing us, and simply angry – I told her I wanted to reconsider our plans to have a child, something we had talked about doing soon.

When I got home the following afternoon, Sasha wasn't there, but on the kitchen table I found two little slips of paper in her perfectly formed handwriting. The first one said:

20 things I like about NYC

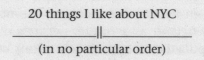

(in no particular order)

1. Maria Torres's dancing classes – of course!
2. Art deco ornaments on the skyscrapers in Manhattan.
3. Plentiful, cheap food.
4. Trees with red leaves in fall and blossoms in spring.
5. Cheap, 24-hour subway.
6. 5th Avenue, Manhattan.

7. The Chrysler Building.
8. Bagels.
9. Generous glasses of wine in the bars.
10. Community radio. Really.
11. Making new friends through mambo.
12. Tiles on the subway stations.
13. The New York Public Library.
14. Fairy lights on the trees by Rockefeller Center.
15. The mix of people.
16. The openness of Americans.
17. The lack of rain.
18. Cool, hip music (inc. salsa).
19. Brooklyn College exercise classes.
20. Hanging out in Park Slope.

The second one said:

10 things I want to do in NYC
———————————||———————————

1. Walk over the Brooklyn Bridge at sunset.
2. Go to the bar at the top of the World Trade Center.
3. Go to the Social History Museum on the Lower East Side.
4. Graduate from Maria Torres's Level 1 class to Level 2 (this might be a long-term ambition).
5. Get pleasantly merry with my husband in a bar in Manhattan.
6. Eat some more Mexican food.
7. Explore Central Park.
8. See Miss Understood (or another drag queen).
9. Actually get to a Manhattan mambo club and dance.
10. Give my husband reason to fall in love with me all over again, and want to share his life with me.

In addition to the ocean too often between us, we were both suffering from something common to academics: the creativity of our early careers was being chipped away by the more mundane requirements of teaching, the bureaucracies of our universities and the increasingly intense demands of publishing for tenure and promotion, in addition to the steady pursuit of grants and fellowships (which were essential in our case if we wanted to be together). The vitality and energy that had been so much a part of who we were when we met were being consumed by all this other nonsense and we were both getting resentful. Had we each been a bit less ambitious, we might have realised sooner and with less trauma that we really did have everything: house, car, supportive families, careers that were good enough (and that would have got better even with less effort invested) and, crucially, *each other*. I apologised profusely for what I had said on the phone and thanked her even more for the NYC love notes. She apologised for not recognising the stress I was under and promised never again to be fazed by a Hispanic clerk in a kosher bagel shop not understanding her British accent.

I'd like to say we resolved then and there never to worry about geography again. But we did. In fact, in these years every argument we had (and we had our fair share) about which restaurant to go to, or how to plan our holidays, or which car to buy, or about insensitivity to cultural differences (from the pronunciation of 'tomato' to the merits of Ricky Gervais) had its roots in the question of where we would make our future, of which one of us would ultimately derail a hard-won career for the sake of the other. It was an anxiety that was always present, simmering just below the surface.

While Sasha was back again in the States in the spring of 2001 on research leave to work in Renaissance archives in Massachusetts, she got pregnant. She was ecstatic. I was delighted if a bit apprehensive about what it might mean for my time. That summer out in Italy our hiking was intense. We clung to rocks on some of the most difficult trails we had ever taken. We discovered new restaurants and ate plates and plates of fish; Sasha craved fish, especially mussels, for weeks on end while pregnant. We renewed our contacts with old Italian friends and worried slightly that it might be an even longer time before we would see them again. We sensed our baby's arrival would change things in our lives, but we didn't want it to change who we were as people. We made a little pact with each other that we wouldn't retreat into a cocoon when our child was born. Sasha would go dancing, I would continue my radio and we would go out to dinner and to concerts as we'd always done (with and without our baby). We would force ourselves to make time for these things and we would make them work one way or another.

Heavily pregnant in Central Park on a bright, late-autumn afternoon, Sasha posed on a bridge, her black velvet hat akilter, black scarf alive in the wind and slightly comic red trainers on tiptoes. I stood next to her with my shiny shoes, my grandmother's red scarf and my leather bag from Morocco over my shoulder. Some random passer-by took a photo of us and we headed back on the Q train to our new apartment on Sterling Place in Prospect Heights, Brooklyn. We loved that part of Brooklyn. And we adored that little apartment: nothing special, but a nice two-bedroom flat with rooms off the street and our own roof terrace with a view of the Manhattan skyline. When I had bought the apartment some months earlier, it was a bit worse for wear. But as we knew this was going to be our first proper home as a family, we took time and made it right, with fresh paint and throw rugs and kitchen cupboards from Ikea.

When the university broke up for the Christmas holiday,

we went to New Jersey to my mother's house. Sasha had decided that she wanted a home birth and, even though we had spruced up our place in Prospect Heights, the house in New Jersey was so much more a home for us, especially at Christmas. Christmas in the north-east is perfect: there's almost always some snow, all of suburbia is lit with flashing fairy lights, the stars atop Christmas trees scrape cathedral ceilings and everyone exaggerates with the presents. On Christmas Eve, everyone in my mother's neighbourhood puts candles along the roads in small waxed paper bags that glow until well after the little ones are dreaming of Father Christmas. In recent years, especially after my immersion in British culture, I sometimes wondered if it all veered slightly on the wrong side of kitsch, but even then I could always get into the spirit.

Our baby (we didn't know if it was going to be a boy or a girl) was due the first week of January, but Sasha went into labour early on Christmas morning in the living room of the house my father and grandfather had built. Sasha phoned the midwife. My mother phoned Nigel and Penny to let them know that it was happening, and I began to fill an enormous blue, spongy-walled tub we had on loan from the midwife. Sasha was planning a water birth. The time between her contractions shortened, I held her hand and tried not to recreate the fear that sometimes flashed across her eyes. She yowled in pain and I massaged her lower back. We lit a fire, and as it started getting dark snow began to fall. She was in labour for 18 hours, and at 1.30 after midnight on Christmas 2001 Sasha gave birth to our son. I pulled him up from the warm water and placed him on Sasha's breast. She glowed with love and our son, eyes already open in the darkness of that winter night, breathed his first untroubled breaths.

'Temporarily Hilarious' was what we called him for the

first few days because of what seemed to be a tiny perpetual smile on his face – we thought we should look him in the eye for a while before contemplating names. Finally, in an effort to find something for the birth certificate, we cracked open our Italian books of baby names and began marking pages. We both, independently, happened across the name 'Lio', which brought us back to sublime sunny mornings on Campo San Lio in Venice. We knew that was it and with hardly any discussion about alternatives our son Lio Felice Spinelli now had his name.

Our lives did change, of course, but true to our promise we remained the same people for each other that we had always been; and Lio simply was, without any thought or effort of any kind, an extension of who we were as people – *the natural expression of our love*. Three days after he was born we bundled him up and took him for a walk in the woods behind my mother's house and snowflakes melted on his red cheeks for the first time. When he was less than a week old, Trudy, Nigel, Penny, Sasha, Lio and I all went out for a meal at a steakhouse nearby. At ten days old, we all went out to the local botanical garden, which my mother had frequented for decades. And at two weeks, Sasha and I took him into New York City for the first time to have dinner at the Ear Inn. But for most of the three weeks after Lio's birth and before I had to start teaching we simply sat in my mother's living room and looked at each other with awe in our eyes.

We settled into our lives in Brooklyn without much difficulty. But for the interrupted nights, it was a time of pure joy in which we found happiness in every moment together, in every walk through Prospect Park or the Brooklyn Botanical Gardens with Lio in his pushchair, in every cup of coffee together in the cafes that line 7th Avenue, in every new expression on our son's face. In May, for Sasha's birthday, my mother had offered us use of her floating timeshare and we booked a place in Pegosa Springs, Colorado, in order to give Lio his first taste of proper mountains. We steamed ourselves in natural hot springs and Lio burbled and laughed as we wandered beneath white aspens and beside streams of melted snow. And for every new gesture and sound that Lio made, we shouted, '*Che bravo!*' ('How good!')

Lio was christened at St Pancras Church back in Lewes in July, by Father Erik Flood, the same priest who had presided over our wedding three summers before. After that we all headed out to the mill in Italy as usual. Lio sat up on the green grass with a view of Monte Pizzocco in the distance. He beat an old multicoloured, wooden and metal xylophone with a cooking spoon. In a rucksack/baby-carrier we took Lio on his first hikes in the Dolomites, where he giggled and clapped his chubby little hands atop the ruins of Castello della Roccia. He spent his first night in a rifugio with us that summer – at Rifugio Boz, the same rifugio that had been the first for Sasha and me together. We saw our relatives in Treviso and friends in Padua and when it got too hot we retreated back up into the mountains, where Lio splashed in the shallows of the river behind the mill, almost always sporting a broad orange sunhat and a huge, open-mouthed smile.

During the days, he pointed at and 'talked' to all the new things in his world. He had learned to crawl and was cheery virtually all the time. Sasha and I joked that when he next cried or got upset we should take some photos because otherwise no one would believe him capable of tears. In the evenings, Sasha and I told him invented stories about Piccolo Mugnaio (Little Miller), his talking horse Mickey, an elf called Pampalin, the brave Cavaliere Lio (Sir Lio the Knight) and a black dragon named Ubaldo who all lived in a shady little valley nearby. He seemed to struggle to stay awake for these tales (or at least the sound of our voices telling them). And each night after he'd lost the battle against heavy eyelids, whoever had put him to bed told the other how the story had progressed so that the next night the adventure could start exactly where it had been left off.

I was completely astounded by our son. Maybe it was just that first-time-parent wonder, but Lio amazed me with something nearly every day. So I did what I had always done when faced with something that impressed me. I started recording. I recorded everything: his giggles, his shouts, his chanting while accompanying himself by banging on his toy blocks, his yodelling in the bathtub, his hiccups, his tiny snores, but above all his rhythm and his pre-verbal sing-song – so utterly remarkable for a boy of six months. He clearly loved the music of his own voice. But it wasn't just music. His enthusiasm for everything in the world around him came in huge waves and his attempts to try to 'speak' about it were unstoppable. As he was approaching his first birthday it sometimes got trying: he could sit for hours just pointing at things, saying, *'Di là!'* ('Over there!') and he would repeat it over and over again until he got some kind of response from us. This was OK for long car rides across Europe, but at 5 a.m. after an unsettled night it was slightly less charming.

That academic year I had won a Whiting Fellowship to collect interviews in the UK for an ambitious radio series I was cooking up. Sasha was back at her job at the University of Kent and working like a demon on her book about *Romeo and Juliet*. We made little jaunts to Wales and France and Sardinia, on the new low-cost airlines. And we took walk after walk after walk on the South Downs that surrounded Lewes. My work was completely my own again, as I didn't have to worry about teaching or departmental admin that year and I, in our small terraced house, with my small perfect family, was more consistently happy than at any other time in my entire life.

After another glorious summer up in the mountains, this one with Lio toddling around on his own two legs, trying to reach the pedals in pedaloes and dribbling his way through *gelato* after *gelato*, we returned to Brooklyn because Sasha had managed to organise another temporary research post in Massachusetts. As she got back to work with fresh enthusiasm, I was more impressed with her than ever. While I was at Buffalo, I had introduced her to different ways of reading modern poetry (focusing mainly on form and sound as opposed to meaning). She had taken these ideas and was running with them further than I could have ever gone, consuming volumes of German Idealists on aesthetics and books by early twentieth-century Russian Formalists.

In my own research, I was hunting for good ways of describing what the new software-based editing systems were making possible for radio speech. Sasha had a look at an early draft of one of my articles and said what I was trying to do reminded her a bit of a writing manual published in 1598. When I found the book the next day on a dusty shelf in the library basement, I danced a jig of delight. Sasha had been right, of course: 400 years earlier this text had detailed poetic tricks in exactly the same way that I wanted to talk about new radio speech. I cited it excessively in my article. In looking back at moments like these, it now seems completely ridiculous that I could have got so excited over such arcane little things, but that's how Sasha and I were – we were connected at the brain. She and I fed each other ideas like grapes on sultry summer afternoons.

I also had a huge new practical project to sink my teeth into: designing and supervising the construction of a brand new radio station at Brooklyn College. Since my start at the college, I had been working hard to develop solid and practical courses that would help my students get jobs in New York radio: I invited radio reporters, sportscasters, commentators, advert producers and programme directors of all stripes to come in and give talks. I set up internships with radio stations around the city. I cultivated relationships with production companies and placed my best students with them when they graduated. But we still didn't have a proper radio station on campus.

I, along with the head of my department, had been courting a wealthy alumnus named Hi Brown. Hi had made millions by producing radio dramas in the 1930s, '40s and '50s and had given breaks to Boris Karloff, Peter Lorre, Gregory Peck, Frank Sinatra and Orson Welles. Our efforts were rewarded by several large cheques and the department finally had the resources it needed to build a new radio facility. This was a job I was born to tackle: while growing up, I had worked on dozens of building sites with my father, my first year at university I had studied architecture and had worked as a draftsperson in an architect's office, plus I had years of experience in radio stations. I set about designing exactly the station I wanted. I worked on floor plans and wiring diagrams, I consulted with architects and with acoustic engineers, I scoured the internet for the right equipment and computers. I even, with the help of my graduate student Miguel, screwed together much of the gear myself. When it was done, we had built the best student radio facility in New York City and we were extremely proud.

Lio was now in a Montessori nursery a couple of days a week, so Sasha and I let a bit more of our old professional ambitions trickle back into our lives. The research, the guest lectures and the projects were exhilarating, but it eventually became clear that the constant bouncing across the ocean would have to stop. Before Lio started proper school we would have to decide which country we were going to call home.

Riding high on my successes with our alum and with the radio station, I went to see the Provost (like the Vice Chancellor) of Brooklyn College to discuss the possibility of a spousal hire for Sasha. It's not uncommon in the States to offer a job to the partners of faculty that a university wants to keep. But I dropped the ball in that meeting: I was too uncertain, too insecure, too frightened of pushing things too far. Or maybe I was just too young and inexperienced in dealing with management to negotiate it. I didn't threaten clearly enough to leave if they didn't find a job for Sasha; I was too afraid of losing a tenured job in New York to really risk it. The Provost coolly advised that Sasha apply for an open 'generalist' position in the English department, but said that any hire would have to go through the standard process and she couldn't give Sasha any special consideration. The job itself was not particularly appealing to Sasha: there was no guarantee she would be teaching in her field, it required more teaching than she had at Kent (and consequently less time for her research), at the beginning she'd have no PhD students and the undergraduates would be much more of a mixed bag than she was used to. All this, coupled with the fact that getting the job was not even a certainty, made her decide not to apply. In the end, the person they hired had half the CV that Sasha did. A better job was out there, for either her or me.

The sun rose and set on another summer in the mountains, but now we had to face separation because neither Sasha nor I had managed to organise any fellowships or leaves to be able to stay together that year. If we wanted to hold on to our jobs, as I did in New York and Sasha did in Canterbury, if we wanted to maintain the upward trajectories of our careers, as I did in media and Sasha did in literature, then I would have to stay in Brooklyn while Sasha would take Lio to Kent. It wouldn't be too bad, we rationalised: British and American academic schedules are staggered so that we'd never be facing more than seven weeks apart, we'd have lots of holiday time and the crèche at the University of Kent was very close to Sasha's office. So we did it. We decided that Sasha and our two-and-half-year-old Lio would find a small house to rent near the university and I would get cracking back in Brooklyn with some articles and conference presentations I wanted to write about digital audio.

We threw ourselves into our work and we started writing to each other again. While her letters talked about missing me, about how fabulous she thought my work was and about the antics of our exuberant Little Lio Lad – chasing chickens one week, getting his finger stuck in the window of a Wendy house and prompting the arrival of the fire brigade the next – I wrote to her mostly of my memories of the year before: about seeing Lio playing in the woods behind my mother's house, carrying armfuls of small logs and tapping the trees with a little stick; about us picnicking in gardens; about our romps in the mountains. I wrote about how these things made me feel warm, sustained me and made me happy. Then Sasha wrote about how insane the admin was at Kent, and about how she had kindly offered to take Lio's friend Brandon for the day and how he and Lio had managed to flood the bathroom by stuffing loo roll down the sink, and about how she would find it hard to manage without her friend Cynthia around for moral support. I wrote back that maybe it was stupid to have decided to live apart at that particular moment in our lives.

Things got worse for her. The combination of pushing herself to produce and looking after Lio was taking its toll. Emails came about her trying 'to dance the doldrums out of my system' and saying 'I love you so much it aches, and I just wish I was with you, and I know if I was I'd be smiling.'

49

After a decade of doing it (and doing it well) the long-distance relationship finally became too much for her and, in spite of the fact that I knew I would miss New York and everything that I was doing there, I decided to look for a job in England. We were both better together than we were apart.

Curiously, a job came up in the Department of Media and Film at the University of Sussex, the place where Sasha and I had met and only ten minutes from our house in Lewes. It was ideal. I knew some of the faculty there from the conference circuit, so I applied and landed a job as senior lecturer. But when I started in the autumn I was slapped in the face with something Sasha had wrestled with for years: the bureaucracy of British universities. In the States, I was completely in charge of the courses I taught; once a course had been approved by the department, I could teach it however I liked and could change whatever I wanted, whenever I wanted, without hassle. In the States, whatever mark I gave a student was the mark they got. In the UK, I was met with battalions of committees that had to approve any course alteration, various complicated systems of the centralised submission of student work, and moderation and double-marking of students' assessments, which was said to foster some notion of the parity across different universities but which existed primarily (it seemed) to double our workload. On the research front, too, the amount of form-filling was staggering and I seemed to spend more time producing reports *about* my research than I did actually *researching*. My intellectual curiosity was being bled out of me and I was getting resentful because simply keeping my head above water was eating up the energy I wanted to spend on my real interests.

My own frustration made me marvel all the more at Sasha for having made it work so well for so long, and for having done it the year before *while looking after Lio on her own*. I understood for the first time why she had to be so organised, with her days structured around little unmissable rituals like tea in the morning and *The Archers* in the afternoons. She, having mastered the system, managed to compress all the necessary but unimportant admin work into less than an hour a day. She also knew what could be put off indefinitely or ignored completely, whereas I sweated about it all.

But I did my best to swallow it for our home life: in the evenings now, Sasha would teach Lio a few notes on his miniature accordion while she played her grown-up one, I would bang pots and pans with him, and Lio's friend Robbie, who had just moved to England from Rome, would come over to play Lego and chat in Italian. Lio and I baked pizzas together and sometimes on Sundays we would go and visit Nigel and Penny for a roast lunch. There Lio would hang onto the leg of the piano and watch transfixed as Sasha played Chopin. We had been trying for a year to have another child but conceiving this time was proving difficult. We changed our diets, got more exercise, started having acupuncture treatments and helped each other keep the niggling sense of failure at bay.

Lio was a shining star in nursery; he was now there five days a week. He chatted with the teachers as much as with the other children. On top of his skill with languages, he was also mature beyond his years and incredibly generous. If he saw another child crying, he would often go offer comfort or a toy before the teachers had time to react. Remarkably for a child his age, he wasn't at all selfish; he shared his games and treats and food. This was so striking that one of his teachers took to calling him 'Saint Lio'. Once or twice I worried about this – I worried that he might go through life not getting enough of what he really wanted, or even his fair share. But that thought never troubled him. For Lio, there always seemed to be more than enough of everything to go around. And I think he was probably right.

In the hope of a second child, I put my Brooklyn flat on the market and sold it. In spite of the fact that I got more money than I expected, it was extremely hard for me – I never told Sasha how gut-wrenching it was for me to sell it. The idea was to buy a bigger place in England and maybe even a little house all of our own in Italy (a place that we could do up exactly as we wanted without compromise). But even as I sold that cosy apartment in the sky in Brooklyn I was thinking about ways of getting us back to the States for the rest of our careers because I just couldn't get used to the way things seemed to run at British universities. I was confused and unsettled. Dissatisfaction was gnawing away at me more each day and I felt myself sleepwalking into a midlife crisis.

That summer in Italy, as we drove from valley town to mountain village chatting with estate agents about access and local planning laws, Lio was in exceptionally fine form, even for him. He charmed the women with his eyes so rich and sparkling blue. *'Che belli occhi azzuri che hai!'* ('What beautiful blue eyes you have!') was their usual refrain. And to the men he offered handshakes and precocious questions in perfect Italian about gardens and tractors and the proximity of ice-cream shops. We all climbed mountains again, and when we did we forgot lots of the other things it seemed we didn't have. We ate with new friends in castles that they had saved from dereliction and Sasha quizzed our old art restorer friends about what makes something 'beautiful' for a new book she was working on. And as the last weeks of August rolled on, we bundled up our wine, our cheese, our books and our golden child Lio and headed off to France for a couple of days more holiday with my mother before driving home to return to work.

The Crash

As Sasha and Lio drove up the hill in front of the station and out of sight between Victorian brick buildings, I had this urge to stop them and to get them to come with me up north somehow. I tried to snap myself out of it and come to my senses. There probably wouldn't have been a room at the hotel because of the conference and I had planned to use the train journey to polish up my presentation, not entertain Lio. Sasha was keen to set up in her office, and – despite my vague misgivings – everything would be fine. Yet as I turned to walk into the station I had this feeling that I would never give my lecture. I even, for a brief instant, began to question the whole point of academic conferences and why I had enjoyed going to them for so many years.

But I chalked those feelings up to the general restlessness I had been sparring with for months. On top of my difficulties with work, when I looked at our small terraced house in our cramped little English town, I wanted more space, a house with my own study and workshop. Sasha was also unsettled. She really wanted to devote her time to her children's books and – more intensely – she wanted that second child. While I did too, I worried more than she did about what another child would mean practically for our lives in our little house already crammed with Lio, his toys and his irrepressible (sometimes demanding) curiosity. I looked at Nigel and Penny's mill house in Italy and started to wonder if I wanted that year in and year out for every summer as we had done for the past 15 years. I worried that I hadn't written Sasha a poem in ages, and wondered if our pretty good sex life was more about making a baby than it was about our own passion and desire. I was discontented and my misgivings about this conference seemed to be just part of that general theme.

I tried to remind myself why I liked conferences: they were fun, subsidised travel. You got to see new places and meet sharp people who shared your interests. They were opportunities to develop a profile, to steal new ideas and to flesh out your teaching and research. Sasha had got a lot out of them too, always double-checking that she had packed both her conference paper and her dancing shoes before heading out the door. But all this didn't really convince me at that moment in front of the station, and I wondered for a second – completely unlike me – if I'd had enough, if I needed them any more, if there weren't better ways to spend my time.

There were two legs of the train journey: from Lewes to London, and then from London up north. When I arrived in London, I had some time to burn before my train left for Newcastle, so I climbed up the stairs to the street in front of King's Cross station to find an ATM. After I'd got my money, I turned back toward the station and almost bumped into a very solidly built, attractive young man who walked past me at a good clip in shorts. I might not have taken any special notice of him but for the fact that he had an artificial leg, not a plastic simulated human leg but one of those much more high-tech devices of exposed metal rods and wires. In spite of his looks and his confidence, I remember taking a breath and feeling thankful that everyone in my family had two good legs.

Back in the station while waiting for my colleague and friend Kate to meet me I got in line to buy a coffee. But then, feeling a bit agitated and perhaps worrying I'd miss Kate, I got out of line. Then back in line again a minute later. I bought the coffee and looked around for Kate a bit frantically and with hard-to-decipher emotions. I really didn't want to miss her. I darted in and out of tall, painted cast-iron columns. I elbowed my way through crowds of commuters. I heaved my bag high up on my shoulder and dashed out along the train platforms under the Victorian glass ceiling. I was desperate to find her, more so than I should have been. I put my coffee on a ledge that ran around one of the train station columns. It fell off, not instantly, but after a minute or two of my continued looking around; it just fell off and spilled all over the ground. I remember planning how I would meet Kate, nervously going over in my mind what I was going to say to her. All of this was absolutely crazy because we had worked together for more than a year at that point and had known each other on the conference circuit for five or six years. Our children often played together on the pebbly beach at Brighton and her partner and I had taught a course together the previous term. There was absolutely no reason for anxiety.

I was also inexplicably nervous about my bag. I'd never worried about leaving luggage before; in fact, Sasha sometimes said I was cavalier about it. I kept checking to see that it was at my feet or on my shoulder. I had been this way on the train up to London too, constantly looking behind me to check my bag, as if expecting it to have disappeared. I desperately did not want to lose something.

The train arrived, I got on board and ran into Kate making her way up the aisle, heading to our seats. She smiled at me and my nervousness receded. There was a large family already sitting in our reserved places, but Kate thought we should leave them, so we found empty seats a bit further up.

'I'm surprised you wanted to take the train,' she said as we finally sat down. 'I would have thought flying would

have been more your style – you know, no time wasting.'
She was fond of teasing me for being a little bit too
aspirational, and this always pleased me secretly.

'Believe it or not, I've just been thinking about ratcheting
down the pace of things a bit,' I quipped, unable to conceal
a slightly satisfied smile. 'You know, slow down, enjoy
more, smell the roses, etc. What do you think?'

'Really?' she said with a smirk of her own. Kate had got
to know me at events where I had liked a bit of spotlight,
liked being contentious, proposing new ways for thinking
about radio and showing off my own radio projects. Kate
knew that I was proud of what I was doing and she was
always good at letting me talk about everything I had
recently said 'yes' to. But for some reason this was not the
chat we had on our three-hour train ride and I didn't work
on my lecture either.

My face relaxed. 'Really,' I said honestly.

Instead, our conversation was wide-ranging and
unexpectedly personal, intimate even. We talked about
getting time off from teaching to do new things, to re-find
ourselves, and about our children and how well they
played together. We talked for a long time about our
partners. I told Kate that I might give off the impression of
being busy but that Sasha seemed to do five times as much
with half the effort.

'The day before we left on holiday this summer,' I said
as I launched into some supporting evidence, 'Sasha was
up before 6.00.' Electric poles were whizzing past the
window and I picked up the pace. 'And before she went to
her salsa class at 10.00 that night she—' I started counting
on my fingers:

'1) finished a draft of an illustrated children's book she
was working on – about a little elf struggling to learn to
sing with the help of some forest animals – and then sent
it off to an editor friend for some suggestions;

'2) took Lio round to his best friend Robbie's house to play for an hour;

'3) revised an intentionally controversial essay about "recreational misogyny" in early modern England for a journal and sent it off;

'4) did some research for a great book she's working on about beauty;

'5) organised car insurance for our trip;

'6) packed up clothes, books, toys for Lio and Earl Grey tea – enough for the whole summer;

'7) teased me about having some fun together when she got back from dancing; and

'8) got tarted up to go out.'

Kate laughed and I went on, 'Just about all I managed to do that day was set my email to auto-reply, pack the car and put Lio to bed.'

As Kate and I went on wistfully rambling about whether or not it was possible to simplify our lives, I told her that my biggest regret since meeting Sasha was deciding to spend so much time apart from her and Lio a year earlier.

'I know it was hard for Sasha,' I told her. 'But my missing both of them day in and day out was excruciating.' In thinking back as I narrated the story it seemed an absolutely insane thing to have put ourselves through. I had missed so many little developmental steps with Lio, and Sasha worked herself ill. I told Kate I would never even think about doing anything like that again. There was a real ease and tranquillity about this conversation. I remember feeling genuine flashes of happiness in it, like I was realising through it that I had so many wonderful things in my life and as I articulated them they seemed to expand before my eyes.

When the train stopped, I made my way to the little hotel on the seaside at Sunderland, brushed up my presentation a bit for the next day, called for a cab to take me to the conference centre and had a shower to wash away the grime of travelling. As I stared at myself in the bathroom mirror, slightly flabbier and slightly greyer than I wanted to be, the emotions I'd been floating on during the train ride evaporated away to nothing. I was overcome by a wave of insecurity and worry. I was profoundly unhappy. It wasn't just a creeping dissatisfaction over my life being stuck in a routine that didn't inspire me any more. It wasn't just anxiety about how Sasha and I were having trouble conceiving and worry over what that might mean for our relationship. It was something deeper and darker that I couldn't quite put my finger on. I looked at the damp figure in front of me and whispered, 'You are a shell of a man.'

The rest of that afternoon and evening are a blur of fragmented details. Policemen met me in the lobby of the hotel as I was waiting for my cab. They seemed uneasy and a bit frightened, lacking the usual policeman swagger. They asked me into the hotel office and told me that Sasha had been killed on the highway outside Canterbury and that Lio was near death. They drove me to the airport with sirens blaring as the traffic parted to let us pass. One of the cars in front of us hit and killed a cat as it tried to cross the road. I was completely numb as I watched it twitch by the kerb. The image was too perfect, too obvious to be real. They took me to an airport lounge and someone offered me whisky; I wanted only water. I got on the plane and worked hard to convince myself that this was all some big mistake, some miscommunication, that it wasn't really happening.

On the plane heading south, I went through some of the traditional phases of grief that I remembered from high school sociology books. First *denial*: up in the hotel, the police had asked me if I was the husband of 'Sarah

Roberts', not Sasha. Sasha's name was Sasha, not Sarah (although I knew full well that Sarah was her first given name and it was Sarah on her driver's licence). Maybe another Sarah Roberts (a common enough name) with a son named 'Leo' had had the accident. *Negotiation*: 'OK, God, if you've really taken Sasha, you can't possibly take Lio as well. She might be dead, but Lio will live and recover and be fine.' And still more bargaining: 'OK, God, if Lio pulls through this, I will dedicate my life to you – I'll do whatever you want me to.' *Acceptance*, however, was not a step I landed on. I prayed and visualised and meditated. But I never once resigned myself to a life without Sasha *and* without Lio. At Heathrow airport an hour and a half later, I was met by more police and ushered to a helicopter. The sun had just set and an enormous blood-red moon was rising over the trees directly in front of us. It was bigger and redder than moons in science fiction films and I wondered in that instant if it wasn't just all a dream.

I was driven from the helicopter pad somewhere on the river Thames by two police officers in the direction of the hospital. My pulse was hammering and electricity surged through me. I imagined I was massive and red like the moon but made of pure burning energy. We screamed through London streets and one of them said something that really did make me want to shriek with laughter.

'Did you have a nice flight, then?' he asked.

What could I say?

He, not knowing the situation, was just making idle conversation – I, on the other hand, was trying not to explode into rage or tears or panic. Eventually he asked, so I answered: my wife had been killed and my son was in a coma. He whistled, as if to say, 'Wow!' I asked if he could find out any information about how Lio might be doing, but after a few minutes of failing to get through to their dispatcher and then to the hospital on their radio they gave up in silence. This would prove one of the very few moments in our entire ordeal in which the police let me down. The police were absolutely marvellous. Never in my life would I have imagined putting the words 'police' and 'marvellous' together in the same sentence. Maybe it was my natural suspicion of authority figures, maybe it was too many films of arrogant policemen involved in arbitrary or unsympathetic justice, or too many humiliating exchanges with the police when I was a teenager, but I had, I will admit, a problem with the police. Not any more. But that evening, as they struggled through the static and cross-talk and eventually quit trying, I felt abandoned by them, completely isolated and different from them, some alien object they didn't understand that they just happened to be delivering somewhere. My chest constricted in the barren urban twilight and even today as I think about this car ride I feel tense and light-headed.

We screeched into the ambulance entrance of the hospital and, as I got out, I was met by a grey-haired motorcycle cop clad in leather. He looked more like a slightly old bike messenger than an officer of the law and it would turn out to be his last day on the job before retirement. He hurried his colleagues along and heaved my bag out of the boot. He raced me to the lift, but then, after waiting an eternity for it to arrive, I told him I wanted to take the stairs and we bolted up.

Making it to the doors of the Paediatric Intensive Care Unit, we buzzed and, eventually, were let in. I remember seeing the face of Sasha's brother Jeff in the entryway, looking like he looked in all those childhood photos of him and Sasha at a funfair or at the beach. I couldn't think of him without her and I struggled for a second to process how he could possibly be there. Jeff was serene. He had a soft smile on his lips and a halo of unkempt curly hair in the fluorescent lights. He embraced me long and hard, the way I remember Sasha had embraced my mother when my father died.

'We've got Lio,' he said in my ear. 'We've got Lio. At least we've got Lio.'

'We've got Lio,' I whispered to myself as much as to him.

I only realise now that I took these words from him as my mantra for the next several months.

I told him I wanted to see Lio and he pointed me to a door. I felt tall as I walked through it. I felt very, very tall and I remember thinking: 'I will face this, and I will face this down. Nothing can touch me and no one will put me off saving Lio. I will face this and I will take it on.' My shoulders were back, my chin tucked slightly under my head, as if showing my horns. I saw the rest of my life unfolding, and unfolding happily even, pulling my son back from this moment. This was the pep-talk that I gave myself; this was how I wanted to see myself and how I wanted to think about what I was entering. However, beneath the surface, there was nothing but fear, simple and absolute. Yet my performance was convincing: I took long, great, quick strides and told myself (and made myself feel) that I was invincible. Far from being crushed by this event, I would be elevated by it, even strengthened by it somehow, and the more frightened I became, the higher I soared.

As I opened the door, I had a vision of Lio playing by my side in the not-too-distant future; I had a vision of us being perfectly fine and happy beside our little stream in Italy. But the instant I stormed into the unit I was completely lost. It was very dark inside intensive care. It was night-time, there were only a few high windows and the lights were low. Amidst all the machines and devices and trolleys and nurses I turned right because most of the beds were on the right. But I couldn't see Lio. Panic rose. I can't find him. I can't find him. I jerked my head this way and that, trying to peer through the webs of medical technology to find my son. Finally, Jeff put his hand on my shoulder and spun me around. Lio was behind me.

There he lay. Tubes down his throat. Hair half-shaved and the rest matted with blood. An enormous wound on the top of his head. A sensor attached to the front of his skull. A giant rainbow of computer screens all around him. His head was the only part of him that was visible. The rest was covered by an air blanket designed to regulate his body temperature. His lips were full and red and lovely. Everyone had always told Sasha and me how gorgeous his lips were, lips like a cherub's in a Renaissance painting. I fished out one of his hands from under the blanket. It was clenched into an impossibly tight little fist. I had to pry his fingers open just to put my thumb in his palm, and like a steel spring they snapped painfully shut on me, but there was no way I was letting go of this little boy now that I had him in my hands again. There he lay, my four-year-old son, smashed to pieces, severe brain damage, mutilated and pulverised leg and knee. But he was my boy and he was going to survive and be all right. He was not just going to be all right, he was going to be the same clever boy who spoke Italian and French, with sparkling blue eyes and a personality that charmed everyone. At least that is what I told myself, the belief that I threw up against the fear.

It was far too dark in paediatric intensive care. At times the children there seemed like creatures still in the womb, at others they seemed like tiny corpses already in the grave. Perhaps like no other, paediatric intensive care is a place on the cusp of things: of beginnings and endings, of life and the hereafter. I did have to let him go. I had to go and speak with the doctors. And letting Lio go was a moment harder than finding him in a deep coma in a hospital bed. I looked at him before I left. I saw him lying there full of total potential; anything and everything was possible for him. I didn't want to go see the doctors because I was afraid of what they might do to that vision.

Doctors in intensive care have an impossible job. It's stressful beyond my comprehension, emotionally exhausting and sometimes thankless. They interpret and treat and too often have to deliver terrible news to parents, and (if they have the wherewithal and the energy) they have to do this in different ways with different parents several times a day. And everything happens so fast for them; they make the kinds of decisions in an instant that it would have taken me days to consider.

I went into the tiny family conference room across the corridor from intensive care like I was about to face a firing squad, but with a determination to face it bravely. The doctor and a nurse followed close behind me. I sat in a too-low, too-soft chair facing three silly flying duck paintings on the opposite wall. The doctor was a young, attractive eastern-European woman – far too young, I thought. When the crash happened, I was 38, yet most of the doctors in positions of authority here looked younger than me. I wanted slightly wizened men with white beards, years of experience and a touch of vagueness about them. What I got was young and too confident in her own assessments. She began by saying that there were two major issues with Lio: his leg and his brain.

As she started telling me about his leg, I barked, 'Forget about the leg, tell me about his brain.' We were a family of brains before legs.

After a difficult pause, she said, 'All right.'

In another tortured second, she continued, 'There are tears in Lio's brain in several places between the grey and the white matter. He's also got several fractures of the skull and bleeding deep inside the brain.'

She paused for a response from me that did not come. 'I'm sorry,' she said, 'but there is a good chance he will die.'

Something was exploding inside me, but still I said nothing. What could I have said?

'If he doesn't die soon,' she continued, 'there is the real possibility that he could remain in a coma for the rest of his life and it's highly likely that he won't ever walk or talk again.'

She paused a very long time, almost insisting that I say something. I steadied myself and breathed out the question: 'Is there any hope of recovery?'

'He *might* recover, yes. But the absolute best I would expect is that he'll be severely mentally disabled. Eventually, though, he could go to a special school. But I have to caution you that that seems unlikely.'

I lost my resolve. I fought tears, but they ran down my face. I fought sobs, but they choked in my throat. I fought hysterics, but at one point had to leap up out of my chair and step towards the door as if trying to escape, only to end up facing the corner for a moment and then to slowly sit again. Her *best-case* scenario was him attending a school for the severely mentally handicapped. This news devastated me, crushed me, forced me into a moment of crisis and doubt about absolutely everything. It was acid burning through my vision of Lio's future.

I had just lost my wife on the side of the road in some godforsaken part of Kent and now I was faced with losing Lio in some dark hospital room. If we were to believe the doctor, we had already lost him even if he did survive. But in spite of my pain and feeling of helplessness in that moment, I didn't believe the doctor. I made a little pact with Sasha in my heart that none of this would come to pass, and from somewhere deep inside me I felt her agree.

This doctor was not a villain. But she terrorised me in

that first encounter. As I composed myself as the final details of Lio's condition were being relayed to me, I told myself that she was simply wrong, that Lio's future was much brighter than she could envisage. She simply lacked sufficient imagination to see the possibilities that I saw, that I needed to see. After she felt she'd explained everything, she took me across the hall back on to the ward to show me Lio's cranial CT scans. As the layered images scrolled past, she would say, 'There's an oedema. And there's another,' with a trace of satisfaction in her voice at being able to – in a clinically correct way, I'm sure – diagnose injuries, observe symptoms and put them together with a textbook prognosis. But my son was not a textbook.

Judging from her slight sense of pride at interpreting the scans, I guessed in that instant that she was not an expert in paediatric neurology. Two aching hours later, when that expert finally came he did have a beard, but he was not very old, maybe ten years my senior. I was nervous when he arrived on the scene, still shell-shocked from my experience with the first doctor. But my apprehensions started to fade as soon as he began talking with a very slight New Zealander accent. He spoke clearly of the symptoms and injuries, in accessible language but not at all in an over-confident way.

While I consciously did not ask him for a prognosis at the end of our conversation, he simply offered, 'No one can say where this is going to end up. We just have to wait and see.'

And then he added, 'The *only* thing that is certain, is that Lio's recovery will be measured in months and years rather than in days and weeks.'

With those words, he gave me a tremendous gift, the gift of uncertainty, the gift of possibility. I clung to those gifts and let them fill me with hope. Time meant that I could pull Lio through. I kept returning to his enigmatic yet drastically honest assessment of the situation. He, the expert, was not interested in demonstrating knowledge or mastery, he was thinking about the work of Lio's recovery, both his work and mine.

As other doctors would come during their rounds and offer their interpretations and prognoses, I simply tuned them out. I religiously did not listen. I focused only on 'No one can say.' If I'm honest, though, I only used that uncertainty as a shield to defend us against all the other 'certainties' that were flying around. I was sure. I repeated to myself over and over that Lio would pull through this, beaten and scarred perhaps, but essentially unaffected. I clung to that and saw myself doing what needed doing to get Lio better. I told myself we had time and I believed it. And this brought me a kind of serenity completely out of place in our surroundings. At times, admittedly, it was a hard-fought serenity.

I really don't know where it came from. Maybe from echoes of my youth before jobs and career and graduate school. Maybe from Sasha, whose presence was so utterly tangible to me around every corner in those early days. Or maybe from the simple fact of the crash itself. But there is something about an event like this one that clarifies things for you, that shows you what's really important, what's really meaningful, what's really valuable. It wasn't just a different perception of the world either. I simply found myself living and breathing in a new (and *better*) psychological space. One of the things I found in that space was tremendous faith in the possibilities for recovery. And when I would feel that faith slipping away, I would take a moment and consciously force it to come back. I could feel Lio's recovery happening and could see him years down the road when this whole ordeal was just some faded scars and a memory for him. I wasn't alone in this. Faith, not just my own faith but the faith of the other parents too, was a strangely palpable thing in paediatric intensive care. You can almost touch it, and you recognise when it's not there. In spite of the darkness and the surreal technology, in spite of doctors who are too politically correct, or too confident or too cautious or too frightened to refer to the divine, there aren't many atheists in paediatric intensive care. The atmosphere of the place had a physical effect on us and my memories of our days in that ward have this floating, almost angelic, quality to them. It seemed as if my feet barely touched the floor. I expect that my attitude and behaviour must have made things hard for some of the medical types. At the beginning, I must have come across as uncomprehending, as ignorant, as difficult even. But I knew better.

A bond developed between me and the other parents in paediatric intensive care, but it didn't develop instantly. While we were there, the PIC unit at King's College Hospital was where most of the paediatric liver transplants happened in Great Britain. At times it seemed like every other bed was filled with a child recovering from a liver transplant or waiting for a liver. One of the staff, delicately and gently, mentioned to me that if Lio took a turn for the worse it might be a good thing to consider donating his organs. I was chilled. After hearing it and after learning the reason that so many of the other children were there, I spent hours in a cold sweat every time I saw another parent looking at Lio – Lio with his frightful brain damage yet a perfectly good four-year-old liver. It's impossible to describe the sea of guilt and longing and fear and hope and condemnation that stretched between the beds. But as the hours passed I saw the other parents were not vultures. They were some of the kindest people I have ever met. And as they said prayers for Lio in a myriad of languages and traditions, I did the same for their children.

Lio's grandparents, Nigel and Penny, stayed with me on the floor of the little family conference room across from intensive care that first night. We pulled the cushions from the chairs and sofa and made a little nest on the ground to lie on. We didn't sleep. We sobbed and got up in turns to stay by Lio's bedside. On the level below intensive care, we had been offered a tiny little prison-cell of a room, stiflingly hot, with two small beds in an 'L' shape along the walls, and one little window about five feet away from a steam vent that erupted every three minutes. We opted for the floor of the small conference room instead.

My mother, whom I had called shortly after arriving at the hospital, caught the first flight she could find from Newark to Heathrow. She told me on the phone that she desperately wanted to be there for us and the next day she met us in King's. She arrived in her multicoloured polyester tracksuit with a single small bag in tow. As ever, she was rock-solid dependable, got herself to London in less than 24 hours after hearing the news and was ready to stay as long as it took. And when I embraced her in the corridor outside of paediatric intensive care, she simply said, 'Oh Martin.' While I knew I would need her strength, I knew also that the intensity of what we were facing would test my patience with everyone around me and I hoped nothing else would get damaged in the weeks ahead.

Almost immediately my mother gave me a break at Lio's bedside and I headed out for some fresh air. I made my way to the lift and when the doors slid open instead of the usual heaving crowd I was met with a solitary, wincing Middle-Eastern man a few years older than myself. He looked very tired and was in obvious pain as he shuffled back a step to make room for me. He was holding up his trousers and he wanted me to see that he was holding up his trousers.

He was agitated and in an accent that it took me a few seconds to work out, he said, 'They took everything. They took everything. I don't even have a belt.'

In my dreamy state of exhaustion and absolute focus on Lio, I didn't understand what he was trying to say and I honestly didn't want to understand either. But elevators are good for forcing conversation (or at least forcing listening) and given the condition Lio was in I didn't want to alienate any potential ally, no matter how strange. I wanted everyone I met to think positively for us, to send us all the good feeling they had to spare, so I nodded and tried to find an ounce of empathy. It transpired that while this man had been in hospital donating part of his own liver to save his young son, someone – someone who knew he was going to be in hospital – had robbed his house. They had emptied it, taking absolutely everything down to the man's underwear. A man goes into a hospital to have a procedure to save his son's life and someone takes the opportunity to rob him blind. The story of this calculated act of cruelty was like a jackboot crushing down on the tiny seedling of hope I was trying so hard to nurture. It was anathema; I couldn't process it, I didn't want to process it. I stepped back into the corner and focused on the floor numbers scrolling by on the panel. In retrospect, I now wish I had offered this man my own belt, but that would have required a lateral thinking that I just didn't possess in the moment.

While our accident had been some horrendously arbitrary act of fate, some tragedy that left me speechless, breathless, reeling with pain, struggling to cope with loss in every direction and with a thousand instantaneous things to do and decide to help get Lio out of a coma, this man's burglary was simply beyond my comprehension. I had relatively little difficulty acknowledging what seemed to be the random cruelty of the universe, but this was a simple, premeditated act of evil. The heartlessness of it bothers me to this day. How could someone be so malicious as to steal from someone he knows is suffering? Did these things happen all the time? Had I somehow just managed to avoid them up until now? I had read about them in books and seen them in films but having an example standing in front of me holding up his trousers was something else. While this was the first cruelty of its kind after the crash, it would not be the last.

When the lift door opened on the first floor to let someone else in, I, anxious and confused, stepped out rather than taking it all the way down to the ground floor as I'd planned. As it happened, the hospital chapel was just to the right of the elevator. I turned and faced its heavy oak door and, with two firm hands, pushed it open into the surprisingly large Victorian church at the heart of the hospital. In the weeks ahead, I would come to adore its Pre-Raphaelite stained glass as much as I would come to dislike its fake electric candles. But none of those things entered into my consciousness that day. It was just me in a big, empty sacred space feeling pushed by the man with the missing belt to say something to God. I didn't kneel. I stood on my toes at the back of the central aisle and stretched out my arms a bit. Anything could have come out of my mouth at that moment.

'What do you want from me?' I said. 'What could you possibly want from me?'

'I'll do anything,' my voice getting louder and quicker.

'Do you want me to become a priest? All right then, I'll become a priest!' I shouted. A nurse who had been lying down asleep in one of the front pews hidden from me sat up, bleary-eyed, and searched around. He looked at me for a second and then lay back down.

I was unfazed and went on, 'You can keep his leg if you'll just give us back his life and his brain. Let him have his mind back!' I lacked the faith to ask for both.

I stood quietly for a few minutes. I put my palms together in front of my chest in just the same way Sasha used to when she meditated.

I gradually let my face soften and I whispered an honest question: 'Will I have the strength to survive this? And if I do, will I have enough left for Lio?' Before the crash I was what I was: an academic with clever dinner party conversation, a well-stamped passport and a fraught but persistent relationship with my family's religious tradition. Since the age of about 20, I liked to refer to myself as a 'relapsing Catholic' (very conscious of the different meanings of the word 'relapsing'). I continued to practise on and off in my own uncertain way; and while I found tremendous peace and comfort in the awe-inspiring ancient churches of my adoptive home, the more rigid aspects of its theology and the cranky way that some Catholic principles are interpreted and applied alienated me much of the time. But it was my tradition, my tether to some distant family origin that had been lost when my grandparents and great-grandparents had emigrated. It also provided a familiar framework for expressing something I felt but could never articulate on my own in a way that satisfied. So, occasionally angry and disgruntled, I persisted.

Sasha, an agnostic when we met, certainly prayed more in her last months than I did. She converted before we got married and, as with most things in her life, she took to it with commitment, more, it must be said, than my own at the time. She converted, I imagine at the start, to make me happy. I never asked her to directly, but she just intuited it. I now think that in our early years together as Sasha was falling for me she must have also been falling a bit for my latent Catholicism. When I would occasionally go to mass, I would never ask Sasha to come with me, but she would often invite herself along. The art, architecture and music (things she had studied) began to take on a different and more meaningful dimension for her and became more attractive. The rituals and the rites of passage also began to resonate with her. When my father died, she was especially impressed at how my family's traditions helped deal with it and process it. Even apart from discussions of eternity, she saw the prayers and the ceremonies that marked and framed his passing as extremely useful in simply living with what happened. They were unquestionably valuable in the present.

This was not so much a great epiphany for Sasha as it was a redirecting of something she'd always had inside her. She, like me, had a spiritual dimension. If I introduced her to votive candles and incense on the odd Sunday morning, then she introduced me to personal reflection and meditation. On days when I was tied up in knots with the stress and anxiety of radio projects or research deadlines or university admin, she would often find little guided meditations for me on the web, give me my favourite headphones and insist with a tiny grin that I sit on the bedroom floor and do nothing but listen for half an hour. I see now that the very grown-up and flexible way she approached her adoptive faith was helping me to gradually evolve out of my own problems with it. Sasha came to it as an adult, not surrounded by the fears and dependency of childhood. She focused on the aspects of it that were meaningful and valuable to her and didn't worry much about the rest. As I marvelled at how she did this so gracefully, I began to loosen my grip on the heavy misgivings I had with the dogmas and orthodoxies of my own past.

We rarely, if ever, talked about any of this explicitly. Sometimes now I can't help but wonder what those conversations would have been like. On two occasions in the months before Sasha died I accidentally interrupted her sitting on the backs of her heels on the floor of our shared study/bedroom with a light smile and a small picture card of a saint in front of her. Clearly, she was wanting some quiet time, so I closed the door quickly with slight embarrassment and as little sound as possible. I suspect her last prayers had mostly to do with getting pregnant again. But I never asked her.

When, dropping down onto the hand-embroidered kneelers in the Victorian chapel at the hospital, I forced myself to calm down even further, I felt a tiny warm shudder and the rush of blood quieted in my ears. With eyes closed but feeling the light from the windows on my face, I came up with my own little prayer.

I breathed out quietly, 'I am here in thanks and in hope for the recovery of my son Lio.' I conjured up a picture of Lio at a graduation ceremony, smiling like his mom, walking tall and proud and straight up the aisle to grab his sheepskin. Next I saw him happy with a wife and child of his own. Then I heard, or thought I heard, a tiny voice whisper, 'I love you.' I opened my eyes and looked around the church. Empty, even the sleeping nurse had gone. I repeated my little prayer over and over and over again until the words seeped out of my pores. I saw Lio getting better in my mind and I saw myself being thankful and deliriously happy for each tiny incremental improvement: a finger twitching, his head moving, his lips quivering, his eyes opening. I had pushed away a grain of the panic and was pleased with this little meditation. I swore to myself I would say that prayer every day until Lio was out of hospital. I believed it would work. I believed it would be an indispensable part of getting Lio better as much as I believed that Lio was a uniquely strong child and that all the brain damage in the world was simply no match for his special capacity to recover.

I don't know how many minutes passed. But all too soon the threads of calm I was holding on to were torn away and I was once again gripped with fear. The fear of losing Lio. I had to see him. I shot up and darted out of the chapel, found the stairs and dashed up. When I reached Lio's bed, it was exactly as I had left it: computer screens flickering, machines beeping, his air blanket inflating and deflating.

'That wasn't much of a walk,' said Penny. It was clear she had been crying.

'I didn't make it out of the hospital,' I said.

'Why don't you really go and get some air? We're not going anywhere,' said my mother. 'You've got your cell phone turned on, right?' She knew I did.

'We'll call you the instant the doctors come,' said Nigel.

So with the words of the neurologist from the day before about Lio's recovery taking 'months and years' still echoing in my ears, I decided to take a few more minutes and regroup with a short walk outside. I was back in half an hour and some minutes later a slight and wiry hospital chaplain from India named Luke appeared at Lio's bedside. As I told him what had happened and about who we were, he suddenly became very animated. In an accent too thick, with speech too fast and a voice inexplicably emotional, he said something frantically about Sasha. I nodded politely. His face wrinkled in worry and he got even more agitated and told me that I hadn't understood – he was right. He tried again and managed to get through to me that he had been one of Sasha's university students a hundred miles away at Canterbury. Only months before, he had been to her lectures and sat in her office and discussed his writing with her. He had laughed at Sasha's jokes, been curious about her readings of poetry and argued with her about symbolism – so, obviously, our situation was more upsetting to him than it might have been. When he understood, the usually composed Nigel let his jaw fall open a little. Penny was a staring blank.

Luke calmed, put on his shawl, opened a small tin of blessed oil, said a prayer and anointed the side of Lio's forehead – the front of his forehead being covered with stitches. My mother shed silent tears and I felt as light as a feather. We'd all just experienced another mysterious happenstance, another strange and intricate little connection or coincidence (call it what you like) and I felt simultaneously startled and comforted. Of all the hospital chaplains in England, the one who happened to be praying over Lio as he lay near death had been touched by his mother. I could not help but feel that Sasha had orchestrated this somehow. I was grateful and allowed myself a moment's reassurance. I thanked Luke and he said he would come to check in on Lio whenever he could. After he left, I remembered that Sasha had been struggling with a keen but difficult foreign priest in one of her classes. I also remember how I told her to take a few steps back from this particularly demanding student. But she didn't.

That evening I saw the man with the missing belt again in the corridor outside intensive care. This time he seemed less surreal and threatening, but the pain on his face was unchanged. I mustered my brightest 'Hello' and told him that I was so sorry to hear what had happened to him. He nodded and I asked about his son.

'So far so good,' he said. 'That's what really matters.' I noticed someone had given him a belt. I reached out and shook his hand; I tried hard but probably failed to manage a smile. He nodded, his grimace gone, and I carried on my way.

My mother kept a journal of her time in hospital. Her entry about the first night she spent with Lio reads, 'I held his hand and prayed all through the night.' Of this I have no doubt. While she sat up with Lio in intensive care, I tried to get a few hours' sleep, this time alone in the little room we had been given on the floor below. It was pointless, not because of the sticky heat, or the erupting steam vent, or the crookedness of the bed. It was pointless because the moment I disengaged even slightly from Lio my mind was completely consumed by Sasha – by Sasha and our lives together. And how that story had been so violently changed. Memories of going out to eat and to films and for walks in the mountains were shot through with images of broken glass and twisted metal that I simply couldn't force out of my mind. Agitated and isolated, I headed back up to the little conference room across the hall from Lio and tried to settle onto some cushions next to Nigel and Penny. But this was even worse.

Penny could not help weeping and sobbed in the dark, 'How can the world be so cruel?'

I knew at that moment that each one of us was going to have to find our own way through what had happened, and Penny's was beginning with different steps from mine. But for the moments when my concentration was pierced by the memory of the man with the missing belt, I was not interested in blaming the world, God, the cosmos or anyone. It didn't seem a particularly useful way to spend my limited emotional energy. I was only interested in making it through the moment and in pulling Lio out of his coma. I had accepted the cruelty in an instant, the instant I walked into intensive care. Nothing was going to be gained by arguing with that.

Rather than cursing the world, I set myself to working with it. The world and every person in it, the universe and all of the positive energy in it I could attract, God and whatever means he uses, were all going to save my son, to heal my son and to return to him his splendidly bright future. I didn't want to alienate anyone or any power, I didn't want to accuse them or force them into impossible situations or demand explanations from them that I knew would never assuage. I was working with them, simply and only asking for help, not insisting on anything else. The world might have its cruelty, and cruelty, like shit, happens. The trick is getting the world to bring you more happiness, and demanding answers to my existential questions didn't seem like part of that trick. I wanted to be productive; that's the course I had set. I left Nigel and Penny without a word after only a few minutes on the floor and went back to Lio's bedside.

I never saw the man with the missing belt again. Perhaps his son was moved to a different hospital. But I thought of him every time I looked at the stained glass and the paintings in the chapel and thanked him in my mind for giving me a new way to think about my situation. He and I shared something, if only for a brief few moments. It was a connection, a way out, a realisation that I wasn't alone in what I was experiencing. I was not alone and I was not going to be driven desperately inward and downward. I had Lio and nothing was going to take that away. And my desire to help Lio, like my too-late desire to do something for the man with the missing belt, pushed back hard against the doubt and despair. If we survived this, I thought, it would be because of that desire and the sense of connection that had sprung out of my encounter with that strange man.

Reviving Lio

After four days of dosing Lio with morphine and staring at his intracranial pressure readout, it was decided to try to take him off his respirator. He had been coughing at intervals and this was the only non-computerised sign that he was still alive. As I watched him there, head surrounded by red foam blocks, it seemed as if he were a newborn infant all over again. His eyes were closed, he had no control over his body, but he was able to cough, he was able to make that one little response to his physical world. A cough meant that he was still with us.

'I think it might be worth a try taking him off the respirator,' our bearded neurologist David McCormick said over my shoulder while I stood mesmerised by Lio's computer monitors.

'What, already?' I asked, excited and afraid.

'He's been coughing on and off against the breathing tube since this morning, which means the part of his brain that regulates the lungs is probably working well enough to give it a go,' he said matter-of-factly.

'Let's do it, then,' I said, not considering for an instant the scene if Lio failed to breathe on his own when the tube came out.

And out it came in the blink of an eye, without fanfare or trauma or even that much preparation. He coughed and coughed some more. His breaths were shorter and shallower because he no longer had a machine helping him get air into his lungs. While I worried that he might choke himself to death with these little coughs, McCormick left satisfied and the nurses seemed extremely pleased. I tried to emulate them as best I could. Lio did it. The tube was out of his throat – he had shown them he didn't need it. The tube was out of his four-year-old bilingual throat. That meant food could go down and words could come out. My mind's eye saw him smiling hungrily over a bowl of pasta and saying, '*Buon appetito!*'

Lio was Sasha's greatest project. It was her tenacity in the face of our own errors and missteps in Italian that made him authentically bilingual. My first words to him were in English. As I held him for the first time – the first time anyone had held him – I whispered in his ear: 'I wish you a life without fear.' And rubbed a pinch of sawdust from his grandfather's workshop into his tiny palm. Sasha's first words to him were simply, '*Ti amo,*' proving in an instant that a love language need not be a mother tongue. And because of her work and commitment to him being bilingual he spoke better Italian than his cousin, who was born in Italy to an Italian mother and who had spent the first years of his life there. He spoke better Italian than his friend Robbie, also born in Italy to an Italian father. He was certainly the most authentically bilingual child of his age I knew. This was Sasha's doing. I had my apprehensions early on and, in my desire to communicate effortlessly and subtly, I would cheat from time to time. But not Sasha: I doubt she spoke ten English sentences to him in four years and nine months, and those ten were only when she was really cross. Because of this, Lio splashed in Italian like a child in a paddling pool at the height of summer. His earliest words were full of Italian Rs, rolled much longer than they needed to be. His eyes would open super-wide and he'd raise his little palms up to his shoulders whenever he said, '*Boh*' (for 'I don't know'). And he would sing repeated vowels over and over to himself in invented, bubbly little arias – the sound of his own voice a pure delight.

By this point in intensive care, our days were divided into shifts: I had the daylight hours, with some breaks whenever relief came. Trudy, Nigel and Penny broke up the nights. I was on in the day so I could speak with the doctors. Our nurses did 12-hour shifts each and Lio had his own dedicated nurse the whole of the time he was in intensive care. Of all our nurses in PIC, I remember a Zulu-speaking South African the best. Marianne exuded kindness with every gesture. She taught me how to say 'Lio will get better' in Zulu, which I forgot a few weeks later. But I'll never forget her most tender moment: a moist towel we had placed on Lio's forehead to keep him cool had dried out and it had attached itself to the wound just above Lio's right eye. Rather than simply rip it off, which would have caused him absolutely no pain because he was in a deep coma and heavily sedated, she spent the better part of an hour gently peeling it back with her left hand while applying water from a sponge with her right until it fell off on its own. I breathed deeply when she was around and let her calm wash over me.

The next day I learned that further neurosurgery had been ruled out for Lio. I tried to feel relieved by this, but the sight of him in front of me made that impossible. Lio's little body remained frighteningly tense, rigid and twisted with muscles like knotted steel. When adjustments were made in his medications, he would have fits of agitation and strange noises would creak from his throat. His grunts and whines were otherworldly and terribly unnerving. I would have given anything to hear the sweet little voice I remembered. The sounds that escaped now were pre-infantile, almost pre-human, yet they somehow made me remember the scene of Lio's birth. Maybe these unearthly cries reminded me of Sasha's voice in labour, but for whatever reason I was simultaneously compelled and haunted by this image of a second birth.

After midnight on Christmas 2001 it was dark, too. We had soft firelight instead of computer screens. We had a CD of choral music instead of beeping machinery. And at his birth, as at his hospital bedside, we had professionals a little bit too eager to tell us what the future held while I was focused on doing what needed doing and appreciating the moment. Less than a minute after Lio was born I remember having the transcendent beauty of it all disturbed by the midwife prying his legs apart and declaring he was a boy. I was so enchanted by the happening, so enraptured, so enthralled, so grateful for this beautiful new creature that I had pulled out of the water and placed in Sasha's arms, that I really didn't want to know what gender it was. I was, there and then, truly immersed in wonder and mystery. To assign the child a gender was to see it in blue or pink at its first birthday party, was to imagine culturally defined possibilities for it in life, was to plan ahead rather than to enjoy what was happening right before our eyes. Similarly, in the hospital I felt a bit of that same resentment as I was made to listen to what boxes would be placed around him in the future. Anything was possible at his birth as it was at his hospital bedside, and there is something marvellous about simply being in the presence of that unknowable and boundless possibility.

Among all the visitors to Lio's ward, I was never sorry to see Paul, our police liaison. While I was focused on the decimal places on Lio's computer screens, a hundred different things needed attention in that other world outside the hospital. And Paul did them: he collected my brothers from various airports and arranged a rental car for them; he went down to our house in Lewes to look for documents that lawyers and prosecutors needed; he was sympathetic, understanding and generous at every turn. I remember very clearly his slightly upbeat tone and reassuring Scottish accent on the end of the phone many, many times. One thing about him stuck with me more than anything else: in all our conversations while I kept referring to 'the accident' he kept referring to 'the crash'. I never asked him about this, but now I'm sure it has to do with the idea of responsibility. Accidents happen, goes the expression; crashes are someone's fault. On the evening of that fourth day after the crash, after we had finished signing forms that the prosecution needed, I walked Paul to his car. He put his hand on the car door handle, but then he paused and turned to face me.

'He's not saying anything, you know,' Paul said. 'We know he understands English, but even through the interpreter he's not being very helpful.'

It took me a couple of seconds to realise that he was talking about the lorry driver.

'Oh, yeah?' I said absently, wanting just to say goodbye and get back to Lio.

But Paul continued, 'He just keeps repeating that he didn't see her. We really want more of a confession. It's frustrating for us, but I can't imagine how that makes you feel.' Paul was always very good about not presuming how I felt.

'But don't worry,' he said. 'We're definitely going to get this guy.'

Something inside me clicked at that moment. I had the opportunity, and certainly every right, then and there, to get violently angry, to lash out about the driver and say, 'Yes! Get the bastard! Do whatever it takes to send him away for a long, long time.' That's what I had seen in movies and that's what I expected to come out of my mouth. And for a second I looked for precisely that bitterness inside me, but it just wasn't there. My composure, however, did start to crumble. Silent tears rolled down my cheeks and as I opened my lips to speak my voice cracked.

'Tell him – tell the driver that I forgive him,' my voice faded away to nothing.

'Are you sure?' Paul said, staring me straight in the eye and squinting.

'Yes,' I said. 'I'm sure.'

'Because that's the kind of thing you might want to take back later,' he said.

Paul's question puzzled me. Of course I was sure. Throughout all of those first weeks in hospital my sense of certainty about my own feelings was rock solid and my regular bouts of self-doubt had all but disappeared. In those days, I had what now seems like an almost super-human sense of clarity and an ability to see, feel and think things in such an absolute way that the thought of second-guessing never entered my mind. I reassured Paul that yes, I was certain. I never asked whether or not he passed on the message.

I understand now why Paul was confused. We were coming at this situation from two very different directions. Paul and his colleagues were working to get an admission of guilt and a conviction. My work was only to pull Lio back to life and to health. I could have got mad, mad at the driver, mad at fate, mad at Sasha even, but that would have been a terrible waste of energy, a distraction from the job at hand of getting Lio better. I didn't want to know about the investigation or even the driver. When I thought about him at all, it only seemed to compound my grief. I instinctively knew that I didn't want to go down that road; I wanted only good and constructive things to flow into our lives, and railing against the man who drove more than his legal hours and caused the crash didn't seem like a part of that. I knew what I was doing.

In fact, I found the whole of the criminal trial process upsetting. I truly did not want retribution. Not at all. In many ways, the only thing I could think of worse than my own situation might possibly be the situation of the driver, aware of the intense pain and suffering and grief he had caused to a young family. Lio and I would come out the other side of this nightmare and the day would arrive in which all of this would be only scars and a distant memory for him. But if I were the driver I would carry the pain of having killed and mutilated with me for the rest of my life. This, I think, would be an almost suicidal burden. But there in the parking lot, tears on my face, I was struggling not to get too tangled up in thoughts like these. I only wanted to get back to Lio.

Lio had been off the respirator for one day. The doctor who had warned me to prepare for Lio's death and to allow myself to hope only for a best-case scenario of Lio being severely mentally and physically disabled had a proposal. Dr Doom, as my family had taken to calling her, said she thought it would be a good idea to try to chemically lessen the severity of his coma. This, she reasoned, would give us a clearer idea of what we were facing and we could change the treatment plan accordingly. If, for example, he got slightly more responsive, we could change his drugs and start thinking about moving and relaxing his muscles. She asked Trudy, Nigel, Penny and I to gather around Lio and had us hold his limbs. She then had me fish the earphones for Lio's iPod down the ear holes in the large, red foam blocks that were immobilising his neck and head. Previously, we had all (including Dr Doom) noticed that if I sang to Lio in a soft voice very close to his ear I could gradually lower his heart rate and his intracranial pressure. She told me to turn the volume up and to play him some of his favourite music.

I don't know what I was expecting. I certainly wasn't expecting him to sit up and smile. But I was completely and totally unprepared for what was about to happen. As his medicinal mix changed, this utterly rigid and barely breathing four-year-old boy began to twitch. The already clenched fists at the ends of his little arms snapped up to his shoulders and his muscles simply began to vibrate and pulsate, as if he were being electrocuted. Everything about him shook in seizure. His little head sprang from side to side even in the tight confines of the red foam blocks. His arms moved faster than my eyes could process and sickening low sounds escaped from his throat. I was kneeling by his side, trying to hold on to one of his hands; my mother was opposite me, and Nigel and Penny were holding his legs.

Alarm sounds screamed from the machines. Penny started shussssh-ing him loudly and repeatedly while rubbing his stomach. My mother couldn't help but say, 'Oh, sweetheart' over and over while holding his other arm. Nigel was rubbing and holding down his uninjured leg. I was whispering to him how brave he was, and all the while Manu Chao was belting out 'Bongo Bong' at him from the iPod. It's no wonder he wanted to stay in a coma.

I just knew the whole scene was going to be too intense with too much stimulation – I knew this even before the doctor told me to turn up the volume. Nothing could have been a more stark contrast with my memory of his home birth. It was horrendous. I understood the doctor's thinking and how she imagined it might work: use his favourite music to invite him out of a coma. But in my gut I knew it was going to be too much for him. He needed to be cradled and calmed, to be held and soothed back into the world. Instead he was being bullied out by a cacophony of voices and technology. I knew this. I knew it should have been just him and me with a minimal amount of stimulation. I intuited this before we started. But I did not have the courage or was too exhausted to say 'no' to the doctor and (which would have been much harder) to tell my family, who were desperate to play a part, that I wanted to do this on my own as quietly as possible. I wasn't brave enough.

I began to get the idea in that moment that for us to reach the end of the journey, for Lio to recover in every way, I would have to trust my own instincts above and beyond anything else. Other people's feelings and professional opinions and personal sensibilities would all have to take a back seat to what I felt was the right way forward with my son. If it had just been him and me alone in a quiet space without anyone but a nurse and a doctor, if I had insisted on that, I might have spared us all that terrible quaking scene, which lasted (it seems now) for hours. I wish I could say I learned that lesson there and then, but in situations like this one, where I was professionally out of my depth, it required supernatural strength of will to tell the white-coated experts that I had a better idea.

His quaking didn't end. It was decided to put Lio back down into his deeper coma. His intravenous drugs were changed again, the tremors slowed and then stopped. He was at peace again. Quiet. I put my own head down on the bed next to him and covered my face; tears fell and the positivity I had been trying so hard to cultivate was seriously dented. Dr Doom laid her hand gently, softly, comfortingly, but formally on my head. I wanted to tear my heart out.

When I had pulled myself together, Dr Doom said she wanted a few words with me outside. I was still too dazed to even sense what she was implying.

She said, in what now seems to me a very self-consciously dramatic way, 'You have to prepare yourself for the fact that this might well be all that's left of your son.'

She paused, waiting for a response which didn't come, and then went on, 'I'm telling you this information and it's up to you to decide what to do with it; whether you tell the rest of your family or not is up to you. But if you don't tell them you'll have to bear it all on your own.'

When she left me, I called in Nigel, Penny and my mother. I told them what she had said simply and without flourish.

Penny, to her tremendous credit, replied without a second's hesitation and with real passion, 'I don't believe her!' And I felt myself smiling.

A few hours later, Dr Doom stopped by Lio's bed. 'So, what did you decide?' she asked.

'I told them. I told them that you said there might be nothing else left of him,' I answered, letting the corners of my mouth slowly curl up just a bit.

'And how did they take it?'

This time it was me who was full of self-conscious drama when I said, 'They don't believe you.'

Dr Doom, this time to her credit, said, 'Good, optimism doesn't hurt.'

No, it doesn't.

Later that day, in an attempt to diagnose Lio's brain damage in more detail, we had to chemically force him slightly out of his coma again. This would involve causing a repeat of the seizures and tremors while Lio was hooked up to an EEG machine that reads the electrical activity of the brain. It took about half an hour simply to attach the electrodes to his head and to set up the little video camera that would sync his physical tremors with the lines being produced by the machine's needles. When the electrodes were attached, his medications were changed. Then, just as before, he began to fit and shake and seize. Watching this second seizure was the single most painful moment of this entire dark ordeal: I could watch my son writhing and contorting and spasming, but I wasn't allowed to touch or to hold or to comfort in any way. Watching my little boy, all I had left in the world, quake and twitch like a fly in a web was unbearable. It was simply unwatchable, yet I watched and I focused, and I swore to him and to myself that I would see him recover. I was not angry, or even confused as I struggled to root out the doubts seeded by Dr Doom. I felt helpless, yes, but my commitment to his recovery kept that helplessness at bay. There was a flurry of activity for a few minutes, not just Lio's flailing limbs but technicians, doctors and Andrew the nurse all flitting about adjusting devices, taking notes, regulating medication, glancing from one machine to the next, reattaching electrodes and so on. And I could do nothing but stand by and struggle to convince myself that we could make it out of this. I gnawed at my fingers, pulled at my face and jittered my leg. My frustration and fear in that moment made my eyes blur.

Since my eyes weren't working I closed them and tried to focus on seeing his recovery unfold in my mind. But I was desperate – forcing myself to find rays of hope, yes, but in an honest panic. I remember fighting to remain calm for Lio and for my family, and even for Andrew the motorcycle-riding, weight-lifting tough-as-nails male nurse. When the EEG was switched off and when Lio's medications were reset to allow him to slip into a deeper coma, Andrew collapsed in a chair with a furrowed brow, limp arms and a pale face. I remember catching his eye and smiling at him; I wanted to go over and put my arm around him and tell him that it was going to be all right but decided that a role-reversal like that might have seemed inappropriate among English people – I wish I had done it now. We were dying inside. But Lio was alive and his future remained an unanswerable question.

About an hour later the neurologist McCormick, the one who had given me the honest, open-ended and uncertain assessment of things from the beginning, came to Lio's bedside with the EEG readout in his hand. He had been seeing other patients while much of Lio's test was going on and wanted to know what I had observed in detail.

'I saw him – "fitting", let's say – at the beginning,' he began.

His voice became a little bit more apprehensive as he continued, 'But can you tell me if he was tremoring here?' He pointed to some particularly intense scribbling on the readout in his hand.

'I think so, yes,' I said shakily.

'Great!' McCormick said and he pumped his fist down as if his team had just scored.

Seeing my confusion at this, he got slightly anxious and started to recontextualise. 'No, no!' he said. 'I don't mean that any of this is great, it's just that if Lio was tremoring at that point, then things might not be so dire. It's a good sign.'

Amidst all the pain and chaos and uncertainty, there was at last some good news. I had liked him from the start – McCormick's new-world delivery and demeanour were very close to my own and we had a good rapport – but now I wanted to give him a tremendous bear hug. I could read and understand him more fully and he spoke with sympathy and with honesty as opposed to the awkward melodrama and detachment that I found in some of the other doctors. I was extremely glad this man was on the case. I thanked him. And before long Andrew's shift was up; I thanked him too, smiled and told him I'd see him the next morning. Now that I had a sliver of hope after days of desperation, I was going to cling to it. Nothing was going to pry it out of my hands. I would sleep a few solid hours that night for the first time since the crash.

In an effort to try to clear our heads at the end of that extremely difficult day, my mother and I went for a little walk in the park adjacent to the hospital. We sat in silence, watching the ducks on the pond, and when it started to get dark we headed for the exit. When we got to the gate, unexpectedly, it was locked – a brief moment of comedy in the most horrible day I'd ever experienced. I did laugh, I smiled and laughed. I called our police liaison Paul. And then I called emergency services. We finally got tired of waiting and were anxious to get back to Lio, so we decided to improvise. I found a low-hanging branch near the fence and my saintly 67-year-old mother climbed up the tree and over the fence and I caught her on the other side. It was a tender moment between us that communicated more than words. Words have never really done us justice. Hers are too real, too clearly attached to things, whereas mine have been too self-conscious, too ironic and too dependent on suggestion. I was grateful to have had that moment. Even our no-nonsense police liaison Paul couldn't hold back a laugh when I finally got to speak with him the next day. He took to calling my mother the 'Park Burglar' after that.

In spite of all attempts to try to impose some semblance of order on our days with bedside shifts and morning rounds and a sleeping schedule, the chaos was uncontainable. When my adrenalin would crash, I was numb with tiredness yet couldn't sleep more than an hour at a stretch; I usually curled up in some uncomfortable chair or sprawled myself out on the benches in the hall outside Lio's ward. Events, even in hospital, seemed to whizz by without me. My brothers Anthony, Paul and Glenn had arrived from Seattle, Virginia and New Mexico and I scarcely noticed. They just set to work dealing with calls from the insurance companies, finding a funeral director, fetching Lio's favourite stuffed animal and a dozen other indispensable things that I had hardly registered. I barely ate anything. Pangs of hunger might come, but usually in the night when the cafeteria was closed, which meant I had to content myself with packets of biscuits I mooched off the nurses or bread from the funny little kitchen unit on the ward – I had no idea who it belonged to.

In the little bubble I inhabited around Lio in intensive care, I lost all sense of time. The outside world simply vanished. It wasn't until one of the hospital social workers mentioned my job a few days after the crash that it dawned on me to call both Sasha's department and my department to let them know what had happened and not to expect us to show up for work. Only days before I had been organising my teaching for a new course and liaising with colleagues about who was doing what lecture. Then, in the blink of an eye, all of that seemed not just utterly irrelevant, but as if it never really existed at all. It even felt slightly wrong to call them and tell them what had happened in the midst of grief and concentration on Lio. It felt almost as if I was risking some part of Lio's recovery to take time to tell them to look for other people to do our jobs – as if it was dangerous to cross the line between the two worlds. But I did it.

A Storm Diary

In the early days of Lio's coma, the doctors asked us to keep something called a 'storm diary'. When someone is in a coma, they will often go through turbulent episodes in which they move and can become agitated even to the point of seizure. The storm diary records the periods of calm and the periods of activity to see if there's any connection between them and doses of medication, times of day, speech or sound or music, therapies and the like.

Keeping a storm diary for your young child is a grisly undertaking. Instead of a scrapbook for recording achievements like bike-riding and school plays and trips on steam trains, you have a sparse and clinical little notebook for charting your child's fits. It's quite a bleak exchange, especially given that once you begin a storm diary you really don't know when it will end. My memory of the anxiety I felt as I scribbled those first entries kept me from opening that diary for more than a year afterwards. Even now the thought of looking at it scares me because I'm worried that it might throw me back to those frightening times when the spectre of Dr Doom was still looming large around every corner. I worried because I was afraid it might distract me from the work I was doing with Lio. But when they asked me to start the diary I took the job on with more enthusiasm than trepidation. Once I started, I discovered that his storms were more frequent than I imagined and were indeed related to lots of things happening around him (like me reading to him). This I took, as did the doctors, to be an excellent sign.

The notebook itself turned out to look almost appealing; it was postcard size with blue, orange, purple and violet pinstripes down its plastic cover. It was innocently and simply entitled 'Lio's Storm Diary' and might have been, in another time and place, a diary of clouds or lightning or wind or moods or anything at all. It starts like this:

11.45	tranquil
1.37	four very good coughs
2.30	very brief bit of agitation lasting a few seconds
2.40	almost awake for occupational therapy movements
3.20	tranquil
4.15	stirring somewhat, less than a minute while I'm reading to him
4.20	moves with pain, almost awake for blood being drawn
5.20	tranquil
5.25	stirring for about five minutes
5.35	tranquil
5.50	eyes open a tiny bit, stirring
6.20	tranquil
7.48	three good coughs
8.30	stirring for six or seven minutes
9.30	tranquil
10.15	stirring after medication
11.00	tranquil

But more troubling entries dot its pages. And when I read 'crunching up face while IV goes in left hand' or 'tense and shaking terribly' or 'very tightly clenched fists and bent arms' or 'wincing at therapy' my chest still tightens.

'Loosening slightly, eyes closed, turned his head to me,'

the diary says when I hugged Lio's rigid body properly and fully in my arms for the first time since the crash. As I pulled him up to me, I tried not to trip over tubes and wires connecting too many different machines in too many different places. I remember how warm his skin felt on my arms and hands. The last time I'd held him properly was the morning of the accident when he'd said his *'J'ai froid,'* with a little shudder. That morning he did feel cold, very cold. I remember, too, holding Sasha at the train station and thinking how cold she felt, and how she reminded me, apropos of nothing, to try to keep the pessimistic tendency of British culture at bay. It was a very strange thing to say. But now I've come to think of it as a little secret message to me, as the last bit of encouragement from my supremely encouraging wife, the very precise and particular encouragement needed during those dimly lit days in intensive care. Sometimes, somehow, I think she must have known, maybe somewhere deep within her, that those were the last words she was ever going to say to me. I repeated them over and over as I dealt with doctors and dutifully wrote my entries in Lio's storm diary.

All the pain the diary brings me is erased in the last entry, written in Penny's neat hand: '6.00 Lio opened his eyes, looked at Monkey and I read *Ten Minutes to Bedtime* – twice I'm sure he followed the pages with his eyes. ☺' Only a few pages later the storm diary is abandoned and I start using the notebook for tallying up medical and legal expenses. Mercifully the storm diary lasted only a few days because Lio was clearly coming out of his coma and his responses were becoming more consistent and more obvious. His long trek back to consciousness now seemed to have taken its first real steps forward.

Still in a coma, but not quite so deeply, breathing on his own, and with fewer machines attached to him than before, Lio was moved from paediatric intensive care to the high-dependency neurological unit called Lion Ward. Nigel and Penny had left the hospital for the first time since the accident to go home and get some rest in their own bed. I was there alone with my mother. A few hours after he had been moved there, Lio's feeding tube got blocked by crushed medication (medication not crushed enough, apparently). Lio's nurse and the head nurse on the ward couldn't get the tube back in. Then they tried with a new one, but it wasn't the right size. Lio's muscles were already tense because of his coma, but now his reactions to their probing around his face made his jaw clench even tighter. I screamed and screamed at him in two languages to open his mouth. I also sensed the nurses' urgency about getting the tube back in. Watching this scene and hearing the awful gurgling, coughing, retching sounds that Lio was making pushed me into a panic. I insisted that they find a tube the right size. They then said that they wouldn't be able to get one until the next day. I was at the end of my rope. This transition to the new hospital ward was threatening to unhinge me. I asked them what the right size tube was and where *I* could find one. They looked at me in puzzled silence.

I couldn't watch any more. I ran out of the ward and began to sweat. I had a vision of myself breaking into closet after closet along the corridors of the hospital to get the right tube, or taking a cab to some medical supply depot, breaking in and stealing one. But they wouldn't, couldn't or simply didn't communicate to me exactly what kind of tube Lio needed; or maybe, after lots of sleepless nights, I was just unable to comprehend. In my hysteria, I went out to the lobby and called Penny and Nigel. I felt terrible about it, but I dragged them out of their own bed for the first time in days to come back to the hospital and help me talk to the nurses. In my limited experience of nice suburban hospitals in the orbit of New York City, when you ask a nurse for something, they usually find it (probably because you're going to pay through the nose for it), but here I remember really struggling to communicate what I needed. It was clear that they wanted to help, but they just couldn't somehow. I toyed with the idea of going back to intensive care and asking one of the nurses there for help, but I was so scared of the darkness and the proximity to death of that place that I didn't want to bring it back into our lives, having only just left it behind.

By the time Nigel and Penny returned, I was back at Lio's side and the nurses had managed to get a tube in him and in the right place. I was glad to see Nigel and Penny again, who arrived looking strong and capable. In the end, the whole distressing scene had a silver lining: after repeated tries to get the tube down Lio's throat, the nurses felt he did (eventually but definitely) respond to the command: 'Open your mouth!' This, the ability to hear and process speech, meant that he was an inch nearer to the end of his coma.

On day six after the crash my brothers, who had flown over from the States four days earlier, returned home. I didn't thank them enough. It seems like I barely noticed them, but I was never so grateful for my family as I was in the immediate aftermath of the accident. The help they gave me in those days meant more to me than anything they had ever done for me in our lives: sorting out lots of Sasha's stuff, moving furniture around the house I wasn't sure I'd ever return to, clearing things out of closets I knew I did not want to face, chasing down documents in Lewes and in London, and simply putting their hands on my shoulder as I tended to Lio. But as I recognised the importance of my own brothers to me, my mind wandered to Lio's future and to his possible life without siblings, without a big, solid family to support him when things went very wrong, a family like the one I had. How would he cope? Indeed, how would he bury me without even a mother to console him? I remember very early after the crash how I started to look at every woman between the ages of 25 and 45 as a potential replacement for Sasha, not that anyone could ever replace her, but I felt this compulsion to give Lio back the happy and normal family life we had had since his birth.

On 14 September, one week after the crash, Lio's favourite 'Bongo Bong' was once again playing on our iPod dock. Lio stirred, stirred some more and opened his eyes. Just a sliver at first, but they did open. Penny, who was making his little stuffed monkey dance at the end of his bed, even thought she saw his eyes move. I looked up through the ceiling when Lio did this and let gratitude beam from me. The neurologists were delighted by this and the other signs of his lessening coma, so much so that they decided to gradually work toward him sitting up with support on the bed. If that worked for several days, then we might even try him in a chair fitted with special straps.

His muscles, however, stayed tightly clenched, which remained disturbing. I was given a series of massages to do with Lio while he listened to some specially designed brain-stimulating music and natural sounds. The basic thinking behind this massage-music treatment is this: hearing is the first sense to mature in the womb, and it's also the first sense to fully revive as you leave a coma. This therapeutic listening combined with particular massages of the face and limbs needed to be done three times a day and it was something I took to immediately with absolute zeal. The CDs we used were designed to create something called an 'electronic auditory stimulation effect' and piqued my interest immediately, as I had come across things like this at various radio and sound conferences in my old life. Back then I had been more than a bit sceptical (or at least uncertain) about the suggestion that these recordings of nature and simple music peppered with pulses of very high-frequency sound could help with brain function. And here they were being offered to me by what had otherwise seemed quite a conservative medical establishment. But beyond my residual professional curiosity, this was something that *I could do.* It was something beyond praying and meditating and imagining; it was something real and practical that I could take on with my own hands to help Lio's recovery. I was finally able to assert a bit of physical control over what was going on. So, at least three times a day, in between doctors' visits and therapists' visits and nurses' visits and counsellors' visits, I put headphones on Lio's head, switched on a CD of Mozart or dolphins or ocean waves with other extraneous noises sprinkled through it, and traced little circles on Lio's face and lines on his fingers and toes. Maybe this was just something the therapists gave me to do to keep me quiet and out of everyone's hair. But I do believe it worked. Within days, Lio's muscles eased and his recovery began to astonish even the white-coated naysayers. In any event, they were tender, physical moments between me and my little boy, and I'm sure that helped as much as the sound effects.

On the next day, his eyes stayed open for nearly 15 minutes and he seemed to follow his nurse at the side of his bed. When the nurse, a Filipino named Dolorio, saw this, he grabbed Lio's toy monkey and started dancing with it and singing at the end of the bed to more 'Bongo Bong'. He was going at it with real gusto, discoing around and bouncing the monkey up with its long arms. Other people in the ward must have looked on perplexed, but I didn't notice, as I was completely fixated on the tiny slivers of blue that began to peek out from under Lio's lids. I'm so glad Dolorio was there and unreservedly, unashamedly, unabashedly pranced from side to side at the end of Lio's bed. After a couple of minutes (I think, possibly, maybe) I saw Lio's eyes move just a little. His eyes did really move, a tiny bit, but they followed his monkey and the gloriously silly nurse holding it. The room shot full with light and there was nothing else in the world except the monkey, Dolorio, Lio and his slowly tracking eyes. It's difficult to express the joy that I experienced in that moment. The fact that Lio was simply opening his eyes like a four-year-old newborn infant was a tiny miracle and I wanted that moment to last forever.

But I didn't get the opportunity to savour it for long. On that same day, he was also scheduled to have surgery on his shattered leg. The bone had been pulverised and pieces of it had broken through the skin. Even though an earlier operation had closed the wound, something more drastic still needed to be done. Various anonymous paediatric orthopaedic surgeons came to study the case. X-rays in hand, they squinted, shook their heads, passed notes to each other and said the word 'amputation' in low, non-native voices. One mentioned fusing the leg so that Lio's knee would never bend again, another broke off from the group and showed me the X-rays, holding them up to the light.

'You can see here,' he began in a Greek accent, 'that his femur is completely crushed.'

There were more bone fragments on the film than I was able to count. 'Yes,' I said dryly and quickly.

'This also has implications for the knee,' he went on, 'because the fracture extends down through the growth plate into the joint, and because of his age it will be hard for us to put a rod in. He'll probably end up fairly soon with an external fixator on the outside of his leg until the bone has healed and then we'll have to re-evaluate things.'

'An external fixator?' I said, a bit annoyed. His leg was distracting me from staying focused on his brain.

'It's a series of metal bars that we put on with bolts.' He pulled out a spanner from his back pocket – a wrench exactly like I had in my toolbox at home. 'Eight-millimetre bolts that we put on with these, like a Meccano set.' A nervous little laugh escaped his lips. 'It might be an idea for you to get a couple of spanners too, so that we have them by his bedside if when we visit he needs tightening.'

The strangeness of what he was saying finally broke through to me. I turned to look at him in the face and said, 'Oh, OK. Tell me. Will he be able to walk?'

'It's early days yet. We can't say for certain. But I think you should probably not expect too much. Even if the fracture heals he will have lost at least two centimetres in length from the femur. If he does walk, he'll need a shoe lift.'

'If . . . a shoe lift?'

'I'll let the proper surgeon who'll do the operations fill you in on all the details. But I think these are all open questions.' He smiled, touched my arm with his hand and left with all the others. His words stuck in me like splinters. While Sasha and I had never dreamt of having a professional athlete for a son, we did climb mountains, and so had Lio. We had taken for granted a lifetime of walks laced with snow high up. These were now darkening in shadow. I remembered throwing a baseball with my own father in our front garden back in New Jersey both when I was a boy and when I was a man and he was much older. He coached me on glove position and eye contact and those moments, so simple and so pure, had always seemed something I would recreate with my own son. Naturally. Obviously. How foolish.

I felt a hand on my shoulder that pulled me up out of

this careening spiral. It was Nigel. He had also been in the room when the gaggle of orthopaedic surgeons had come and gone.

'So,' he said. 'Shall I go and get us some then? I've seen an ironmonger's near the coffee shop we go to a couple of blocks away.'

It took me a second to realise that he was talking about spanners. 'Yeah, that's a good idea.'

Nigel's furrowed brow had relaxed a bit, and a tiny flicker of a smile had pulled up the corners of his mouth for an instant. He was glad to be on familiar turf. He knew all about spanners and ironmongers. It was something real and tangible that he could do to help the situation, and it appealed to his deeply practical streak. Glad of the assignment, he turned on his heel and left me with Lio.

The surgeon slated to do the operation arrived an hour later. He was a good human being; I sensed that from the start. His name was Daniel Warren and it was clear that he really identified with us and felt for us. He was only a few years older than me, with young children of his own. Over the ensuing weeks, he brought Lio presents, spent lots of time with us and was completely unguarded with his advice later on about how and where we should have Lio's future leg surgery done – advice which he knew conflicted with his boss's. But, if I'm honest, one of my biggest regrets in those early days is not finding another, more experienced paediatric orthopaedic surgeon to do Lio's first operations. But how could I have done? There was no time, I was in no position to find someone else and the thought of doctor shopping on day one after the crash never even crossed my mind. At the end of our discussion about attaching the external fixator, he asked me if I had any questions and wanted me to sign the consent form.

I signed and he said, 'We're going to do everything we can.'

I looked him in the eye and said, 'I trust you.' As I spoke, I saw a tiny bit of uncertainty flash across his face, as if he was weighing up his limits against my hopes. (It was, it turns out, not the best leg reconstruction that could have been done.)

I said again quickly, 'I trust you,' simply to give him the confidence to do what he needed to do. Daniel, like me, did his best in the moment (which is what I must always tell myself whenever I start slipping into second-guessing – Sasha always and rightly got at me for second-guessing).

'Lio will walk,' I told myself. He will walk tall and straight and proud up to the podium to get his degrees one day. He will walk straight and steady and true down the aisle to take his wife's hand one day. And one day he'll walk long and steadily in the mountains with his own sons following after him. Lio would do his best, too.

When Lio returned from surgery, Dr Doom paid us a visit. She was simply astounded with Lio's progress and later admitted to my mother that she was badly wrong in those first days. I took that to mean that the sky was the limit in terms of his recovery. After the surgery, Lio was crying proper cries when medication was injected into his lines: these were not the unsettling animal-like grunts of a deep coma patient, but the cries of a child, a real child with real reactions to real pain. I never would have thought that a natural-sounding cry could have been such a tonic.

I always saw life going in a certain direction, following a certain path. You grow up in a loving family and spend most of your childhood in the same nice neighbourhood, maybe even near your grandparents. You live in a sweet, comfortable house with some green spaces nearby, nothing too big or glamorous but pleasant enough. Maybe you share a room with your brother and argue about whose music gets to be played while you're doing your homework.

Your family goes to church on Sundays, but as you grow your own beliefs evolve. You go away to university and see a bit of the world. After some adventures, maybe in graduate school, you find the girl of your dreams. You write poems to each other. You buy each other the books you loved when you were children. Then you find jobs, you get married and you have a family. Your careers blossom, nothing too grand but you have your moments when you feel like you can do no wrong. Your children grow up, you marvel at their accomplishments, they go off to uni and then another link in the chain stretches out through time. You retire and have some more adventures or even a second career without the pressures of the first. You creep into your late 80s and then you die quietly and peacefully a few years apart. You're buried side by side in the same family plot, where your spirits smile down on the lives of your descendants and on your bones turning to dust together slowly over the centuries.

That was the unstated plan, the series of normal and beautiful events that my life fell into. My actions were organised to make these things happen, my decisions propelled me along that path, but those things, exactly as I've described them, seemed to fall into my hands without too much effort. It wasn't something I dreamt: it was a way of life and it was so natural I didn't even think about it. I never once considered how tenuous it was. Beautiful and pleasant, it was a life with more joy than pain. And then, one thoughtless September morning, through no fault of my own or my wife's or our son's, everything was blasted apart. That sweet and natural life exploded into thousands of pieces, like the tiny shards of glass that were still coming out of Lio's scalp months after the crash.

After more than a week of hospital food, my mother, Penny and Nigel agreed to sit beside Lio while I went out for a meal. I found a little Thai restaurant on Cold Harbour

Lane just two blocks away. It was yellow and green with golden elephants in the window and was called the Su-Thai. It promised real food. Inside there was a large fountain just to the left as you went through the door, a door that swung shut too quickly and too forcefully after you let it go, with a loud bang that followed if you weren't careful. There were large lounging Buddhas scattered around and the tables were from Ikea. It was perfectly comfortable.

This was my first opportunity to order alcohol since the accident and I remember, oddly, not wanting any. The thought of a glass of wine was completely unappealing and even made me a bit queasy. Sasha and I always had a glass of wine when we went out; it was something we did without even thinking about it – unless there was a reason not to. But here, for the first time in nearly a decade, I simply did not want a drink. It wasn't as if I made the conscious decision to not drink (which I might well have made given the circumstances and wanting to stay absolutely clear-headed about the medical goings-on all the time), it was more as if my body was rejecting it somehow. It was as if my organs themselves recognised something new about my situation, physically and emotionally, and simply said 'no'.

I ordered the Penang chicken curry with brown rice and a small bottle of sparkling water. When my glass arrived, I sat there staring at it, thinking about all those evenings out with my wife: the choosing a table, the decisions about what to order (she had a real knack and I often regretted not getting what she did), the talk about Lio, the planning our holidays, the intense and serious academic conversations we had about romantic poetry, Shakespeare, capitalism, advertising, the culture industry, language, German idealism, radio, Henry Moore, sound poetry, Joan Miró, aesthetics and (above all, in recent months) the idea of beauty – of what constituted something beautiful and how we appreciated it. She was working on a book about beauty and every night we went out and every time we met friends, in England, Italy and America, she wanted to talk about 'the beautiful'. She was, in most of these conversations, intent on saving beauty from the critical rubbish heap, wanting to reclaim it and salvage it from those who said (as most academics might) that beauty was a worn-out concept, something best left to fashion magazines and to people without the critical faculties to see beyond their own cultural constructions. She wanted to save it as a category of living and sophisticated adult appreciation, of physical pleasure, of joy and of life over death. The best and most confident writing of her life, about beauty, was done the week before she died:

> Death is our common end; our conclusion; our ultimatum. But death is not our *raison d'être*. Life, by contrast, is not only worth living for, but worth dying for. And so it is not death that makes the beautiful flower possible, but life.
>
> And yes, love grows as our understanding of death deepens. But love's growth also exceeds death. It's not just that love continues beyond the grave; that love outlasts death (this we know), but love can grow in ways other than through the comprehension of death, in all its limitation and expansion. Love can also grow with love. I risk loving more and I am loved back; and so I have more love to give. And all the while, I have not been thinking on death.
>
> Is it only death that makes life meaningful? Only in the cruel present: in the confrontation of the death of loved ones and strangers, in beds and streets. And death does not have the reach to explain the meaningfulness of life, love, and beauty in all their infinite variety.

For instance: when does consciousness of mortality begin? Is a child conscious of mortality? If not, by your argument the child cannot perceive beauty or love. This cannot be right. A little boy who does not yet understand death (it has not been part of his cruel present) still tells me: my love for you is strong, and good, and beautiful. Is he wrong?

And so let me give you death, if you give me change.

And let me give you pain, if you give me joy.

These words written days (maybe even hours) before she died are utterly uncanny. When I'm faced with them, I can't help but read into them a prescience about her own death and an echoing message to me about the importance of living a beautiful life not in the face of death but in almost the erasure of it. As I sat staring at the bubbles climbing up the sides of my glass, those hundreds of dinner-table conversations about beauty ran through my mind and reverberated softly in my ears. I missed her company excruciatingly in that moment. She was clever and witty, with penetrating insight and an intense and honest commitment to wrestling with big ideas. This was Sasha, my wife, out at dinner over a glass of Côtes du Rhône and a plate of mixed mezze. I matched her as best I could, most often playing devil's advocate to her more elegant and sustained lines of thinking. She was passionate, and once she got going it was hard to stop her – occasionally, I'll admit, to my own exasperation.

I looked over at the vacant chair across from me. With tremendous effort, I mustered a smile, and raised my glass to the emptiness. I believed then as I do now that she was there with me, that she is by my side helping me, guiding me, working on Lio's recovery and delighting in all our joys and accomplishments. I long to do those things that we did together, even if I have to do them on my own, because when I do things that we enjoyed – going out to eat, climbing mountains, walking in the woods, visiting tiny Italian churches and chapels, speaking Italian, sledding in the snow, eating sushi – it makes me feel closer to her. In doing these things, I'm in contact with her and that lightens me. When I experience something beautiful that we might have done together, like listening to some small choral group singing in some little Italian mountain town, I smile because I feel her presence. Understandably though, others cry at these same moments because they feel her absence.

While I was out at the restaurant and trying to sleep later that night, according to his grandparents, Lio got extremely agitated. As had become our routine, my mother stayed until 2 a.m., then Nigel came, and then Penny took over at about 5 a.m. As they sat by him and tried to comfort him, he would jerk and fit and clench, or, worse yet, simply stare at them blankly through half-opened unblinking lids. The agitation, a late-night neurologist doing rounds assured us, was a completely natural part of the recovery. It was a sign of the brain trying to sort itself out and to heal itself. Ghastly as it was to watch, it was a good thing.

It was around the middle of the second week after the crash that I began to feel a positive energy flow back to me from the nurses, therapists, doctors and other parents. Sasha's inexplicable last words to me – 'Don't let these pessimistic Brits get you down' – had been steadily ringing in my ears and I made an effort to keep them in mind every waking moment. My smile, my tall pose, my gliding on air were all a part of it and just might well have been infectious. One of the nurses, Lio's favourite, Nurse Amy, took me aside one morning.

'Do you know how well he's doing?' she whispered almost furtively.

'Nicely, I hope,' I said, not knowing how to respond.

'No,' she said. 'He's making *amazing* progress.'

'You have no idea how happy I am to hear that,' I smiled and focused on her words.

'Really,' she continued, 'he's giving us positive sign after positive sign and your whole family is doing everything right. Absolutely everything.'

My heart bounced and I felt a tiny bit dizzy. This little grain of encouragement and validation of all our reading to him and singing to him and telling him stories and massaging him was beyond heartening, especially coming as it did from the hyper-cautious medical establishment (albeit from the mouth of a junior nurse). If Lio was to be saved, he was going to be saved by his family as much as he was by any medical intervention – a formal medical report written several months down the line would say exactly that. Shortly after my chat with Amy, Marianne, Lio's Zulu-speaking nurse from intensive care, came by and said that from what she'd seen and heard she was expecting phenomenal things for Lio's progress. Apparently, the doctors and nurses were talking amongst themselves about how well Lio was doing. After a horribly difficult night I was being flooded with positive impressions and feelings. It was a turning point in Lio's recovery, ten days after the crash, and I felt like everyone who approached him now shared my vision of his full, happy and rewarding future. With Sasha's last words swirling in my mind, and with evidence lying in the bed in front of me, I became convinced, unequivocally there and then, that outlook influences outcome.

After it was clear that Lio was going to survive and also clear we were going to be in the hospital for a very long time, a social worker offered us a flat owned by the Rhys Daniels Trust, a charity that maintains houses near paediatric hospitals in the UK for families to use in situations like ours. It was a tiny one-bedroom place with a threadbare sofa, dingy grey-beige carpet, posters from Woolworths on the walls and plastic cutlery in the drawers. I have never been so grateful for an accommodation in my life. It was our little bolt-hole away from the stress of the hospital. I wanted to be home again, but I didn't at the same time, knowing that returning would be immensely difficult. So our little apartment, our little beleaguered one-bedroom wedged in between sweet Victorian terraced houses and a brutish high-rise of council flats, was a limbo I accepted with all the grace I had. Every morning on my way to hospital I would pass a small primary school. And every time I passed I would think about Lio in that school. Each week saw more and more rainbows and sheep and paper houses added to the windows and walls inside, and each week I would imagine Lio cutting and pasting and colouring with classmates.

He had been scheduled to start school only four days after the crash. And, if the reports from his nursery school teachers were to be believed, he was meant to be at the head of his class. This was one of the hardest images to keep in my mind, seeing him day in and day out in a coma. Shortly he would be going to school, yes; but it would be the school in the hospital, with other children from the paediatric neurological ward. In between therapies and doctors' visits, I did want him in school, certainly, but I was unsure about the school on the fifth floor of King's College Hospital. When I eventually met them, the teachers there were very friendly, but I didn't know if I wanted Lio identifying with other children suffering from other neurological issues. This was the dilemma that tests, and sometimes makes hypocrites out of so many well-meaning, socially progressive people: educational inclusion is a wonderful thing until it threatens to put downward pressure on your own child's development. But then I thought again about Lio going to the school he was meant to go to near home and about how he might be one of the ones that other parents were concerned to have around their children – I lost myself for hours in these mental acrobatics. Given that only a week ago a doctor had told me that there was no chance of Lio ever attending a normal school, I decided to simply slow down my racing worries and, when the time came, embrace the school at the hospital all the while keeping the vision of Lio doing fantastically well one day at university firmly in the front of my mind.

As a small child, he had (often annoyingly) an unrestrained curiosity. And while this sometimes led to tears, like when he touched one of those electric ribbons around a small enclosure of baby goats up in the mountains, it also led him to experiences beyond his years and to try new things that very few small children try. During our last holiday together as a family on an island just off the west coast of France, I had ordered some oysters for dinner – fresh, local, *raw* oysters. Lio, far from being put off by these slippery grey globs on half shells, was fascinated by them. He simply had to try one. So I put one on his tongue and, after it slid down, he smiled and said, '*Mi piace*' ('I like that'). His eager eyes flashed around my plate, but I wasn't going to offer him another. Now, as he lay still twitching slightly in his hospital bed, I had to believe that the boy with wonder in his eyes, with the desire to try new things, and with the desire to simply *try*, remained.

On Sunday, 17 September, ten days after the crash, while Lio's bed was about to be changed, I manoeuvred myself around the remaining tubes and wires and slid my hand under his back up to his neck. I put my other arm under his knees and gently lifted him up onto my lap as I sat down in the chair beside his bed. The warmth and the softness of his skin on my hands were reassuring. Then it happened again. I was just holding him and thinking about how nice it would be when the IV tubes finally came out of his arms, about his therapy session later to loosen his muscles, about what I was going to ask the neurologist when I saw him next, and a thousand other things. I don't know whether they were focused or not, but he did open his eyes again. He looked at me. Everything else in the world stopped and I was looking clearly and directly into his deep blues for the first time since the crash. His eyes had always been so alive and expressive, yet today I was overjoyed simply in their colour. After seeing me hold him, my mother wrote in her journal that the sight of Lio draped in my arms reminded her of the *Pietà*, the famous Michelangelo sculpture of Mary holding Jesus after the crucifixion. She wrote, 'Lio will come back to us too.'

At times it's extremely hard for me to read her words when she writes like this. It's as if the writing and the reading of them make the thing they suggest less true or less possible. It's almost as if that most famous Christian miracle, like the miracle of Lio's coming back from near death, are undone somehow when you put them into words. This is perhaps my problem more than it is my mother's. But in her attempts to describe the ineffable, the indescribable, she can bring me a little crisis of faith because my education (or maybe over-education) had taught me that words are slippery things that often conceal as much as they express. Penny had a less complex reaction to seeing Lio in my arms: she wrote in her diary simply how beautiful it looked. There is something spiritual in that as well.

Part 2

We should have confidence in being. We don't always need to think our being. The beautiful can strike us, touch us, precisely in ways we cannot theorise – except in retrospect. In the after-being of the beautiful moment your hairs stand on end. Tears fall out of my eyes when the cathedral stones sing, and I don't even know how I began to cry. And at that moment, at that sensation – for the aesthetic is sensation – I and maybe even you are not thinking, reflecting, on death or change.

This is why the beautiful doesn't always need consciousness of death, or change. The beautiful is, and should be above all, an act of being; not an art of theorising. Sometimes the beautiful does not need the intellect.

– Sasha Roberts

Chocolate Mousse

Perhaps it was the result of the music we were playing during his massages, perhaps it was the result of the Italian songs I was singing to him over and over, perhaps it was simply his brain slowly and naturally healing, but ten days after the crash Lio's muscles seemed less tense, his fists were less clenched, his arms were less rigid, he was much more relaxed and supple than he had been. But he was also more alert; in fact, he was showing the first signs of real consciousness since the accident. In one of his more switched-on moments, I slipped the iPod headphones on him and scrolled down to 'Bongo Bong' (again). Penny held up Lio's monkey and moved it around at the end of the bed. Lio was, without a doubt this time, watching the monkey and following it! There was absolutely no doubt about it this time. His eyeballs moved left to right and then up and down. The whole scene had the feel of some bizarre laboratory experiment. The strangeness of it, shot through with pure elation, was almost too much for me to process and I felt light-headed and slightly tense in the chest. We buzzed around and told everyone on the ward, we grabbed nurses and other parents and dragged them over to Lio's bedside to see his eyes move. It was almost as if we were kids ourselves and had created a machine with moving eyes; we wanted everyone to know about it and to congratulate us. And they did.

That afternoon saw another decrease in the morphine. While this meant longer periods of alertness, it also meant more pain for Lio. I tried to distract him by telling him stories – his eyes now wincing shut or cracked only a tiny sliver. I told him the tales of Piccolo Mugnaio, Cavaliere Lio and Pampalin that we had spun at bedtimes when we were out at the mill. I was reweaving a storyline that Sasha had started about Pampalin finding magic berries that soften the hearts of cruel kings when the corners of his mouth rose into a little smile. It was a tiny thing, but it happened. Beyond a shadow of a doubt, it happened. He smiled. He smiled for the first time in more than a week. His little face was happy. At times over the past days even I, when consumed by doubt and fear, wondered whether or not I'd ever see him smile again. But he did and he was. It was such an awe-inspiring reward after days of fret and anxiety and of sheer force of will exerting itself to be positive. Such a little thing: a four year old's smile. This time serenely, with less urgency and more simple, sweet confidence, we told the nurses about Lio's smile. I knew in that moment (even if others might have needed a bit more convincing) that Lio would be all right. In fact, he would be more than all right, he would be exceptional. His recovery was already exceptional. The nurses, for their part, seemed now to expect it too. They were happy with us and happy for us.

From the beginning, I was torn about what I should be reading. From the very first days in intensive care I swung between wanting to learn everything I could about Lio's medical condition and wanting to see Lio recovering in my mind. These two needs often didn't sit well together. In the end, the more I read and the more I searched the internet about paediatric brain injury, the harder it was to hold on to my vision of Lio's future. I was an academic. I had lived by books and my curiosity about what they might have to say was eating at me. But I was also very frightened about what they might expose us to. I don't know where it came from, but I believed somehow that I could *think* Lio better, that my image of him as a fit, active, clever little boy among his friends was as important to his future well-being as anything flowing through his intravenous lines. I worried that poking around too much in the literature might jeopardise that frame of mind. But I gave in. And, precisely as I had feared, the more I learned about oedema and brain haemorrhages and axonal injury, the more my vision of a completely healthy and happy Lio graduating at the top of his class took a beating.

These books were beyond scary. They were torture. They described profound and irrevocable changes the likes of which were too horrifying to contemplate fully. For example:

'Severe brain injury may result in paralysis, lack of motor control, lack of language function and continued seizures.'

'Patients with severe traumatic brain injury can occasionally be left in a persistent vegetative state.'

'Although the child may improve with time, significant impairments will be a permanent feature.'

'The result is the immediate loss of the function of the neuron and its death.'

'If certain of these limbic structures, particularly the hippocampus, are destroyed or even damaged, no new declarative memories can be formed.'

'The consequences of frontal and pre-frontal lobe injuries include consistent lack of emotional control, lack of an ability to self-regulate and an inability to control impulses.'

'If there is a concern that a brain-injured child might attempt to leave the home unsupervised, then dead-bolt locks should be installed on all external doors.'

The list of dire inevitabilities and terrible future scenarios in writing on brain injury is endless. As I read the words about permanent impairments, about the lack of reasoning and self-control, about the violent behaviour associated with Lio's type of frontal-lobe damage, about the language deficits in his type of left temporal-lobe damage, about the shortcomings in abstract reasoning as a result of his type of corpus callosum damage, my belief in Lio's recovery began to wobble.

It was a mistake to read too much. And beyond that, it was a mistake to let it interfere with my feelings and my vision for Lio's well-being and recovery. Obviously, I needed to know what was going on at some physical, material, medical level. Obviously, I needed to know what the doctors thought, but I needed to know as well that there was a possibility that he might recover. Doctors don't know and can't know everything. They have the impossible job of being half scientist and half interpreter; books are even worse in that they can never appreciate the nuances of a given situation; they aren't standing over my son reading the subtle signs. Predictions in these books only map on to his coma scale reading and his intracranial pressure. They really can't help to understand the particularities of your specific case. So, in spite of the fact that I knew Lio had a severe brain injury, I also knew as certainly as I knew his birthday that the things I was reading did not apply. At least they did not apply for Lio. That's what I told myself and that's what I tried to hold on to.

But having braved the research, I then had this gnawing compulsion to put the precise numbers and precise details of Lio's medical reports together with what the books were saying. I knew it would be painful, damaging even, but I couldn't resist.

When I started, it was as if I was reading a novel; it was as if the text in front of my eyes was about some other child, in some other country, from some other time. I recognised the wounds on my son's head and leg as evidence of the injuries written about in the reports and intellectually I knew that he was the subject. But the detachment of the language made it impossible for me to put Lio's face on the printed words. Now, as at so many other points along this journey, these scientific calculations seemed self-evidently incomplete. They seemed an almost totally irrelevant way to relate to and come to terms with what was happening in our lives. An early neurologist's report starts like this:

Severe head injury secondary to motor vehicle accident 7.9.06, GCS 4/15 at scene, peak ICP 33, lowest CPP 29; extubated Day 4, seizures on PICU.

Evidence of diffuse shear injury on neuro-imaging, early EEG consistent with diffuse encephalopathy.

Comminuted fracture left femur requiring external fixation and subsequent out-patient orthopaedic surgery with residual leg shortening.

The numbers themselves, without their contexts, are meaningless, like scores for a sports match you've never seen before. GCS, Glasgow Coma Scale, is perhaps the scariest. It ranges from 3 to 15, with 15 being fully awake and alert and 3 being absolutely unresponsive to any kind of stimuli: speaking, shouting, causing pain, shining a light in the eyes, bending and hyper extending joints, etc. Lio's score was a 4. ICP is Intracranial Pressure. After a brain injury like Lio's, there is usually a small sensor inserted to check the fluid pressure inside the head. Optimal ICP is between 7 and 15. An ICP of more than 25 for an extended period of time is fatal. Lio's peak ICP was 33. CPP is Cerebral Perfusion Pressure and is a measure of blood flow to the brain. Children require a consistent CPP of 60 to stay alive. Lio's lowest was 29.

119

Page three of this report summarises the details of Lio's CT scans – the layered images that give a three-dimensional picture of what is happening inside the head. It says, in short, that Lio was facing injuries to: the right frontal lobe, the left thalamus, the left hippocampus, the right parietal lobe, the corpus callosum and the left temporal lobe.

I had reached a point of no return. After sorting out what all the numbers meant, I went back to the neurological textbooks. Here's what they say about damage in the places where Lio had his injuries:

Right frontal lobe: There are a variety of different centres here which are involved in a wide range of functions: emotional responses, reasoning, planning, creativity, problem solving, judgment, initiating social encounters, impulse control, concentration, interpreting the environment, rule following, sexual behaviour and risk assessment. Damage to the right frontal lobe tends not to affect traditional IQ but can affect learning from experience, a sense of propriety and social conformity.

Left thalamus: The thalamus is found deep in the brain and is a relay station for stimuli that come in from the outside world. The thalamus sorts these stimuli and sends signals to other parts of the brain for a response. Damage to the thalamus can affect levels of arousal and alertness, motor skills and coordination, and can cause an inability to sense things in the world and hyperactivity.

Left hippocampus: The hippocampus plays a major role in short-term memory, spatial navigation and (according to some) inhibition and the regulation of negative behaviour. It is sometimes referred to as the 'cognitive map' and is used in locating yourself in the physical world. Damage to the hippocampus can result in disorientation, hyperactivity, the failure to lay down new memories and in some cases amnesia.

Corpus callosum: This is the connecting bridge between the two hemispheres of the brain. The corpus callosum works in memory retrieval as different parts of the brain on different sides communicate with each other. Damage to the corpus callosum can cause difficulties with abstract linguistic thinking later in life, as language tends to lateralise to one side of the brain or the other at some point from four to six years of age. This lateralisation is necessary for more complex language development to occur. (Lio was four years and nine months when the accident happened.)

Left temporal lobe: Above the left ear, the left temporal lobe is responsible primarily for language and speech. In addition it's used in the generation of meaning, categorisation of objects, verbal memory, narrative memory and comprehension, organisational skills and the regulation of aggression.

Right parietal: On the right top of the head, the right parietal lobe is used in handwriting and drawing, hand–eye coordination, spatial reasoning and perception, building things and processing information about the state and position of parts of the body.

Completing the equation of *Reports + Textbooks = Lio's Future* left me sleepless again and pale with fear.

But it shouldn't have. I need only have looked at the

little Lio in front of me to realise that there was a mistake in the calculus. Neither Lio nor his future could have ever been the sum of case notes and textbooks. And after several days of anxiety the Lio I knew began to eclipse once again the Lio of medical formulas and bar graphs. Although my mind remained troubled by them, I worked tenaciously hard to not let the reports and the books cripple me. I took to meditating, as Sasha had introduced me to it a few years before. Nearly every morning I would sit on the floor at the end of the bed in our little borrowed flat, cross my legs, straighten my back, put my hands on my knees, close my eyes and force all thoughts about doctors' comments and medical reports out of my mind. I would conjure up waves of good feeling at the sight of my future Lio, happy and healthy, running with great strides and thinking great thoughts.

Yet I would be lying if I said my defences never slipped and, try as I might, the combination of Lio's reports and the existing research continued to gnaw quietly at my imagination. I was a person of the written word – and the written word, especially coming, as it did, in hard-bound, conservatively illustrated medical textbooks written by people with spoonfuls of letters after their names, intimidated me. But in the end I took a lesson from graduate school and found I could read them not as infallible sacred documents but as texts that could be pushed, interpreted and challenged in lots of different ways.

In getting to grips with these books, it was very useful for me to remember who their authors and audiences were. They were written by medical professionals for medical professionals – extremely stressed, extremely over-worked medical professionals. They were written to guide them through these types of injuries, to make their jobs easier and even (occasionally) to help them interface with families experiencing intense crises. Although I'm sure neither the authors nor the intended readers would articulate things this way, and I'm certain this isn't anyone's intention, part of making their jobs easier is lowering families' expectations. If parents' expectations are low, goes the unstated assumption, parents will demand less of limited resources and make fewer impositions on doctors' scarce reserves of time.

This tendency to lower expectations *is not in any way* a doctor's fault; the doctors we came into contact with were among the most well-meaning people I've ever met. But some of them realised their own limits too readily for me as a father of a child with a fractured skull, limits of what they had the time, the expertise and the technology to do. Compounding the doctors' problem is the dense and sometimes conflicting forest of research out there and how best to apply it to a particular child. To complicate things, researchers are expanding that forest all the time. Work on the human brain is certainly the most ambitious and most complex frontier of medical science. This stuff is really difficult. I empathised with Lio's doctors as I began to try to crack it myself.

It wasn't too long before I found some research published in electronic journals that cried out for me to understand it. While orthodox interpretations of existing data have said for many years that most of the brain does not regenerate itself, there is an increasing body of work which argues against that conventional wisdom. And there is already widespread agreement that the brain can 'rewire' itself for messages to find new pathways where other pathways have been disrupted, as well as evidence which suggests that the brain is much more like a muscle than previously thought, in that exercising parts of it can make them stronger.

But the orthodoxy remains difficult to shift. Take, for example, a recent study about the hippocampus, an area where Lio had damage. Reputedly, the chief function of this part of the brain is locating yourself in the world, remembering the location of things, and physical orientation and navigation. The study looked at the hippocampi of hundreds of London taxi drivers by taking scans of their brains and revealed that their hippocampi were slightly larger and had a slightly different shape than the hippocampi of the general public.

I read this study and thought, 'That's great! Through "exercise" these taxi drivers had developed the part of the brain they use the most. Their job was like a "workout" for their hippocampi and they were physically more (or at least differently) developed as a result.'

But in the last paragraph of the article the authors warn against exactly this interpretation. They said that their study should not be read to imply that the hippocampi changed as a result of the cabbies' jobs. An equally plausible reading, they suggest, was that people with well-developed hippocampi, with a good ability to find themselves in the physical world, are simply drawn to work as taxi drivers. This interpretation certainly follows the rules of 'good science' and 'good statistical analysis' – we can't *necessarily* make a connection between taxi driving and a particular kind of brain development. But where the science of this study might follow the rules, its cultural analysis is very naive. It's naive because it doesn't recognise a pretty basic reality about the career of taxi driving: driving a cab is not so much a 'calling' as it is a job people do on their way to or on top of something else that they really feel drawn to do. Most of the taxi drivers I've spoken with over the years are or were something else *before they were taxi drivers*: immigrant professionals in other things who couldn't get licensed to practise their specialities in their adoptive countries, or inventors, or artists, or musicians, or actors, or football players, or radio producers, or dancers, or entrepreneurs squirrelling away money to start their own businesses *doing something else*. At least that's what they've always told me through the glass. It's not so much a vocation as it is a catch-all. This study's authors hadn't understood this and it reminded me that science alone would only ever take Lio and me so far.

I should have left the medical books and journals to the doctors, especially in those first weeks. Instead I should have read books on meditation and visualisation, books on the power of the body to heal itself and books about the astonishing recoveries of others. These are no more or less correct, no more or less abstract, than the books that catalogue physical signs and tell you what to expect. Lio was never a statistic, never a compilation of data or the sum of a mathematical equation. And there, on his hospital bed in the high-dependency ward, he had already proved it by living when doctors were preparing us for him dying; he proved it by getting out of intensive care when others were preparing us for a never-ending coma; and he would keep proving it in the months to come – of that I convinced myself I was certain. What made me so sure? Lio had been exceptional since the day he was born and no amount of brain damage was going to change that. He was, in some disastrously bizarre way, the perfect boy to be in this situation.

The next day, after Lio's EKG leads were removed, an impish-looking character with bright eyes and spiky red hair arrived. She was to be Lio's speech and language therapist. From my point of view, speech and language seemed a very long way off, but I was delighted that people were thinking about that possibility so soon.

'Hello, Lio,' she said, batting her thickly lined eyes at his expressionless face. 'My name is Miranda and I want to check how your throat is working.'

She put her stethoscope in her ears and put the business end up to Lio's neck. She listened with real concentration for what seemed like minutes.

'Lio, what's your favourite thing to eat?' she said and, oddly, waited for a response.

'Chocolate,' I said, bemused. 'Lio really likes chocolate.' But then I could have sworn I saw a tiny flicker of recognition flash across his face.

'Oh yeah? So do my little boys,' she said as she faced me. 'Well then, maybe one day soon we can try a little chocolate mousse experiment.'

'Wow!' I blurted out. The thought of Lio eating *real food* (or at least the cafeteria's chocolate mousse) *with his mouth* instead of the grey formula going down his nose through his feeding tube sent shudders through me. I didn't know how it would happen; he wasn't moving, his face was almost completely non-responsive, but just the prospect of it coming from this Miranda lifted another shadow. It was another step towards the door.

All of the little milestones that he'd passed through in his first four years of life he would pass through again in that hospital. He opened his eyes, then he focused and then he smiled. And each time he did one of these things my heart raced and I felt the same wonder that I'd felt when I'd seen him do these things as a newborn. The feeling was virtually identical, except this second time around the joy was multiplied because I took nothing for granted. As the parent of a new baby, you're thrilled when your child smiles for the first time, but you expect it to happen and it is perfectly natural that it does. This time that expectation was shot through with apprehension that he might not be able to take the next natural step, that he might not be able to do the next natural thing. But as he reclaimed his abilities, like eating real food, I was grateful in a way I couldn't possibly have been before.

On Tuesday, 19 September, 12 days after the crash, they removed the stitches from Lio's head and washed his hair, which was still matted with blood and tiny bits of broken glass. As they did this, he began to look more human, less like some little ghost. As we prepared for the soap and water, Nurse Amy was talking to Lio in her bubbly and slightly cartoony voice while making funny faces at him as I held him in my lap. He laughed; he laughed his first proper and real laugh in nearly two weeks.

Other little medical adjustments continued to happen: this day saw the last of his antibiotics. They altered what went down his feeding tube, switching him on and off between milk formula and electrolytes; and they continued to lessen the morphine, which meant he was 'awake' a good part of the day – sluggish and unresponsive and still in a coma, but he was regaining consciousness, with tiny tortured expressions splitting his face. I did what I could. I tinkered with his position on the bed and his acoustic massage treatments. I adjusted the way I stroked his skin and my grip on his legs. Hundreds of times I changed what I read to him and what I sang to him and the stories about what we were going to do when he got out of hospital. The only thing I didn't adjust was my vision of him as happy and well. Throughout all of this I kept reminding myself that this was not just an average brain injury case, this was Lio Spinelli, remarkable boy of life and languages and curiosity and joy. And I believed fully that he was going to leave this terrible episode an even greater person than he was before. Maybe because of the emotional experience he was forced to gain, maybe because he'd now have unwavering faith in his own ability to heal and to pull himself out of horrendous places, or maybe because of my absolutely undivided attention, but he was not going to come out of this simply OK, he was going to come out of this amazingly well. Together, Lio and I were going to make the best of this situation and turn it into something good and positive, something worthy of his mother. That's what I said to myself and it had got us this far.

The next day, they took Lio off the steady morphine drip but left him with a system of controlled morphine-on-demand. Then Amy got him ready for a sponge bath. Smiles were coming to his lips and his face showed a flash of surprise when the cool water hit his skin. Later the occupational therapist came in and put him in the chair with straps to hold him in and upright. She held his purple dragon in front of him and moved it from side to side. He followed it with his eyes and head. The physiotherapist Nikki came in later and sat him (held him) on the edge of his bed. He could support his head for a few seconds, but when it fell forward it was impossible for him to lift it up again. He seemed to really concentrate on a story while Nikki was doing some muscle coordination exercises. All the therapists heaped praise on him when they put him back into bed. And at that moment, I thought – vaguely and through muted expressions – that he looked proud of himself. He beamed a tiny little bit. He was positively pleased to have done something and to have been congratulated for it. My eyes misted.

But equally emotional for me were the obvious traces of frustration on my little boy's face when he wasn't able to do things that he'd previously been able to, like communicate or even raise his head. This, worse than his winces of pain, was the hardest thing for me to watch day after day. It tore my guts out to see him struggling and getting angry with himself. However, when the nurses told the neurologist McCormick about Lio's bouts of frustration he seemed pleased. This was an encouraging sign in that it showed he was trying. It was another little gift to me. I had been radiating good thoughts about his recovery and expecting improvements and projecting those feelings in every breath I took. And now a little of that had come back to me when I hadn't expected it.

Two weeks after the crash, before Miranda was scheduled to come by the next time, I asked my mother to go down to the cafeteria and buy a little tub of chocolate mousse in the hope that Miranda would be ready for what she had proposed the day before. When Miranda came in, I must have been smiling a bit, I must have been letting a bit of childish excitement show.

She grinned at us and said, 'So, what have you two been up to, then?'

I couldn't contain myself and just blurted out, 'We've got some chocolate mousse and a spoon.' Her face blinked from puzzled to concerned to gently warm and comforting in a matter of seconds.

'OK,' she said. 'Let's see if it's worth a try.'

While she checked Lio's throat again with her stethoscope, I peeled back the lid on the mousse and held it and the spoon out ceremoniously for her. But the scene didn't unfold at all as I had expected. Miranda put a bit of the dark brown gloop on the end of the spoon and held it, teasingly, cruelly, about a half-inch from Lio's unmoving mouth.

'This is chocolate, Lio. Would you like some?' she said.

Lio clearly saw it and knew what it was but couldn't quite reach for it. A tiny squeak of exasperation passed his lips. After a couple of minutes, and considering all he had been through, this scene struck me as callous: offering him chocolate, tempting him, taunting him with it almost, but not properly giving it to him. I shifted my weight from one foot to the other and Miranda could see that I was agitated. After about a minute of this teasing, she put a tiny amount on his lips. He did manage to suck a bit of it in, but he wasn't able to lick his lips. Getting it in his mouth was a good start, of course, but I desperately wanted him to be rewarded with a bit of chocolate mousse. And he desperately wanted it too. The throaty rattles that came out of Lio at that moment were not recognisable four-year-old sounds; they were wizened and piercing in their yearning.

Miranda certainly wasn't cruel: she was just doing what needed to be done clinically, using Lio's desire for chocolate to spur him on to more progress.

She turned to me, put a hand on my jittering forearm and said in a soothing way, 'So far, so good.' She gave me a warm smile and left, looking pleased.

I stared down at the floor and couldn't wait for her to go. After I made sure she was on her way down the corridor, I picked up the chocolate and the spoon, looked around to check that no one was watching, pulled down Lio's jaw with my fingers, put about a teaspoon of it on his tongue and closed his mouth. His bruised eyes opened fully and I'd like to say that he smiled. I wiped his face clean and held his cheeks in my hands.

During medical rounds that day, McCormick led in his entourage of nurses, therapists and junior doctors, who all crowded around Lio's bed. McCormick asked Lio to try to follow his finger as he moved it in front of him, the nurses made little gasps of delight and some of the other doctors looked at me with a mix of astonishment and satisfaction as Lio managed it for a few passes. I raised an eyebrow. Miranda then told them about how he had managed to suck in a drop of chocolate. This also impressed them. I, however, was not completely satisfied. I knew he was going to improve and was expecting more. His recovery, startling in its pace to the professionals, wasn't happening fast enough for me.

But when they left Lio and me alone again I leaned over him and softly whispered in his ear, 'I am so very, very proud of you.' I smiled and he looked at me.

Later that day one of the junior doctors was with us when Lio shakily attempted to scratch his head where his stitches had been.

'Look at that,' she said. 'That's incredible.'

She then explained to me the complexity of the neurological processes in which his brain had to first recognise where he was itching and then manage to get his fingers to that spot and scratch. Today, she also noted, Lio was recognising voices and faces and smiling more readily. His arm and leg movements were no longer wild and violent but more purposeful. He pulled his feeding tube out and it had to be replaced – another good sign. But all these movements and all the therapy were wearing him out. Both physiotherapy and speech and language therapy had to be truncated on day 14 because he would just fade back into being totally catatonic. Part of the reason for this might have been that he was no longer getting any morphine at all. Chemical withdrawal was making him tired. He'd been having difficulty settling at nights, which may also have contributed to his relapses back into deeper coma during the day.

The following morning Lio seemed to have regained his therapy groove. His actions were coordinated enough to reach for a toy that the occupational therapist was holding out in front of him. She would say 'bear' or 'monkey' and Lio would reach out and touch the correct toy. Later in the session he could even grab it and then give it back when asked. And at the end of physical therapy that day he managed to give the thumbs-up sign. I danced, spread my palms and looked up at the sky. I was ecstatic.

On Sasha's initiative, she and I had managed to teach Lio pre-verbal toddler sign language. We started with signs for 'hungry' and 'tired' before he was one year old: closed fingers of one hand going up to the mouth indicating hungry; a hand on the side of the cheek with head tilting slightly for tired, stiff fingers of one hand repeatedly poking the open palm of the other to sign for 'more'. I must admit I was unconvinced at first because she seemed to be signing to him for weeks without result, but it finally took hold and I remember how thoroughly impressed I was (with both of them) when he first signed for hungry. Only then did I really get into it. Now, beyond easing frustrations, reducing tantrums and generally lowering stress while Lio was a toddler, this signing proved absolutely indispensable in communicating with Lio while he was still in his non-speaking recovery phase. It was something that I came to think of as another little gift Sasha had given us both to use after she'd gone; it was as if she knew we were going to need it again some day. To see him, if not happy, at least spared the humiliation of not being able to communicate his most basic needs, to have him (a little boy who proudly spoke two languages well above his age level) spared the indignity and difficulty of not being able to speak at all, was a blessing beyond words. And we embraced it. I was proud of Lio as he managed these gestures, prouder than *any father* had ever been at the first words of their little child. My mother's diary says simply, 'Today was a big day.'

Yet after more than two weeks of pain and extremely hard work, the war going on inside Lio between what he wanted to do and what his muscles would let him do became increasingly upsetting. One lunchtime he whined after I'd put a spoon in his hand and he couldn't make it find the bowl. So I brought it down to the custard for him, and brought it up again to his mouth. He did manage to open his mouth a little bit and pucker his lips. He sucked it in and swallowed, and although he still wasn't able to lick his lips, he did what he needed to do. Later that day my mother asked him if he would like an ice cream and he smiled, wide this time. When she returned, she sat in front of him with the cone and spooned a bit of it toward his mouth, but instead of opening his mouth he reached for and grabbed the whole cone. He actually grabbed it! Trudy held his hand on the cone and brought it to his mouth. But when he couldn't quite make his mouth work to get the ice cream in he broke into tears. After so much excitement at his progress this came as a sting: to have him really want and struggle for one of his favourite pleasures in the world and to have his own body rebel against his efforts, to reject his wishes after all he had been through, must have seemed to him hideous and unbearable. And for me as well; imagine how it might feel to have your perfectly capable four year old not be able to eat an ice cream, something that's every four year old's birthright. But, I tried to console myself, he had managed to reach out and grab something that he wanted, without any prompting or expectation from anyone. Given where he had been only the day before, this in itself was a monumental achievement.

The rest of the day was calmer because the therapists didn't work on the weekends, but it did see another huge milestone. He was moved out of the high-dependency unit (two nurses and four beds) into the general paediatric neurological ward and was placed in his own room. In spite of all the hospital/industrial noise outside (from both the corridor and the rooftop below our window) I came to think of that tiny little room as a sanctuary, tranquil and quiet. It was a refuge away from the cries and pain of other children. We could close the door, draw the curtains and be alone, which we did immediately. He slept better, we got more out of his therapy and the room generated a bit of peace in us. We started decorating it as if we were moving in permanently. But perhaps the most important new asset in our little room with Paddington Bear pictures on the windows was a fold-up cot. This meant that whoever was staying with Lio at night could have a real lie-down (if not sleep) instead of sitting up all night in a chair next to his bed, as we had been doing every night since the crash. But in spite of getting our own room, Lio seemed quite sad on the day, with bouts of unexplained crying. There were a host of potential reasons: pain from his leg or his head, ongoing morphine withdrawal, frustration at not being able to physically do what he wanted and do what he remembered doing well, fear at his situation, confusion over where his mother was and simply not wanting to do all the painful and humiliating things that I and everyone else around him were asking him to do ten times a day.

The next day, in order to avoid a repeat of the earlier chocolate mousse therapy session, Penny bought a chocolate mousse and she and I simply fed it to him. He hadn't choked on it before, so there seemed little harm in increasing the dose. This time he opened his own mouth, licked his lips and ate the whole thing. He was happy. I wheeled him across in his special supportive chair to the next room and he watched a DVD of Winnie the Pooh for nearly a half-hour with the little boy staying there, named Jack. Jack, who came from a village not far from Lewes, had a brain tumour and had been going in and out of a coma, and in and out of surgery, since he had arrived. He had been Lio's neighbour for a couple of days and his mother Franny had taken a special interest in Lio and smiled whenever she passed. Lio and Jack had been the two most serious cases on the ward. I was pulling for Jack and would help Franny as best I could to decode the doctors' words, just as she would do for me.

We met so many people during our months in hospital (Americans, Germans, Saudis, Iraqis, South Africans). The intensity of your experiences fools you into thinking you'll remember them all forever. But, with time and the desire to put the pain of those days behind you, their names and even faces do fade. There were tragedies and triumphs, agonies and accomplishments, screams and the most joyous laughter. There were open people, aloof people, middle-class people, working-class people, the sons of doctors, modern London families with 12 children, proud people, ashamed people, intellectual people and people who never read anything. Yet between us all something grew. Between this completely random cross-section of society there was a connection and an intimacy. We radiated hope for each other's children, we cared about each other, lit candles for each other and wanted to see the best happen. All the children, too – bright, generous, caring children, wise and gentle beyond their years – formed their own little support network. One boy in particular, an eight year old with severe epilepsy, came to Lio's bedside almost every day for two straight weeks. He played with Lio and would always, very politely, ask me how he was doing.

After Winnie the Pooh with Jack, Lio got even more into the sign language, pulling it up from the depths of his very early childhood: there were affirmative thumbs-up for food, thumbs-up for stories and a thumbs-up for trying to feed himself, which he did this time with only a bit of help. I put the spoon in his hand and he shakily delivered it to the container of strawberry mousse, getting a bit of the pink, gooey sweetness on it and then slowly directing it to his waiting mouth. After a few mouthfuls I felt emboldened to try a bit of shortbread biscuit on him. I broke off a corner and gave it to him (the therapists and the doctors had not allowed solid food, but he seemed keen and I didn't want to lose momentum). He chewed, swallowed and smiled. So did I.

Given that Lio's feeding tube (inserted down his nose)

was now not attached to the nutrient bag most of the day, we were free to roam the hospital in his special orthopaedic wheelchair. We got him in his chair, went down in the lift and out of the hospital front door. It was very easy to fantasise about leaving hospital for good, walking out of it all and never coming back. It was a tantalising image – just leaving – and I often used it to keep me going throughout our stay there. We stopped just outside the front door, breathed some smoky air for a few minutes and then headed back to Lio's room.

After a little rest, Nigel brought him a toy rocket attached to a truck. He was able to take it and hold it in his hand. Penny drew some pictures of him. He ate some more strawberry mousse and had a taste of macaroni and cheese for dinner. This little scene of almost domestic bliss was disrupted, though, when Penny showed him his favourite teddy bear (called Luigino); he fumbled for it and, not being able to grasp it as he would have liked, broke into tears. On seeing this, Betty, Lio's large and striking Afro-Caribbean nurse, came in and did a silly little dance to cheer him up. He laughed and succeeded in giving her an unsteady high-five on her way out the door. Not for the last time a nurse had restored peace and hope to our little room.

After a very good night, McCormick came in and examined Lio. He asked Lio to squeeze his finger and to follow a stuffed animal with his eyes and head. Lio did it all. We asked him about Lio's tendency to suddenly burst into tears and McCormick said, reassuringly, that these episodes of 'emotional overspill' were due to the fact that he had simply not regained control over his emotions yet. Strong, even exaggerated emotional responses could, he said, be triggered by the tiniest of things. Lio gave him another high-five before he walked out of the door.

Time with Sasha

Day 19 after the crash was a turning point. To my eye, Lio was truly and completely out of his coma – although I now understand a coma's end is a very grey area, much more precise on TV than in reality. He washed his face by himself – with a bowl of soapy water – washing his chin when asked, washing his cheeks when asked and washing his ears when asked. Then, after having his special chair put in front of the sink, Lio was able to brush his teeth all by himself. Today, 25 September 2006, less than three weeks after the crash that nearly killed him, that nearly left him a vegetable, that nearly erased his future, my son had returned. With every advance he made, I was able to shore up my defences against the fears, the doubts and the worries that still sniped at me, and the more I was able to keep those thoughts at bay, the more progress Lio seemed to make.

After lunch the therapists took him to the gym to work on his sitting and standing balance on his uninjured leg. This seemed quite a dangerous undertaking. But it only lasted a few seconds and we supported him continuously. We all clapped and the therapists were pleased to see that his lower-body muscles were working. They told him that he should give himself a clap. And he did clap himself; halting and imprecise, but he did it. Lio tried so hard at everything that was asked of him; in spite of his brain injury, he was acting like a well-mannered boy of seven or eight most of the time. I was sure this would be a tremendous asset to his recovery, which, it was clear to me in that moment, would happen in a series of small steps, with some steps forward and some steps back. Painfully slowly perhaps, but it *would* happen. Today's little step forward was clapping himself. And as I applauded him too, like I never would have done before, I also spared a few claps for my new-found appreciation of small accomplishments.

After a nap back in his room, Lio ate nearly a whole banana. I watched intensely as his little fingers curled around the soft white fruit. There is a thrill – yes, certainly – when your infant first reaches for and grasps a banana; there is a feeling of joy. Even though you were expecting him to do it, you are proud almost beyond measure if you're a new parent. But now imagine if there was some doubt about whether or not he would ever be able to do it, if you had been cautioned not to expect it, if things like this were to be approached as rare and unique triumphs, tiny little miracles unto themselves that defied the expectations of the experts. Lio and his banana brought me feelings of elation that I'd never felt before. It sounds a bit silly now, even to myself, talking about these simple, mundane events, but those were the feelings I had. They were deep and transcendent feelings of the most profound happiness. After the banana I asked if he wanted ice cream – he did not hesitate for an instant, gave the thumbs-up sign and ate it all by himself.

Post-ice cream Lio's proper wheelchair arrived, a cool kid's wheelchair called a 'Blade 2'. It was navy blue, with planets and stars on it, and it was such an improvement on the very strange, Martian-looking orthopaedic contraption he'd been using. This was a proper wheelchair that we could take outside to the park, which is exactly what we did with it that very day. Spurred on by his small steps earlier, Lio even managed to turn the wheels himself a few times in pursuit of ducks and pigeons. Recovery – that is full, complete, absolute, total recovery – seemed in that instant more than a vision I had trained my mind to see; it seemed as if it was actually happening before my eyes. In fact, it seemed like it had happened already.

I struggled to fit Lio's new wheelchair in his little room. In spite of my best attempts to rearrange things, I ended up having to park it in the corridor outside. Penny and Trudy had positioned a couple of armchairs out in the hallway on either side of the door to Lio's little room, guarding it like a couple of stately bookends. The wheelchair kept them company when not in use.

I arranged and rearranged Lio's room so many times. I moved the piles of stuffed animals, the cards and postcards and the drawings. I put some at eye-level on the wall facing his bed. I put a picture of him playing cricket above the sink, to remind him of the boy inside him. I put pictures of his mother on his bedside table. I perched the purple dragon my brother Anthony brought him on top of the paper towel dispenser. I put Penny's print of a Modigliani painting with empty eyes a bit higher up on the side wall. I put the photo of all his classmates at school (his school down in Lewes) in front of him, so he could see all of the friends he didn't even know he had who were all wishing him well. Next to that I put the hand-drawn card they had sent him, which I would take down and read to him from time to time. I wanted his room to be vibrant and alive, inspiring him and engaging him, as his perception returned and interests evolved. The tiny little permanent images of Paddington Bear on the walls were completely covered by our own stuff. As more gifts and cards arrived, things were shuffled and rotated to make new views for him.

On Wednesday, 27 September, 20 days after the crash, Lio began to speak. He was rediscovering his ability to talk. He had been watching a DVD of *Monsters, Inc.* as Miranda came in. We switched it off and she started asking him about characters in the film and Lio faintly managed 'Boo', the name of the little girl lost in the monsters' world. The feelings of pride and of delight from this little expression lifted me for days afterwards. Now that speech had come to his second childhood, walking had to be just around the corner. When we put him in the wheelchair for another spin around the park, he reached for his seatbelt as he had learned how to do in the car. With a little help, he managed to do it himself. And once in it, he reached down for the wheels and started pushing harder than before. These days remain, in many strange and unbelievable ways, the happiest of my life.

From the very first weeks, I was inundated with cards and calls and questions about how Lio was doing from friends and family all over the world. I wanted a nice and efficient way to thank everyone for their love and support as well a means of keeping them up to date. So I asked Ken, my old friend from Buffalo, if he could sort out a website for us – he was very anxious to make some kind of practical contribution to what was going on and he had done a lot of website production already. Initially, I would send him emails, maybe with some photos attached, and he would just fashion them into a web page. The first of these posts went up on 28 September and read simply:

> Lio has already exceeded the initial expectations of most of the doctors (although it must be said that the nurses were always more optimistic). He has fully woken up, he is feeding himself (his feeding tube was removed this morning), he is smiling and laughing, he is helping us wash him, and although he still lacks coordination he is grasping toys, playing with large Lego blocks, operating his bed controls and even

pushing himself in his wheelchair. While he is not yet speaking, he has begun making some vocal sounds and is communicating using sign language. We are all buoyed by his progress and the doctors (at least the honest ones) now say anything is possible. Lio's recovery will undoubtedly be a very long one but I am confident it will happen.

Your cards, letters, calls, thoughts and prayers have brought us all tremendous comfort and strength during the past weeks. We are extremely grateful and consider ourselves very lucky in you all.

Love,

Lio & Martin

Over the months I would draw huge reserves of energy from Lio's website. It was a place where I worked out my hopes and my fears, where I struggled with difficult medical and legal issues, and where I felt like I was communing with a global interchange of good feeling. The notes and reassurances in the comments left by people who read the site, mostly people we knew but also people who just stumbled across the site while searching for this or that and became fascinated by the story of one little boy's ordeal and astonishing recovery, were heartening beyond words. It really was a perfect feedback circuit for me: all the passion and good feeling I put into those entries came back to me tenfold in the replies.

Lio had been pulling out his feeding tube for several days. Finally, one of the nurses decided, on her own initiative, to definitively remove it because he was eating so well on his own. As each piece of medical kit was removed Lio began to look so much more natural, so much more like a four-year-old child. The feeding tube, nearly the last bit of alien apparatus, was gone. He was also saying far more words today: *papà, ciao, nonna, Trudy* (*grandmom* being still too difficult for him) and *yes*. Miranda said because he had regained his speech so (relatively) quickly his improvements should continue at a great pace. The quicker the recovery in this phase of his rehabilitation, the better the overall outcome would be. In my heart, I had known this would be his path all along. After rounds, at McCormick's suggestion, we went for another walk in the park, this time with some bread for the ducks and squirrels. I didn't realise it, but McCormick had proposed this outing as a test of sorts.

When he came into our room later that day, he asked, 'So, how did you manage out in the park?' He squinted and looked a bit too interested for this to be small talk.

'When we got to the pond, Lio seemed happy,' I said. 'He tried to throw bread to the squirrels, but it didn't go very far. The squirrels came right up to his chair and almost took it out of his hand.'

'And how did he react to that?' McCormick asked. 'Was he overly frightened or emotional?'

'No,' I said. 'He seemed relaxed enough and quite interested in seeing them up close.'

'That's great,' he beamed. 'Often patients with the kind of injuries Lio has had can have very intense and exaggerated responses to a lot of the quick, random, close-up stimuli like the animals in the park. They can get overwhelmed by it.' McCormick gave us a thumbs-up on his way out the door. I turned to Lio, who was pushing a bit of banana around on his hospital bed table. I thought for a second that I should have washed his hands after feeding the animals in the park.

Instead I just said, 'Lio, you're doing great, so absolutely great.'

The next day the therapists and doctors agreed that Lio was well enough to attend school for the first time. This was not the lovely little village school Sasha and I had visited, vetted and chosen for him. It was not the school of our proud middle-class imagination, surrounded by rolling hills with sheep and white chalky cliffs in the distance. Instead it was the school in the hospital. He was puzzled when he first arrived. The two cosy rooms opposite the physiotherapy gym with cheery teachers and magazine racks filled with colourful books climbing up the walls seemed out of place in the hospital. But he acclimated very quickly and gave a broad smile in the absence of a 'hello'. After fiddling about a bit to get the external fixator on his leg to fit under one of the tables, the teachers set him up with a large bowl and a wooden spoon. They added flour, sugar, milk, egg and vanilla while he mixed gently and methodically. Sometimes they had to hold the bowl for him and sometimes he managed to do it himself. While things baked in the oven, one of the teachers read him a story that he seemed to follow fairly well with his eyes. After about an hour he went back to his room with a paper bag filled with cupcakes. Pride mixed with simple childish pleasure rose on his little face as he opened his bag, reached in, grabbed one and shakily offered it to his grandmother Trudy.

Later that day he had the opportunity to give both his self-esteem and his generosity another outing in the physiotherapy gym. He had brought the slightly stained bag of cupcakes with him on his lap. As soon as he saw his favourite physiotherapist Nikki, he grabbed the bag with one hand and unsteadily but earnestly fished around with the other for another cupcake.

'Oh, Lio! Is that for me?' she said with pure delight. She danced in a little circle in front of him, unwrapped it and took a huge bite.

Lio's eyes flashed their old familiar sparkle for a second. He was proud to have made something himself and prouder still to have offered it to Nikki. He was rediscovering the power of his smile, the power of his gestures and the power of his own goodness. His charm and charisma were flowing back into him, and he felt it. He smiled a toothy smile as she finished the cake and nearly pulled himself out of his chair to start his physio; his eyes lit up again as I shot over to make sure he didn't fall. It really is all about Lio's eyes for me. While I could help him eat and wash and get stronger and perform better in almost every way, I was fairly powerless in the presence or the absence of that sparkle in his eyes. Every day he was more 'switched on', as his neurologists called it; he was inching his way back to alertness and clarity. When I saw that spark, I blew on it, kindled it, nurtured it and tried to keep it going as long as I could in whatever direction it wanted to go, even if it wanted to tap fingers to 'Bongo Bong' for the one-billionth time.

Early next morning, well before the chaos of rush hour, Penny and I walked down the lonely steel steps of Denmark Hill rail station opposite King's College Hospital. My mother was with Lio and Nigel had gone back home to Wandsworth to deal with accumulating bills and paperwork. It was dark and cold, with London's dreary low-hanging morning mist. Nigel and Jeff had gone to see Sasha's body in the police morgue; now it was our turn.

'It was tan and strong. I didn't want to let it go,' Nigel had told us when he recounted his visit. While waiting for our train, I thought about nothing but Nigel holding his daughter's brown hand and sinewy arm. I imagined my own fingers slipping between hers, our wedding rings clicking together.

As I looked out the window at the passing green hills, all the times Sasha and I had told and embellished the story of our first proper encounter at the cricket match flickered through my mind. The train pulled into Lewes and we headed for the undertaker's. Penny and I both spent time alone with Sasha's body, an experience she would later describe as 'unbearable'. I was sitting on a flower-print armchair surrounded by flyers about sympathetic cremation services and eco-friendly burial options when Penny opened the door of the viewing room. She sobbed and hid her face in her hands as she came out and sat down across from me. My turn. I had second-guessed my decision shortly after the accident to not visit Sasha's body in the morgue. I had thought then that I wanted to remember Sasha as I remembered her: alive and happy and meeting life head-on every day, rather than a broken corpse.

There, on simple wooden saw horses, on beige carpet with very low light in a windowless room, was a simple oak coffin containing what was left of my wife's body. It was smaller than I had expected. The lid was screwed down tightly with brass screws all around and on the top was a brass-coloured plastic plate that read simply:

Sasha Spinelli

1966 – 2006

I was fazed a bit because she wasn't 'Sasha Spinelli'; to me, she was 'Sasha Roberts'. My Sasha, and I wanted to hold her so very badly in that moment. I knelt in front of her body and put my head down on the oak. I had this absolute, desperate, angry desire to touch her again. I did the only thing I could: I stretched my arms out, one over the lid and the other under the bottom, and squeezed. I squeezed so hard that the edges of her coffin cut into my neck and arms. I squeezed so hard my fingers went numb. I would have given anything to have touched her skin one more time. Tears.

'I love you so very much,' I whispered into the wood.

After a few minutes I let go my embrace. I sat back on my heels and tried to compose myself.

'Your son is amazing everyone,' I said in my normal speaking voice. 'You should be incredibly proud of him.'

Silence.

'He's talking again and just about feeding himself and all the nurses adore him.'

Silence.

'The one doctor that I really trust says the sky's the limit in terms of his recovery.' I couldn't help but put a positive spin on McCormick's completely open-ended prognosis.

Too much long, still silence.

Then I finally gave in to the pain.

'Why did you do it?!' I shouted. 'How could you? How!' Once I started sobbing I couldn't stop. I pounded the carpet, 'How could you have let this happen?! How could you have left me with such a shitty mess to clear up? It's so unlike you!'

The adrenalin ebbed away. I was left silently kneeling with my head in my hands. I eventually felt some paper on my forearm. In my shirt pocket, there was a poem written for Sasha by Luke, the chaplain of the hospital, the Indian priest who had been a student on her course on Shakespeare's sonnets. When he had given it to me the day before, I told him I would read it to her remains. That's just what I did there and then. Hand on her coffin, I pulled myself up and dried my cheeks.

'We're going to give you one hell of a send-off,' I said with a tiny smile. 'Try not to be late. OK?'

With that I left her. I touched Penny on the shoulder as I walked past into the office. I gave the funeral director the sheet of paper with the poem on it and asked him to put it in her coffin before the funeral.

I called my mother Trudy on the train ride back up to London and she couldn't wait to tell me all the things she and Lio had done that day: they had read books, taken a spin around the new wing of the hospital and built a tower out of Lego. In the afternoon, she had worked at getting the knots out of his hair, still matted with some blood despite two earlier attempts to get it clean.

In the evening, when I returned, Lio was speaking in short sentences. 'You back,' he said when he saw me. I was so grateful in that instant I didn't even fret that I had missed him speaking properly for the first time since the accident.

Friends and more friends arrived; almost every other day there was someone new now. These were good people moved to tears by what had happened but also lightened by Lio's recovery, feeling as if they were also a part of something beyond themselves somehow. Perhaps they were simply curious or perhaps they were drawn to us because they sensed something special was happening; some of them almost seemed like pilgrims, quiet, and slightly awe-struck. And I was glad for every visit.

The most regular of these friends was Rene, a German colleague from seven years earlier who had remained in touch. She would come and bring little presents for Lio – a children's book one visit, pirate pyjamas the next. Then she would take me out of the hospital and let me offload for half an hour or so – gentle, informal therapy. On her third visit to see us she took me out to a little coffee shop slightly too trendy for the surrounding neighbourhood.

'He looks fantastic!' she couldn't resist. 'Absolutely transformed from when I came a week ago.'

'It's hard for me to judge because I see him every day,' I said with a sigh.

'But Martin, if he looks great, you look terrible!' she said wryly. 'I mean it, you have to take care of yourself, too.' I had heard these words before from the hospital counsellor. I'd resisted them the same way I had always resisted the instructions they give you before your plane takes off about putting your own oxygen mask on first before helping others. 'That's ridiculous,' I'd always said to myself. 'Of course I'd put my child's mask on first.' And while I still wasn't about to change my approach to Lio's recovery, having Rene poke a bit of fun in my direction made me focus for a second on my own body for the first time in three weeks. Her expression of concern at first made me feel good, but then I got a flash of paranoia about ageing and about not being able to do what needed to be done for Lio physically in the absence of Sasha. I withdrew a bit and dried a tear before it fell. When I looked again, I noticed Rene's eyes were red and two tears trailed down her own cheeks.

'I can't possibly imagine how hard this is for you,' she said.

On 1 October, Lio had breakfast in the hospital cafeteria and then a spin in the park. In between ducks and bagpipe players, Penny called Nigel on her mobile phone and Lio spoke to him for a few seconds. Two weeks earlier those words would have seemed impossible to some, and, if I'm honest, occasionally a distant hope for me as well. His speech was very, very soft, abbreviated and completely monotone, but Lio did speak on the phone.

That afternoon, after practising some breathing exercises that Miranda had shown us, Lio started whistling. He learned to whistle there and then in the hospital. He just did it, without any prompting. This was something he had *never* done before. What a glorious sign: he was teaching himself new things less than four weeks after he'd been nearly killed. In the evening, we took the nurses in intensive care some chocolate to thank them again. They were astounded at how well Lio was doing. Their faces lit up with an incandescent pride, they passed around the chocolates (I pushed the boat out and got some nice continental ones rather than the familiar Cadbury's), they took a photo of him and pinned it on the wall next to the exit like a little icon of what lies beyond for all those parents and children on the wrong side of the door. It remains there to this day.

On 2 October, Lio wrote his name for the first time since coming to the hospital. Penny wrote it on a bit of paper and Lio copied it underneath. Again, when the doctors and the therapists came round, it was difficult to describe their surprise.

They kept saying, 'Given the severity of his original injuries, we would have never expected this.'

And, 'You have to be extremely happy at this.'

Again, I wanted to dance for joy.

They took the stitches out of his leg that day and with them went the last of his intravenous lines. He was patient and calm throughout both of these uncomfortable procedures; on top of that he sat up by himself while much of this was happening. Things were racing ahead and I saw in my mind's eye Lio walking tall through all the big days of his future, the same big days that he had coming before the accident. I saw him walking tall and straight and gracefully up the aisle at his wedding to a beautiful girl whom he'd charmed with his cleverness and wit. I saw him happy in mid-life with his own children in tow, striding over soft, green and curving hills. I saw him at meetings and assemblies of all kinds, where he was speaking eloquently and forcefully. Less than four weeks after the beginning of it all, I could already see the end of it as if it were happening right in front of me. We still had a very long road ahead of us, though, and part of me didn't honestly know if we'd be walking down that road or rolling in a fancy blue wheelchair, but I knew we were heading in the right direction.

'I've got a great game I can lend you to play back in your room,' said one of the hospital schoolteachers as Lio started to lose interest in the blocks of Lego in front of him and looked towards the door.

'It's called Snap,' she said in a slightly Mary-Poppins-y way. 'Would you like to try it?' Lio gave a half-hearted thumbs-up.

'Good,' she continued. 'You play it like this.' She dealt each of us out a small pile of cards with cartoon animals on them.

'We go around in a circle and we each turn over a card. When you see a card that matches another card, you have to yell "SNAP!" as loud as you can.'

'And the first one to yell "SNAP!" wins all the cards,' I couldn't help chiming in.

'That's right,' smiled the teacher. 'Let's give it a go, shall we?'

She began and, after a few long seconds, I prompted Lio to turn over his card. Before too many turns, there were two elephants showing. The teacher and I waited a long time.

'You know what to do when you see two cards that match, don't you?' I said. 'You have to say . . .' I paused.

Lio looked blankly. Finally, the teacher leaned over and whispered in his ear.

A long, low, soft, sad 'Snaaaaaaap' escaped from his lips. I struggled to hear him as I bent forward and cupped my ear. My heart ached. My gifted little linguist could barely speak at all and couldn't even recognise a pair of cards. My head dipped a bit as Lio continued to stare at nothing in particular. I hoped he hadn't picked up on my desperation.

As I readied Lio's wheels to take him back to his room, the teacher leaned over and whispered to me this time, 'Early days yet, early days.'

Almost immediately after the accident people started talking to me about suing, about bringing a claim for damages to court. This upset me to the point of shaking. I remember a social worker broaching the subject with me. I broke down in tears and croaked out, 'Nothing will ever compensate me!' The thought of 'profiting' from my wife's death and my son's mutilation was disgusting. The shock of it was more than I could bear. But even in the state I was in, somewhere inside me I suspected that if we were ever going to be able to put our lives back together it was going to be very expensive.

It was Penny, with a good head for money, who took some steps in the middle of her own tremendous pain only weeks after the crash to try to find me a lawyer. She asked one of her old friends, an attorney who eventually wound up doing a stint as the head of an airline, to suggest someone. Penny reasoned that as he shared a social circuit with high-court judges he might be able to steer us to someone who was a good combination of compassionate and very capable. Lio's neurologist also gave me the card of a lawyer who specialised in cases like ours.

Meeting them was terrible. All the lawyer jokes and stereotypes that I had ever heard swirled around with my grief and I found myself simply feeling sick. I was not prepared for the first meeting. I was not prepared at all to hear the solicitor talk in terms of 'worst-case scenario' – something he assumed as a point of departure for our conversation. I needed to remain focused on 'best-case scenarios'. I needed to see my son as recovering and living a normal and happy life. I needed to think that we would come out of this not just OK but really well. And yet there I was, sitting at a table in the hospital coffee shop across from a lawyer who was talking about severe and permanent disabilities, who was talking about long-term care, who was talking about the need for permanent special accommodation. I had just pulled myself from the brink of that abyss and here was someone pulling me back into it. Having to hear stories about completely incapacitated but completely conscious people while my son had only just put a coma behind him made my stomach lurch. But in the end I told myself that he simply needed to talk his talk and adopt his attitude for strategic reasons: he had to think about Lio in his terms because that would be best for Lio and me financially. And I had to think about Lio in my terms because it would be best for Lio's recovery. Yet I found myself stuck in this contradiction, in a frightening psychological balancing act.

At one interview I showed a calm and well-dressed 'neuro-lawyer' called Eric a handful of photos of Lio playing cricket and riding his bike the previous spring. Before I got through the small pile, my throat tightened and I broke down.

'So the little man likes his sport then,' Eric said soothingly and sympathetically, as I tried to steady my voice and rein in the tears.

'I can't imagine I'll ever be able to go back to my old job, or would even want to,' I said, thinking aloud.

'Lio will have the best treatment that money can buy, no matter what you do about work,' he reassured. 'But hopefully we won't need to spend fortunes on care. From what I've seen, he's already beaten the odds. And age and time are certainly on his side.'

'The police tell me that he's not talking,' I said about the lorry driver, trying to compose myself a bit more by shifting the focus from Lio. 'They say he's not cooperating – they think he's too scared.'

'He should be scared, and so should his insurance company,' Eric said with a very natural confidence.

'They want to do an autopsy on Sasha's body.'

'They're grasping at straws,' said Eric. 'Your wife is dead and your son is in the state he's in for one reason only: someone fell asleep at the wheel.'

'I could never do your job,' I told him, my voice cracking again, my mind flying from one thing to the next.

'Why's that?'

'I couldn't immerse myself in these nightmares, in this pain, day in and day out, year in and year out. I couldn't do it.'

He looked down into his coffee and reflected for a long time, adjusted his glasses and then said without a trace of irony, 'I do it for the pay-off.' Adding quickly, 'Not the pound and pence kind. I get my real pay-off when I see that I've been able to return a little comfort and a little security to families struggling with the most difficult situations I can imagine. My pay-off comes in knowing I've helped people re-build a life.'

I was convinced.

'Regardless of who you choose, you don't need to waste time thinking about the driver or what his lawyers are doing. That's not your job. Focus on Lio, get him better, get him out of here and let whoever you instruct worry about details like those.' He got up and shook my hand.

A few days after I met Eric I called up another lawyer that I had interviewed – another very good person – to let her know what I had decided. She was a sole practitioner and I wanted a lawyer with more backing and more resources. I phoned her from the little Thai restaurant that had become my regular, the place in which I'd had my first meal alone, where I'd toasted Sasha's presence. I told her that I had chosen Eric and she said with complete candour that I had chosen well. She knew of him and his firm and had been impressed with them over the years. She also said that if there was ever anything she could do to help us, personally or professionally, all I needed to do was call.

While I might have waited until things were a bit calmer, I am glad I made contact with the lawyers in the first few months after the crash. I am glad because the financial realities of Lio's recovery, even in a country with a good national health care system, are staggering. I knew the savings I had from selling my Brooklyn apartment would evaporate in appointments with private specialists, extra therapies, supplements and flights to foreign hospitals; I knew my income would diminish to a trickle because I wouldn't be able to work because all my waking hours would be spent caring for Lio and finding the best possible treatments for him. These things can have a funny effect on grief. They force you to deal with practicalities instead of symbols regardless of how crucial those symbols are to you. A good solicitor is one who figures out ways to let you grieve and to let you focus on recovery while he goes out and gets you some money to make that happen. This is what I hoped I'd found in Eric.

Nissan Micra v. Scania Lorry

We were living in our small top-floor apartment in a slim and elegant Victorian stone building in Brooklyn. Lio, then two, was spending the evening with his grandmother out in New Jersey. Sasha and I had some friends over for a dinner of orange chicken and spinach salad that we had spent most of the afternoon preparing. By the third bottle of wine, the conversation had somehow joked and meandered its way to funeral arrangements.

'I don't believe in much of anything,' said Tom, a videographer colleague of mine. 'So when I go, I don't want any kind of religious service at all. What I want you to do is to lead a procession into the funeral parlour carrying a big black plastic bag taped to a broom handle and then put it over my coffin,' he laughed. 'That way no one would get the wrong idea. I'd be really upset if there were any religious images anywhere.'

'But you'll be dead,' Sasha said, her words laced with irony. 'Dead – and, as you take it, completely gone. You won't be around to see it, so what does it matter to you how we send you off?'

I turned to Sasha with a chortle of appreciation and said, 'I trust you with the details, darling. Just see that my remains end up in the mountains.' We had always assumed that I would die before her and she had always seen herself walking up above the clouds well into her 80s.

Exactly one month after the crash, on 7 October, we held Sasha's funeral at Saint Pancras Roman Catholic

Church in Lewes. Erik Flood, the priest who had married us and baptised Lio, came out of retirement and said the funeral mass with the new priest, Richard Biggerstaff. Richard was someone Sasha had admired; when we had occasionally gone to mass, his homilies were always carefully constructed bits of rhetorical gold, poetic almost. They were intelligent, reflective and probing rather than dogmatic; they were never just cobbled together. Sasha related well to them and to him. He did not disappoint on the day, delivering a haunting eulogy about Sasha and 'the month's mind' on which, according to the medieval Catholic tradition, one month after someone's death special time is taken to think about them and their passing.

At the funeral service, the sun shone beautifully through the stained glass and made transfixing little patterns in the incense-filled air. Four years earlier, I had stood in exactly the same spot amidst the front-row pews for Lio's baptism. I remembered how, back then, for an instant, I was hit by a wave of doubt. I looked at my child, my perfect little infant, and I worried for a bit about what it might mean for him to enter the church as I had done. I thought for a moment that it might be better if he came to this as an adult by himself, if he were to come to it at all. In the past I had questioned whether or not the church had helped or hindered my development as a spiritual person and I had those same thoughts for my little child. And while I know that even the most devout people have their wavering moments, I couldn't help but wonder, as I sat on that oak pew at Sasha's funeral, whether or not my flash of apprehension at Lio's baptism might have set our course for the accident and for my rediscovery of my own faith. But now, after months and months' more reflection, I don't believe the divine works that way, and I've come to think that 'evolution' is a better word than 'rediscovery' for what I'd been going through metaphysically since the crash.

My spiritual development was not unusual. I came from a family with strong religious roots yet in a thoroughly modern and urban part of the States. It was simply a part of the fabric of my childhood. We went to an unassuming suburban church, a church that my architect father had designed, with an altar that he and my grandfather had made in his basement workshop – like they'd made desks and bookshelves and other things for us and for our friends.

As normal, I came to a point as a teenager where I became increasingly ambivalent about it, where I wanted to define myself for myself as something other than my family. This meant questioning and rejecting most of those familiar religious ideas and mindsets. In college, I read widely and curiously about other traditions and other philosophies, trying to gain something from all of them. Like many of my age and upbringing, I was happy enough, comfortable enough and content enough to consider myself vaguely spiritual and culturally Catholic. But there at Sasha's funeral service I was no longer adrift, I was grounded to something greater than me, something that put me in a head-space that I liked being in. I was not the Catholic of childhood, the Catholic of 'because-I-say-so' dogma and fear; I was not the atheist/agnostic of a teenager rejecting all structures and frameworks because all structures and frameworks are oppressive. Now, I was a Catholic who could recognise the support and value that even a tradition with an imperfect history could provide, I was a Catholic of meditation and the imagination of the possible in everyday life. And my meditations put me immediately closer to Sasha, immediately closer to the Lio still too often trapped behind half-closed eyes, and (most vitally, I thought) they were playing a part somehow in his astonishing recovery. The familiar and transcendentally beautiful forms of mosaics and frescos and stained glass and sculpture and cathedrals and plainsong moved me more profoundly than ever and could give expression to faith, but its real essence, I had realised, was to be found somewhere in the space between people – between Sasha and me, and between Lio and me.

At the funeral, I read the two passages of scripture; Richard Ward, a friend of Sasha from her university days, read a poem, and Father Flood reminisced about the first time he'd met Sasha at the annual arts festival in Lewes. We had originally planned after the service that the hearse would take Sasha's body alone to the crematorium, all of us being too tormented by the finality implied in burning her remains. We would say our last goodbyes in front of the church and then make our way to a reception at the White Hart Hotel, where Sasha used to go salsa dancing every week – we would drink and dance and hold in our minds the image of a living Sasha, rather than something in a box screwed shut. That was the idea; that was what I imagined she'd want – two years earlier in our apartment in Brooklyn she never did say precisely what she'd have liked for her final arrangements. But there, underneath a cloudless, deep-blue autumn sky, I just couldn't stick to the plan. Absolutely nothing about me was ready to let her slip out of sight.

The service itself had been too beautiful to come to an end and as our friends began to disperse off down the hill outside our serene little Victorian church, my heart began to pound. If this was going to be goodbye, I needed it to last much, much longer. I changed my mind about what should happen next and decided that I would accompany her body to the crematorium. I followed the hearse in a car driven by one of the pallbearers through the bright autumn sun to the crematorium behind black iron gates on a green and wooded hill just outside of Brighton. Like soldiers, the pallbearers got out of the hearse with straight steps and stiff arms, opened the back and gently, silently, slid her out. Heads slightly bent, they walked her coffin past the studded oak doors and through the stone arch into a beautiful Pre-Raphaelite chapel filled with stained glass and marble. They placed her coffin on the rollers concealed in a large, smooth stone slab at the front. It lay alone, with only me, the funeral director and his pallbearers.

I'd been asked to choose some music to be played as her body was pulled back behind a curtain into the crematorium proper – I picked Palestrina's 'Kirie', the same music Sasha had chosen to welcome Lio into the world as he was being born. The funeral director and the pallbearers stood stiff and silently. I stood as well, but I was crying. The funeral director told me to sit down and I did even though I wanted to stand. By this point, I was too tired to resist. I wanted that music to keep playing forever and ever. It was as if as long as the music was playing I would still have her in my life. As the piece was coming to an end, the curtains opened behind Sasha's wooden coffin and it slowly began to roll backward without a sound into the tiny stone room behind. As Palestrina finished, the curtain closed and I sat in silence, like a statue. In the most demanding days of my life, at the moment when I needed Sasha's help the most to save our son, I saw her slipping away forever behind a red velvet curtain.

For reasons that I never fully grasped, any remaining bits of melted metal would have to be removed from the ashes before they could be presented to me. Because of this the funeral director had suggested that he remove all Sasha's jewellery. I agreed, but because these things weren't just accessories, they were physical and meaningful emblems of our life together, I wanted her body to enjoy them as long as possible. In preparation for the funeral I had taken Sasha's wedding ring and her favourite necklace, a modern silver and moonstone piece (moonstone being associated with fertility) to Jonathan Swan, the local jeweller who had made our wedding rings. Both the necklace and the ring were hideously bent in the crash and I'd asked Jonathan to repair them so that Sasha's body could wear them up until the last moment. Just before the service in the church the funeral director took off the ring and necklace, along with the earrings and the several other rings she had been wearing before the crash. Outside the crematorium, the small, shiny box of jewellery he handed me dazzled my eyes in the bright afternoon sun. I opened it. One of the rings still had a bit of dried blood on it. I didn't know what to do with it.

Sasha was always a flurry of activity. The days before the crash were no exception. She was busy taking on a big project to edit a new edition of a little-known Renaissance play, writing and rewriting pages for her beauty book, and dancing whenever possible. Hers was a life devoted equally to pleasure and accomplishment. But in those last days she seemed even more intense, if that were possible. She was driving herself like crazy. On top of the professional writing, she was re-working her illustrated children's book, researching old houses that we might buy, fix up and rent out, trying to get pregnant and gardening, lots and lots of gardening. She hadn't touched her garden in months, but, two days before the crash, Sasha, clippers in hand, filled seven large bin liners with cuttings from roses and fuchsia and boxwood all from our tiny garden, maybe 15 feet by 20 feet. She went at it for nearly one full day.

In the late afternoon, I went out back with a cup of tea for her and said, 'Sweetheart, don't kill yourself. This doesn't all have to be done today, does it?'

She smiled, but I could tell that she was a bit annoyed. 'I've got my office to sort out, we've got loads to do to get

Lio ready for school and the poor garden needs seeing to. When am I going to get time to do it if I don't do it now?'

She kissed me 'thank you' and I went inside.

Even our sex life, it now seems to me, had an edge and intensity about it in that last week that I can't explain, and I wonder if in this buzz of activity she sensed at some level she was going to be leaving. The pace of her life in her last days was staggering, even for her.

Those seven bags of clippings lay there, the most prominent feature of our little garden, for weeks and weeks while we were in hospital. I asked our neighbours Pascal and Michael if they could deal with them for me because I didn't want to have to look at that particular unfinished project of hers when we returned home. They did and I was grateful. Her other projects were all crying out to be finished, though. Some of them I would give away to friends and colleagues anxious to have some way of connecting with their own dear Sasha. I told myself I would pick up some of them when I had time. But I never got terribly worried about it because I knew that in many ways my life would always be about continuing what she had started. As I was reminded once in the aftermath by a friend, I was one of Sasha's projects too. I even had a vague and fleeting idea that perhaps one day I would take up some of my own old work and make it into something truly remarkable as a way of communing with her. But in those early days my mind was focused exclusively on the single project we shared: Lio.

The evening after the funeral my brothers, Anthony and Glenn, who had flown back over for the service, came to the hospital to visit Lio. Anthony in particular was a gem. He couldn't believe the transformation he saw in his nephew – the last time he had seen him, Lio was deep in a coma.

He said simply and incredulously as he came out of Lio's

room, 'That's Lio in there. That's just Lio with a broken leg.'

After weeks of thinking and worrying and praying about Lio's injuries, it was as if the injuries had almost *become* Lio somehow in my mind. So it was exquisite to be reminded by my brother who Lio was. There is no 'Old Lio' and 'New Lio'. Lio is Lio. And that blessed little four year old who managed to prop himself up on his bed all by himself and turn his head slightly to watch me come in the door was the same astounding and astonishing person that he had always been. While I had been telling myself precisely this for weeks as a way of battling panic and doubt, it was glorious to have my brother remind me of it so casually, so matter-of-factly. Anthony caught a flight the next morning back to Seattle; he left Lio a large hand-puppet knight whom we named Bruno.

According to the police report, Sasha's Nissan Micra was parked on the hard shoulder of the M2 – that's the side of the four-lane motorway that leads in and out of Canterbury. She had chosen a Nissan Micra because of its fuel efficiency. It weighed about 1,500 pounds – 110 stone, 700 kilos. Her handbrake was on. She was turned around, facing Lio in the back seat, watching him or tending to him or protecting him or comforting him – we will never be able to say for certain. Her car was several feet on the correct side of the white line and (she obviously assumed) safe. The police assured me several times that she was well within her rights to be there. Lio was in his properly fitted booster seat behind her. His seatbelt was undone and her seatbelt was undone and was slack, meaning she had probably just unlatched it.

At 10.21 a.m. on Thursday, 7 September 2006, a Scania heavy-goods vehicle – an articulated lorry, a tractor trailer, a really big truck – returning to Belgium empty after delivering its load of mail but still weighing at least 12 times Sasha's Nissan Micra, was travelling at 55 miles per hour along the same motorway. The driver, Yvan Vandermeulen, a fifty-four-year-old father of two, had not taken his required breaks and had been driving more hours than his legal limit for three days prior. The police report suggests driver fatigue as the most likely cause of the crash. At 10.22 on a bright, clear, dry late-summer morning, that Scania truck hit that Nissan Micra with enough force (144 kilonewtons, according to the police report) to send it spinning into the air until it came to rest 230 feet away – that's one and a half lengths of an Olympic swimming pool.

As Nissan's website boasts, with its 1.2 litre engine and aerodynamic three-door design the Micra gets 47.9 miles per gallon (combined driving). It was good for the environment and easy on the wallet. Sasha always took this car for her 100-mile commute to a job she didn't need. Yvan Vandermeulen fell asleep at the wheel doing a job he certainly did need. His Scania truck was outfitted with all the latest safety features because at Scania 'safety is always a priority'. Scania was the first, its website says, to introduce 'front underrun protection' on all of its trucks to protect car drivers and passengers because 'unfortunately accidents and collisions do happen'. Front underrun protection is essentially a bar mounted on the front of the truck cab at roughly the same height as car bumpers to maximise the absorption of impact energy in the event of a crash – think of it as a cow-pusher for young families in Nissan Micras.

So upbeat is the material on the Scania website that after reading through it a few times I almost wanted to become a truck driver myself. The 'new Scania truck delivers – big time' and 'also measures up to what your drivers are demanding'. 'You get high-torque engines with easy driveability and outstanding fuel economy.' But Scania always has an eye on safety: 'Scania has taken a hard look at vehicle control and handling, brake performance, and the driver's work environment all with a view to minimising risk.' Yvan Vandermeulen's cab was cluttered with paperwork, even on the dashboard. But nothing obscured his view of Sasha's Nissan Micra on the side of the road for at least ten seconds prior to impact. The high-performance brakes, applied only after the crash, were working as well as the day they'd been installed; and the truck itself, unburdened by its heavy load of mail, was without mechanical defect of any kind.

The design of the Scania heavy-goods vehicle, according to the website, is one of the safest in the industry. In a crash test involving the Scania truck and an Audi A3 passenger car at a collision speed of 40 miles per hour both car passengers and truck driver should be able to walk away from the accident without serious injury. At a collision speed of 55 miles per hour, according to one of his medical reports, Lio was thrown from the car 50 feet across traffic until he landed on the other side of the road. Sasha's body, her slender, supple, beautiful, healthy, tanned body, was pierced by the metal and plastic that was her Nissan Micra. Her skull, with her brain so alive with ideas and words and passions, had been fractured as she turned to tend to her child in a theoretically safe spot in a supposedly safe world.

But 'humans make mistakes', acknowledges the Scania website.

These are just words on the internet, technical specifications and mechanical details. The photos of the crash site tell a different story. Most of them were pulled from my copy of the police report to spare me the sight of them. These were, however, precisely the photos included in a TV documentary about 'killer lorries' that came out a year later. The photo of Lio's splintered wooden push-bike at the back of the car was the most troubling for me. Lio loved that bike and asked about it hundreds of times after the crash. His new bike is better, a big boy's bike.

On Friday, 13 October, McCormick said that because Lio was doing so remarkably well, and that since there was no therapy scheduled for the weekend, he could spend a night out of the hospital at our little flat nearby.

This was an opportunity not to be missed. The next day was my birthday; I was going to be 39. A more poignant present I could have never imagined. In the hospital early in the morning we had the bandage changed around the pin sites of the external fixator attached to Lio's leg. Two of Lio's former nursery school teachers from Lewes came in to visit him. They were both extremely gentle and compassionate and promised to spread the news of how well Lio was doing back in town. After lunch we managed Lio's first serious excursion out of the area of the hospital.

After hefting Lio in his wheelchair down some 50 stairs, we hopped on the train at Denmark Hill and took it to Victoria Station. From Victoria, we walked in the direction of Westminster Cathedral, the Catholic cathedral of London. It's a striking William-Morris-style, Italianate 19th-century church with stripes of red brick and white marble. Inside the acoustics are magnificent; there was a boys choir practising and the black-and-white marble domes and arches extended, transformed and caressed each note in such a way that I couldn't help but tear up. On my previous birthday Sasha had taken me to Canterbury Cathedral to hear a new John Tavener choral work and both moments rang around together in my mind. It was magnificently beautiful. I spent some minutes alone just soaking it all in while my mother, Nigel and Penny roamed with Lio amongst the saints and the votive lights. I lit three candles on that day and it's been my practice to do the same nearly every time I've entered a church since: one for

Lio's complete recovery, one for Sasha's spirit and presence in our lives, and one for the deep reserves of strength I found after the crash. It was a transcendent hour or so in that cathedral, not the largest, oldest or most ornate cathedral in London, but it spoke to me on that day like no other.

After a coffee across the street it was getting late so we decided to head back to our little flat. At Denmark Hill Station, as Nigel and I were preparing to hoist Lio in his chair back up the 50-odd stairs to get to street level, a dishevelled and possibly drunk man offered us his services.

'Here, little mate. Let me help,' he said quietly in an accent I couldn't place as he grabbed one of Lio's front wheels.

'Thanks, but we can manage,' I said a bit louder than I needed to. He ignored me and stared Lio in the eye.

'No, really,' I added nervously, but he held on nonetheless. I could tell Nigel on the other front wheel was nervous too. But Lio just turned his head and looked at me placidly.

'You should insist!' I said to myself. 'You should just stop and insist he lets go.'

'But we're already on the fourth step,' came the internal response.

'If this guy trips and hurts Lio and sets you back weeks of recovery, how are you going to feel?'

Step 10.

'He's just an innocent stranger trying to do something nice. You can use all the good feeling you can get.'

'To hell with some stranger's feelings! Protect your son!' I was now angrier with myself than I was with the man. 'How are you ever going to keep him safe on the road ahead if you can't even see off this inebriate?'

By step 20 my internal shouting had stopped and I had decided it best to just keep everyone calm and focus on getting up the stairs. 'OK!' I barked. 'Keep the front level.'

Step 27.

'Fine,' I breathed.

By the time we were nearing the top, the man hadn't stumbled at all and even I relaxed a bit.

'Thank you,' I said a bit too slowly and clearly. The man looked at Lio, his face cracked a slight smile and then he was off without a sound. No harm was done, but the doubting self-talk over this moment rattled around in my mind for days afterwards.

We headed back to the little flat, where, for my birthday, I cooked a simple tomato and onion pasta sauce just the way I had always done at home. I love to cook and this was the first time I'd had the chance since the crash. Penny brought me in a birthday cake with a candle on it, and Lio, my miraculous, marvellous, amazing, recovering son, who only two weeks earlier was still in a coma, gave me a birthday card that he had lettered with his own shaky hand. In black ink, huge across the front (and over the faintly pencilled letters written by my mother), was the word 'Daddy'. And inside on orange construction paper he'd drawn me with a beard, pasted on a little pom-pom for my nose and two bangles for my eyes, and managed to write faintly but unaided 'x x x lio'. As he handed it to me from his wheelchair, tears flooded down my cheeks for the second time that day. Never in the history of birthdays has a child's gift to his father meant more than that little card meant to me. It was as if he was giving me his future back in one neat gesture, and even more so, it seemed for a second, as if Sasha, watching over our little scene and guiding Lio's recovery from the start, promised me in that card that our son would come back completely whole and undamaged.

After dinner I made a little nest of sofa cushions at the side of my bed for Lio and covered it with sheets, blankets and a pillow we had stolen from the hospital. Being close to the floor seemed a good idea – no risk of him falling out of bed. There, in that anonymous little apartment, on a makeshift bed, I covered him with a beige cotton blanket. He was asleep in very short order. I got changed into my customary shorts and T-shirt for sleeping and slid into my bed. It had been a long and exhausting day for me as well, but I couldn't sleep. I hung over the edge of the bed for hours and stared at him, concerned that he was still breathing, thinking about my birthday card, wondering what I was going to do if he needed a nurse in the night, and in simple awe at the fact that he was sleeping out of hospital. It wasn't home, but it was almost normal.

On the day after my birthday my mother, Lio and I had planned another trip away from the hospital, but the trains were not running from Denmark Hill that Sunday. We took a long walk instead and we ended up at a Turkish café for lunch. Lio's reactions were slow and his speech was even slower, but his face was lit with a perpetual smile. We talked to the waiter about Lio, his situation and how well he was doing. Lio tried some Italian on him and we asked the waiter how to say hello in Turkish. He said '*Mehrhaba*' and we all copied him, slowly saying 'mar-ha-bah'. Lio was very pleased to add a new foreign word to his arsenal and decided to put Turkish on the list of languages that he could speak.

On the day after my birthday I sent my friend Ken an update for Lio's website, with some photos. It read:

> Lio is doing remarkably well . . . at least that's what the doctors are now saying. Although I must admit it makes me a bit uneasy when they stick their heads in the door and simply say 'Amazing', or when they tell me how much he's 'exceeded our expectations'. I get a bit anxious because I'm prone to read into those

comments the subtext of 'he might not get any better than this'. But he does continue to get better every day: he's talking in both English and Italian (he even corrected his grandfather's Italian yesterday); he's asking about things (especially his mother); worrying and crying about this week's operation to remove the metal external fixator on his broken leg; playing with his cousin Tyler and other friends on the hospital ward almost as if he's his old self; and kicking a football from his wheelchair with his good leg in the park.

He's still got some coordination problems, which means his drawing and writing are painfully imprecise; his speech is a bit slow and breathy (but getting better); his voice is a bit higher than it was and is often shaky; he sometimes speaks in charming non-sequiturs (Q: 'Why do you like your speech therapist Miranda?' A: 'Because I have relatives in Italy.'); he squints as he tries to remember what he had for breakfast or what his nurse's name is (which he can't often do); but most troubling for me is his lack of concentration and how quickly he gets fatigued. The therapists regularly remind me that his recovery will be measured in months and years rather than in weeks but I get from them an optimistic vibe. I am filled with hope.

In a few weeks we will probably go to a rehab centre. One of the doctors there was very positive about Lio moving to outpatient treatment relatively soon and even about him gradually integrating into regular school (the school he was meant to start at four days after the accident), which is of course marvellous news.

Thank you all so much for everything you've done for us in this impossible time. Every visit, every card, every email, every thought and even every unanswered phone call has helped us go a little further.

Telling Your Child

I put it off and off for days and days. Part of me feels like I should have never told him – at least not when I did. As he was coming into consciousness and more and more aware of things, he began to ask about his mother. I had put lots of pictures of Lio together with Sasha around his hospital room. Her image was in every direction you looked and her presence was there tangibly. And naturally, as Lio's senses returned to him, he got increasingly curious about his mother. I told him that she was in another hospital and that she was badly hurt in the accident, she was sleeping but that she wasn't doing as well as he was. I made sure the nurses and the hospital staff knew my approach and in the beginning they were extremely good at working with it.

For several days, the doctors and therapists danced around the issue of Sasha's death with Lio. But his questions to me about where she was and when he was going to be able to see her again were getting more and more coherent. I knew I would have to tell him eventually, but it was going to be torture. It was also not without its risks in my mind. Lio had had such a tremendous blow, he had had such a brutal physical shock, I didn't want him to suffer a second emotional shock on a par with the first. I remembered how the news of Sasha's death delivered to me by the two policemen in the hotel up in Sunderland had simply crushed me, had been like a physical beating. My worry was that, after such a remarkable recovery, Lio might suffer a similar blow, a similar trauma. If I could have put it off indefinitely, I would have done.

The psychotherapist on the ward had weekly meetings with me that were often quite useful. She told me that young children don't process the news of death in the same way that we do and that I shouldn't worry about him suffering emotional damage in the same way I had. As Lio was asking more and more about where his mother was, I started to take some of the pictures of Sasha down from the walls in his room. I also removed the large image of Lio and Sasha from the desktop background of my computer (we were using my laptop to watch DVDs). But this only proved a catalyst for more worry and more questions from Lio – now he was asking me where the photos of Mamma had gone. It was becoming increasingly difficult for everyone to be consistent with their stories about where Sasha was, what state she was in, if she was nearby, whether or not anyone could see her, etc.

Something finally forced my hand. A few days after Sasha's funeral, Cynthia, a dear friend of Sasha, and her three-year-old son Brandon visited us in hospital. Lio and Brandon often had fun together but their history was chequered, and Brandon's difficult behaviour had riled me more than once. Yet Cynthia and Sasha had been extremely close for decades, and Cynthia was nearly as stricken as the rest of the family at Sasha's passing. And the few bedside visits they had made while Lio was in a coma had been welcome.

Lio, speaking slowly and not functioning cognitively very well, asked me again about his mother. I told him again that she was in a hospital in Kent. But as soon as I did, Brandon piped up, 'No, she's not. She's dead.' I calmly repeated that she was in another hospital, but Brandon started insisting that she wasn't. In desperation, but as gently as I could, I grabbed Lio up out of his bed with his leg and external fixator dangling. I carried him to the lounge out in the front of the ward, where I put my arms around him and fumed.

Lio hadn't heard or hadn't understood. He didn't react to Brandon's insisting. He didn't or couldn't process what his friend had said. In the lounge, Lio stared passively at nothing in particular, but I was struggling to contain my rage. It had been a long time coming. Ever since Lio was two years old and Brandon was one, our sweet and sociable boy too often came out the worst in their encounters. If Brandon's pushiness had frustrated me before the crash, now, in the context of everything we were going through, it could prove utterly unbearable.

Some of the emotion and pain that I hadn't found a way to vent properly for more than a month were now seeping out in anger directed not just at Brandon (who was being sweeter to Lio than he had ever been) but at Cynthia too. Why was it *me* who had to take *Lio* out of *his own* hospital room? Why couldn't Cynthia intervene and do something about her son? How many times had I been told just to accept moments like these as part of the boy's nature? And as Cynthia tried to avert her eyes from the scowl I shot her way as she and Brandon scuttled past us towards the exit, I'm sure that's the explanation she would have apologetically offered then.

Now, reasonable people can certainly take different positions in the nature/nurture argument, but at that moment I had absolutely no patience for talk of the determining factors of biology. It seemed beyond absurd to me. Hadn't Lio and I been fighting and winning a tremendously hard fight against 'the nature' of his injuries? All of this was also interfering with my relationship with Cynthia, whom I had always liked for her quirky charm and for the way she supported Sasha while we were doing our stints on opposite sides of the ocean. This added to my anxiety.

I stayed awake all night, pacing through the corners of Camberwell and Brixton until dawn, from ghetto to affluent suburb, in an absolute state about Brandon. With the best intentions, Cynthia had organised a birthday party for Brandon to happen the next day in the ward lounge. It was her effort to try to remind us all that life's little pleasures might still be available to us. Initially, I had thought this was a brilliant idea, a way of turning the corner after Sasha's funeral and an opportunity for Lio, his younger cousins Tyler and Chris, and his occasionally challenging playmate Brandon to share some sweets and maybe even a few giggles like they had always done. Cynthia was extremely invested in it and I knew that this party was a crucial part of her own healing. But after the encounter in Lio's ward room I was terrified of what might happen if Lio and Brandon were put together again, and even more worried about what would follow. As I roamed the lanes, I saw myself yelling at Brandon, holding him by his curly red hair and slapping his chubby face. I was practically foaming at the mouth as I shouted and gesticulated through the dark streets. I half hoped a police car would stop and put me in the back seat before I hurt some random passer-by or did myself harm. I was exhausted after weeks and weeks of dealing with the aftermath of the crash and I was channelling my rage and frustration at one innocent little boy who might only tell the truth.

Cynthia had promised to keep Brandon from speaking to Lio about Sasha at the party, but I was not convinced that would happen. I should have just cancelled it. But Cynthia and the whole family were so looking forward to it and we had all developed an incredibly effective system for supporting one another emotionally. We carried one

173

another, and when our desires managed to find a way to articulate themselves through the fog of grief and pain and exhaustion we worked to realise them for one another. But I knew what would happen at this party: Brandon would say something again about Sasha and Lio would hear of his mother's death from his aggravating little companion and not from me.

Clearly, some of the pressure to tell Lio about Sasha from both hospital staff and family was born of self-interest. It certainly would have made everyone else's lives easier if I had just told him as soon as he was conscious; it would have made the system flow more smoothly. But I had no interest in *the system* or how to grease its wheels: my job was to help Lio, not to make things easier for other people, especially if their desire for efficiency was going to hurt my son. This was definitely the case early on when I felt tremendous pressure to 'accept certain limitations' for Lio's future. The number of times I was counselled to simply 'come to terms with the fact that he will have disabilities' or that he will be 'permanently affected' or that he would 'have to go to a school for severely handicapped children' was simply outrageous. It would have made life easier if I had accepted these limits – easier for the medical institutions, in that I would have expected less from Lio and therefore less from them; and it would have been easier for me as well not to risk believing in his recovery – but this would have done Lio a terrible, terrible disservice because he would have picked up on those negative expectations and internalised them. I don't know how I came to realise it so profoundly, and I certainly didn't think this way before the crash, but I believed in that moment and believe it still that your perception affects your results. And I didn't want anything interfering with Lio's perception. I chose the less convenient path. Now the pressure was the same to tell Lio about his mother. This time, however, I was not as strong as I would have liked.

Jeff and Nigel thought Lio must have known already, that he must have figured it out, and that my delaying was just making things harder for him and everyone else. Nurses kept asking me (in a supportive and well-meaning way) if I had told Lio about his mother and wondered whether he might be thinking the worst already. Exhausted as I was, intensely focused on the day-to-day work of his recovery, holding on to each little tangible improvement, all the while knowing that this party meant a lot to Cynthia and everyone else, I didn't have the strength to pull the plug on it. Fortunately, I didn't have to. Penny, often extremely intuitive, just knew I wasn't going to be able to handle a party. She called me the next morning and told me that she had spoken to Cynthia and cancelled the party. I thanked her.

The following week I gave in. I reserved one of the rooms in the child psychology ward nearby for when Lio had finished his therapy for the day. The room contained a wooden doll's house with toy people in it, stuffed animals, three sturdy chairs and an old leaded window that opened less than two inches. The sun shone in and made little criss-cross patterns on the carpet. I wheeled him inside and pulled him up onto my lap – the prongs of his external fixator poking me in the ribs. I held him in my arms as we sat in front of the wooden house and played with the people.

'Lio,' I said, putting down the wooden boy with pink freckles and shorts that I had in my hand. 'I have something to tell you about Mamma.' Lio remained focused on building a tower of toy furniture for the toy people.

'It's something very, very sad and very, very hard.' He didn't say anything.

'Lio, Mamma has died. She died in the accident.' It didn't sink in at first. He didn't understand it. He continued

175

to play as if nothing had been said, as if nothing had happened.

'Lio, I need to tell you that Mamma isn't here with us any more. She's died. But her spirit will always be all around us and in our hearts.' He still didn't get it, and I considered holding off for a few more days or even weeks, but then decided to push on – we'd got this far.

'Lio, please listen to me.' My own voice, calm up until this point, was starting to creak and tremble. 'I'm telling you something very important and very sad. Your mother Sasha has died. She was killed in the crash. She's not on earth any more but up above the clouds in heaven with Granddad. But she'll always be near to us and you'll always be able to feel her. She's looking down on you every day and is so happy that you're doing so well.'

Then Lio went still. The toys slipped from his fingers yet his arms remained outstretched in playing position. And then he started to cry. He cried and wailed inconsolably and with hardly any breaths between the sobs. He cried for what seemed like 20 minutes and I tried to hold him close but the damn external fixator kept getting in the way. There was nothing I could do to comfort him. I couldn't even hold him as he wanted to be held, as I wanted to hold him. My guts turned to ice water and I re-lived that horrible moment when I first learned about Sasha. I put my hand under his chin and my forehead on his.

'I will always be with you,' I said. I repeated over and over and over again to him what I had told him in the car as I left him and Sasha that final time. 'I will always be with you. I will always be with you, and Mamma will always be in our hearts and in our lives together.' It was the best I could manage.

After a long while he calmed a bit and, gasping in between each word, he said, 'I wish you were dead and Mamma was still alive.'

At our wedding
reception at the
Grange in Lewes.

Sasha mountain
climbing while
pregnant – Lio's
favourite story
about his mother.

Lio with his grandmothers Penny and Trudy
on the day of his christening.

Lio at seven months, having a bath at the Mill.

Passo Duran: Sasha and Lio walking on the same mountain trail that Sasha and I hiked on the first time we were in the mountains together.

Lio in the mountains north of the Mill, just prior to meeting some baby goats.

Campo San Lio, Venice.

Lio plays in woods
behind his
grandmother's house
in New Jersey.

Lio and Sasha together in the Dolomites for the last time.

Lio in a French field two weeks before the crash.

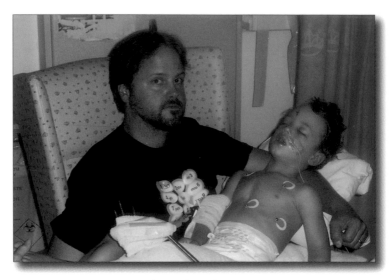

Ten days after the crash.

The cast
comes off!

Lio rides his bike again for the first time since the crash.

With Tony Blair at No. 10.

Lio and me on his sixth birthday in Lewes.

Climbing the Tofane in the Dolomites, Italy.

'Oh Lio,' I winced. 'If I could change places with her, I would in an instant.' And I would have done. I meant it. I myself had wished the same wish more than once in the days prior. Having been able to exchange places with Sasha would have completed my experience of loss. It would have finished it. I had lost so much but not the one thing that could have taken away the pain of that loss – I was alive. But, somehow, so was my son. We had each other and that was something.

Eventually, the crying gave way to silent tears. When they abated, we went back to playing with the wooden house. Lio laughed a choked laugh when I pretended to flush the head of one of the toy people down the toilet. We played at silly stories of people dancing on the dining-room table and stacking up all of the furniture implausibly high in the living room and having some of the grown-up people yell at little ones for jumping on the sofa. Before too long, though, his silliness had ramped up into hysteria, a kind of wild big-eyed laughing that I had never seen in him before. I recoiled in fear and I felt like he was really slipping away. I felt like the psychological blow I had been trying to avoid I had instead succeeded in delivering. Down past his tear-stained cheeks, through his wide, wide open mouth, I was sucked into an abyss. This, like the moment when we were not able to revive him in intensive care, was a deep, dark place I was afraid we might never escape from. I was terrified. I had lost him, too.

But both Lio's mania and my despair passed relatively quickly. He began to play more calmly. I gave him the best hug I could, smiled shyly into his eyes and put him back in his wheelchair. We returned to his room and were greeted by concerned-looking grandparents.

'We'd like a little nap,' I said. Their eyes looked at the floor and they shuffled out. After I settled Lio to sleep, I came out into the corridor.

'Martin,' said my mother. 'How was it?'

'He didn't know,' I said, trying to mask that I was shaken. 'It took a lot of work to get him to understand it.'

'Listen,' said Nigel, looking earnestly into my eyes. 'We will, Penny and me, speak to Lio about Sasha in whatever way you want, in exactly the terms you think best.'

'Thanks, Nigel,' I said and I hugged him, collapsing slightly into his arms.

But it didn't end there. For days afterwards, Lio continued to ask me where his mother was, and I had to tell him again the terrible news, and he would cry all over again. Sometimes, worst of all, he would laugh when I told him; and other times, troublingly, embarrassingly, he would say silly things about his mother being dead or sing silly songs about Sasha dying. These moments did eventually subside and evolve into gentle remembering – sometimes happy, sometimes melancholy – of the things we had done together as a family. Lio, like most children his age, had a hard time with the idea of mortality, with understanding the finality of death, yet – remarkably – he wove his living memories of her into something beautiful that served him somehow. He would reminisce like an old man at the adventures the three of us had had together in Brooklyn and in our mountains as if these things were neither real nor unreal, neither past nor impending. The simple telling and re-telling, hearing and re-hearing of these stories as we looked through old photo albums would comfort him deeply, make him smile and look backward and forward at the same time.

I think, in the end, I suffered more from telling him about Sasha than he did. When I see a child now of a certain age, I am at the mercy of this nervous compulsion to ask him how old he is. And if he says 'four', I am instantly transfixed, my breaths become rapid and short and my hands start to sweat. I can't do anything but re-live that moment in the little room with the wooden doll's house. Four year olds – normal, healthy four year olds – are so tender and fragile, they need so much care and protection. How on earth can they be expected to process news the likes of which Lio received?

The following day, a Saturday, was Nigel's birthday. We all went to Nigel and Penny's house in Wandsworth to spend the night. This was our first night in familiar surroundings and it was magically pleasant. Like all re-entries into places we had known well before the crash, there was something poignant about it. I kept expecting to see (and maybe did see) Sasha in corners, at tables, on the top of the stairs, and kept feeling her behind closed doors. These moments were uncanny, natural and filled with trepidation all at once. I really wanted to see her, and to hold her, and to let her know everything was going to be all right, but more so I wanted her to do and say those same things to me. Still, I felt her by proxy through her family and every second through the boy whose recovery continued to defy all expectations except our own.

After the external fixator on Lio's leg was replaced with a nice blue plaster cast Lio was able to spend more nights in our little flat near the hospital, which helped relieve the boredom of his room on the ward; it was also a bit more comfortable. The end was in sight now, at least for this part of our journey. Most mornings as I lay in bed for a few minutes before getting up I created a little picture in my mind's eye of the hospital doors opening with us walking through them, leaving never to spend a night there again.

On Friday of that week, we went to the Tate Modern and then back to Penny and Nigel's house for the weekend. We saw Lio's cousins, Tyler and Chris, and all went to the Wetlands Centre and Kew Gardens before returning to hospital on Sunday afternoon. Despite one little scene about biscuits in a café, the children played very well together. I don't remember thinking it at the time, but it was incredibly normal: four-year-old kids and their parents and grandparents and uncles and aunts and cousins get together and do things like going to gardens and parks and wildlife centres. Lio, teetering only slightly on his yellow walker, didn't just want to play with the other kids, he actually did it. He was actually getting in there and having fun with kids he didn't know. He dragged his blue-plastered leg up the giant fibreglass flower and slid down just like his cousins. He pulled himself up the cargo net to get into the little tree-pod house. And he laughed a real, genuine, authentic, four-year-old laugh while slithering around on his stomach in the giant mole tunnels underneath everything. And other kids laughed with him. Sometimes other children would withdraw as Lio tried to interact with them, but he was in there trying and doing. I was so stunned by how well he was managing that I didn't fully appreciate what a typical scene it was. Would that all parents, myself included, could take such daily pleasure in the simple playing of their children. He had moments of genuine happiness that weekend, real, normal, everyday childhood happiness. I gathered up a few more pieces of my heart.

On Monday my mother, patient, generous to a fault and showing very little sign of her own health issues, flew back home to the US for just two days to sort out some necessary paperwork and to see her own doctors. My respect and love for her during the preceding two months had been greater than at any time since I was a small child. She never complained about anything, she was there to support me whenever I needed it but never pressured me, and rarely (this is the most remarkable thing) invited me to question my judgement. It would be a lie, though, to say she never wound me up during her stay. Parent–child tensions can run very deep and in spite of everything I found myself caught up in the old currents once or twice.

One morning, in the kitchen of our little flat, I was cutting up a banana for my cereal and going over in my mind questions for my two meetings that day – one with the neuropsychologist and one with the lawyer.

'You know,' she said, 'we'll have to get more bananas if Lio is going to be here this evening.'

On that morning, those innocuous words hit a nerve that had been scraped raw since childhood by statements of the obvious that I didn't need to hear: 'If it's cold, wear a hat.' 'Don't burn yourself in the kitchen.' 'Remember to make a good impression.' 'Check to make sure you have enough gas.' But as these perfectly normal mother-to-son communications continued in various forms into my adulthood my tolerance for them had eroded rather than improved and her simple, throwaway comment there in the kitchen finally broke me. I dropped my knife with a clatter on the countertop and raised up my hands to the ceiling. I lifted my head and shook as I opened my mouth and let out a silent scream. Out of the corner of my eye I could see a wave of anxiety cross her face as she bent her head down and pretended to concentrate on buttering her toast.

'Mom!' I exploded. 'Has it occurred to you that I have more important things to think about right now than bananas?!'

'I was just saying—' I didn't want her to go on.

'All I do all day long is worry about really important things for Lio. It's my job now.' What I heard in her innocent comment about fruit was a subtle criticism that I was somehow not doing right by Lio. I wasn't taking care of him as I should.

'OK,' she said hastily. 'I'll go to the store and get some bananas later this morning.'

I left my bowl of cereal untouched on the counter, walked out of the kitchen, got my coat and left the flat without saying a word. I was exhausted, nervous and, I freely admit, irrational.

She returned on Wednesday, 1 November, in time for Lio to have his cast taken off.

On Friday we went back to Nigel and Penny's again for the weekend. After she'd first met Lio, Miranda had lovingly made a cardboard rocket with 25 little spaces for stars on it. Every time Lio did good work in one of his therapies or at the hospital school he got a star sticker to put on his rocket. When he got to the top, he was going to get a 'fabulous prize'. That day had arrived. Lio had reached the top of his rocket and I wanted to organise something special, more than a gift, a memory to mark another great milestone in his recovery. I decided to take him on the London Eye, the giant panoramic Ferris wheel on the Thames in the heart of London. Sasha and I had often talked about taking a ride in it, but the weather was never right, or it was too crowded, or it was the wrong time of the year; there were always reasons to put it off. I like to think now that she might have put it off to make this first experience of it more special and more memorable than it would have otherwise been for us. On Friday night I booked tickets online for all of us at sunset on Saturday: Lio and me, my mother, Tyler and Chris, and their parents Margherita and Jeff. Lio in his wheelchair got us to the front of the line and the attendant, perhaps because of Lio, gave us our own cabin, a giant bubble floating high above London all to ourselves.

'Do you want to get out of your wheelchair and hold on to the rail?' I offered, seeing Lio excitedly using the armrests to push himself up and then flop back in his chair over and over.

'Yes, yes,' he said softly, but his smile was broad and his eyes were wide. He slid out of his chair in a second, grabbed on to the rail with both hands and off he went shimmying around our sphere. I watched without a worry. I was serene, I was transparent; it was as if I was watching him fly from a distance.

My eyes drifted from my son to the city receding below: St Paul's, Green Park, the Globe. Each one of those landmarks was filled with a memory of Lio's mother that I lingered on and re-lived as we floated.

Thump. Thump. Thump. My dream was pierced. Lio had manoeuvred himself round to the concave doors of the bubble, his nose touched the glass and he was looking straight down at the river below. He was banging hard on the glass doors as he grinned to himself and leaned perilously. I was over to him like lightning and put my hand on his chest. There was absolutely no danger – this was a major tourist attraction and I knew the doors were perfectly well sealed – but the sight of it scared me nonetheless.

I left my hand there and felt his heart beating under my palm; it was quick and steady and warm. Everyone else in our floating ball faded away. I held Lio for a long time. I was tempted to start pointing out the sights, the Tate Modern, Millennium Bridge, the Gherkin, but I checked myself before I started, preferring just to let the scene envelop us. It was almost exactly like one of my meditations of our future: Lio and I together and unstoppable, doing anything, even flying above a city at sunset. Very near the top Lio turned to face me and started to pull on my cheeks with his free hand.

'Did Mamma do this?' I didn't know whether he was talking about my cheeks or about the Ferris wheel ride, but I assumed the latter.

'No,' I said gently. 'But she really wanted to one day and I like to think she's with us now.'

He looked quizzical, then delighted. 'We have wings,' he said. 'Can we do this again?'

'There are going to be loads more rewards in your future, champ. And you can choose to do whatever you want.' In truth, this particular reward worked out to be as much mine as it was his. We floated down like angels from wispy clouds ablaze with colour. With a gentle hiss, the doors of our glass bubble opened and we fluttered out along the Southbank, drunk on vertigo and memories. A curtain of pigeons parted and we were surrounded by jugglers and acrobats and musicians and living statues. Lio seemed intrigued, if a bit surprised, by a pirate statue who assaulted his wheelchair, clapped him in irons and insisted we take a photo. Which we did.

On Monday, 6 November, Lio learned how to manage stairs. The therapists showed him how to go up using his backside and his arms. It was slightly degrading, seeing a boy who used to dash up mountains at lightning speed reduced to this odd and dirty manoeuvre. But it needed to be done and it would turn out to be only necessary for a few weeks. I consoled myself with the more wholly positive aspects of his recovery, like his work with Lego. After his re-education on the stairs, Lio went to the hospital school, where he managed to put together a Lego car with very little help, finding all the right pieces and putting everything where it needed to go. I made one, too, and we raced them down the corridor ramp outside the school. It wasn't long before the other two boys who were meant to be in the hospital school were out in the corridor with us, racing cars down the ramp. One of the teachers came out and mocked a frown, which made us all giggle.

On this Monday, Penny and I had an almost comical

meeting with Dr Michael Kahn, one of the head paediatric orthopaedic surgeons at the hospital. He took Penny and me into the interview room on the ward and in a Middle-Eastern accent, with very serious tones and melodramatic phrases, he told me that Lio would likely never bend his leg more than the 45 degrees he was able to at the moment. He told me further that because the growth plate on his left leg was damaged he would need to have the growth stopped on that leg, as well as the growth stopped on the *good leg*. Still further, because Lio had lost nearly an inch of length on the injured leg as a result of the way the bone had healed after the crash, he might have to have his *good leg shortened*. That was *the way it was going to be*, said the paediatric orthopaedic surgeon. Beneath his short sentences and matter-of-fact expression he was saying more than that Lio's childhood would be marked by a shoe raise, it would be deprived of football and basketball, of games of tag, of running over hills and hiking in mountains, of bike riding and skateboarding, and probably even deprived of friends.

He consoled us in a soft voice rendered even more surreal by his thick accent, 'I think it best if I leave you now with this information. I know it is an awful lot to take in.'

I, for my part, had a smile ear to ear. It must have seemed very odd to poor Dr Kahn, unsettling even, and perhaps my smile was the thing that prompted him to bid for a hasty retreat rather than any sense of allowing a parent to come to terms with terrible news. I was thankful that Lio's leg had been saved (very much an open question at the beginning), but more than that I simply did not accept what he had said, so much so I almost laughed out loud when I heard it. It wasn't just that I didn't believe the good doctor, I simply knew that he was utterly wrong.

We had been down this road before and I had learned how to play the head games that were a necessary part of medical relationships. I was also now well versed in the general language of the medical establishment. It was a language of pessimism, preparing families for the worst. This has the effect of lowering expectations (for recovery and for treatments) and can, if you're not very careful, lead to a deadly and self-fulfilling spiral of hopelessness (if something is hopeless, then there's little point in trying). This language has the additional effect of ensuring families are most often pleased with the results because the results they'd been led to expect were far worse. As I grappled with this way of thinking during our months of Lio's rehabilitation in Britain, I began to hatch a little theory: maybe this attitude, this tendency toward pessimism (as Sasha warned me about), or cynicism even, might be a deeply ingrained cultural condition that stretched back to the Second World War. During the Blitz, it might have been a way of preparing for the bombs to hit. The thinking goes like this: if you know what to expect, you'll be prepared and not surprised when things start exploding all around you, and therefore picking up the pieces will be a bit less painful and traumatic. Obviously, this is not a character trait confined to Britain, and not everyone is afflicted by it, but I do find that here the glass is usually half empty. The problem with this thinking is that, while it may prepare you for disasters, it doesn't particularly enable you to avoid them. You become resolved to the worst happening because that's what you're preparing for. It poisons your thinking in a way that infects all of your actions. It distracts you from finding alternatives. You're told what's what and, it seems, it's the sensible and grown-up thing to do to accept what you're told and move on. When imported into the field of healthcare, however, this tendency has potentially devastating consequences. If your expectations are lower, you won't try as hard at therapies, at self-improvement, at making your life or your family's life better.

It may be stoic, and even 'rational' in some masochistic

sense, but it shows a deep lack of faith, even the non-religious kind, of simple positive thinking, which might prevent you from visualising and working towards the best possible future. All of this, you would have thought, makes pessimism self-evidently bad medicine. Bad outcomes are presented as Fate and great literature is littered with fools who chose to argue with Fate. This fool smiled across at Penny, who was looking flustered, perplexed and angry in the chair by the door. As Dr Kahn was getting up to leave, she started firing panicky questions at him. I held up my hand for her to stop. She did stop, her head sinking to her chest, and Dr Kahn left.

I smiled again at her and said, 'That's not going to happen. None of that is going to happen.' I don't know how to explain my certainty other than to say I simply knew this in my heart and I saw us going down a different path in my mind. And my vision prevailed.

As with Dr Doom earlier, I'm sure Dr Kahn was a good person. Beyond that, I'm sure he was describing the situation as he saw it, doing his best, and doing a very hard and unpleasant part of his job. I can't imagine having to give parents news like that on a regular basis. It must age you prematurely and you must develop strategies to make it easier for yourself (like preparing families with worst-case scenarios). You couldn't pay me enough to do his job and I'm sure he doesn't get what he deserves. But nevertheless, his strategy for self-preservation and the slightly melodramatic way that he chose to present his message were completely inappropriate for me. Perhaps he, like the others, was trying to show gentleness and sensitivity, but I found it infuriating in the first instance and laughable in the second.

It must be said that not all our doctors felt the need to employ the same strategies. Daniel, the orthopaedic surgeon who worked on Lio under Dr Kahn, had a much more open-ended approach. After I told him about Dr Kahn's prognosis, he, showing tremendous courage and probably complete disregard for hospital protocol, said there were other options to look into. I'm grateful to him for his honesty, and also his bravery because (as he must have known) the consultations with other doctors that followed from his advice led to some critical appraisals of his surgical work on Lio's leg.

On 9 November, two months and two days after the crash, the end of our stay in the hospital was well and truly in sight. An enormous party was held for Lio in the physiotherapy gym with all the nurses, doctors, teachers, interns, secretaries, administrators, therapists and even some gatecrashers I didn't recognise. Virtually everyone Lio had met during his stay in hospital had been charmed by him and practically all of them were there, each bringing a plate of something. My mother supplied the cake: chocolate with white icing and strawberries on top because that was the kind Lio had asked for. Someone had brought funny flying balloons that only I seemed to have enough lung-power to blow up. Lio loved them and had me doing them until my face was red and veins bulged out of my forehead.

The kindness of the staff was staggering. But in the end I got the idea that they were merely returning a favour somehow. I sensed that they genuinely wanted to do this for Lio because he had done something for them. I'm not sure exactly what it was, but it had something to do with his resilience, his tenacity and his irrepressible smile. It also had to do with restoring their faith somehow, or giving them an opportunity to express it. He came to them having lost his mother and nearly dead, with very dire prognoses. They first met him with solemnity and compassion, some of them uncertain whether anything they might do would help him. Others were simply exhausted and burnt out after years of limited resources and very hard work with sometimes disappointing results. Their work with Lio, though, when taken together with his own courage and strength of character, his dedication to his own recovery, plus the constant attention and profoundest love from his family, had brought him back, had made him what our local newspaper took to calling him: 'Lewes's little miracle'. Maybe Lio reminded them of why they had chosen to become doctors and nurses and therapists and hospital teachers in the first place; maybe he gave them back a bit of belief in their own ability to work wonders. Lio was their reward and their promise of more of the same in the future. He was their poster child for things going right, for everything happening as well as it could. And at his party (aside from me) the person who was the happiest to see him pursuing recovery so well was Dr Doom. She glowed with something, exactly what I can't say: pride, love or simple joy. I was very glad she managed to drop in.

On 9 November, I posted this update on Lio's website:

> The rest of this week will be bittersweet: we leave the hospital on Friday and head back home for Lewes and Charleston, where Lio will be in rehab. I have such tremendous faith and trust in the people who have been caring for Lio in the hospital; I really feel they are profoundly invested (on a personal and emotional level) in his recovery. Maybe it's just that we've been around far longer than anyone else in the place (more than two months), or because they saw him when he was close to death, but it really does seem like they love him, an impression I don't always get as I watch them interact with other children. I worry that it will be difficult to build relationships like these in the rehab centre.
>
> It's also a bit bittersweet because even as Lio

189

continues to make progress every day, the pace of his recovery has slowed down: we're taking small steps in speech and concentration whereas before he was making great leaps. When the therapists were cautioning today about long-term problems and difficulties, my own spirit took some bruising. Also, after seven weeks in a cast or covering of one form or another, Lio's left leg has finally been unveiled, unfortunately it's two centimetres shorter than his right leg. This means lots of quite scary surgery is probably in his future. We were all so focused on his brain injury that his leg seemed like it would take care of itself somehow. But everyone has always said, as they continue to say, his recovery (in all its forms) will take a very long time.

Lio's leg aside, he does seem much of the time like the boy he was before the accident.

He is a witty little comedian with a tenderness and an empathy far beyond his years: last week when he said out of the blue, 'I expect the lorry driver is a bit sad too,' I couldn't hold back the tears. The promise of him returning to his regular school, which is imminent, makes him extremely excited and fills me with hope. Given all that we've been through in these past eight weeks it's sometimes hard for me to remember (and a bit daunting when I do remember it) that we're still only at the beginning of his healing.

And I am heartened on a daily basis by little comments from everyone at the hospital: from the psychologist on his social skills: 'You don't usually see that until they reach eight or nine'; from a doctor when Lio translated a sentence from Italian to English: 'There aren't many four year olds who can do that'; from a physiotherapist on Lio using a walker to get around: 'We never even try this with children as young as Lio.' I will miss them all.

Please keep us in your thoughts as we take this next big step in his recovery.

Love & love,

Lio & Martin

The next day was Lio's last in the hospital. We spent that night at the flat, tidied it up and returned our keys. We rolled into the hospital in his wheelchair to find another child in his room. This was a shock because it was 'Lio's room': we had been there so long, that's what everyone called it. The nurses must have spent an hour pulling all our photos and posters and postcards and pictures off the walls, collecting his menagerie of stuffed animals, finding all his books and then packing everything up in big green hospital sacks for us to take. We didn't know they were going to do this otherwise we would have done it ourselves. All that remained were the Paddington Bear stickers that were on the wall when we moved in. Lio pushed himself into Jack's room, reached out and touched his sleeping foot and said goodbye. I hugged Franny and told her I'd be thinking of them. She smiled slightly, thanked me and invited Lio out for ice cream when we had all made it home. We headed towards the exit of the ward teetering under the load of presents everyone had heaped on Lio. These people were more than just caregivers; they were like an extended family, and it scared me a bit to be leaving them.

We walked out of the hospital, Lio on his bright yellow walker, light as the balloons we were holding on to. My son walked out of the hospital under his own power two months after he was nearly killed in the crash, two months after I was told he might be a vegetable or might never speak or might never walk again. He did it. I don't know who was prouder, him or me. We went for one last meal at the Sun and Doves, our serviceable local pub. Lio took a pen and one of the pub menus and sketched a beautifully precise drawing of a person under an arch. I asked him what it was and he said, 'It's me leaving the hospital.' It was another of those hundreds of moments throughout this journey when emotion overtook me and tears stung my eyes. We would spend that weekend at Nigel and Penny's house and then go down to Lewes to settle back into our home.

Part 3

And so, as well as giving me change, and joy, give me sensation in all its colours, sounds, smells, tastes, and touches.

Oh, and our communal imagination; sweet miracles of humanity.

Beauty may not always have a wider purpose. Sometimes, beauty may be more about playfulness: the play of colour, of sound, of sunlight; of water, of words, of a smile. In empiricist, embarrassed, and anxious times, playfulness – like beauty – seems frivolous. This is both a failure of confidence and of discernment. Playfulness is what unites the child and the grown-up. Playfulness is part of the human condition.

– Sasha Roberts

The Media and
the Victim Statement

While we were in hospital, the lorry driver was in police custody. At the initial hearing, he pleaded guilty to causing death by dangerous driving and a date for sentencing was set for some weeks later. As the date approached, Paul, our police liaison, asked me to write a 'victim statement' for the court, describing how the accident had affected our lives. I almost laughed at the idea. Our lives were so completely transformed it was impossible to know where to begin. But Paul encouraged me to write something and said that these statements were usually just read by a judge privately before sentencing.

I wasn't at all apprehensive about doing it. In many ways, I looked on writing a victim statement as an opportunity, my first real opportunity, to try to make sense of an impossibly senseless situation. It was my chance to force some skeleton of structure onto the chaos and insanity of the event and the aftermath. It was as if putting it all into words, writing a story that I could tell to myself, would help me cope somehow. It was also an opportunity to communicate to someone, if only the judge, the pain I had been forcing down every day in order to maintain my outlook. I wanted empathy, even from a stranger, and I was going to draw on all my years working in journalism to get it. I was going to write a solid, honest, cathartic, moving statement. My mother, Jeff, Nigel and Penny all wrote statements as well. Penny's focused on the moment of the accident in which Sasha's last act was to try to protect her son from the oncoming lorry. Her last act was saving her son. No one can say for certain this is what happened, indeed I like to think that she didn't notice anything at all, but Penny's was a useful image to her.

This was my victim statement, dated 11 November 2006:

> To whom it may concern:
> I write to relay to you how the events of 7 September 2006 have changed our lives.
>
> On 6 September I had a perfect life. I had a wife who loved me and whom I loved with all my heart. Every day I told her how much she meant to me and every day she told me how wonderful I was. We had the same tastes, the same interests, the same passions and the same big and wonderful plans for our future. We were hoping to have a second child this year, Sasha was going to publish her first children's book, we were going to collaborate on a radio play, act together in a local charity pantomime and do all the small but wonderful things that a couple in love approaching middle age is meant to do – things that are now just dust and memories. At the centre of our lives was the profound love we shared for our marvellous son Lio.
>
> Lio was an exceptional boy; these are not just the words of a proud father but the words of everyone who knew him. At the age of four he would introduce himself to other children and adults alike by saying, 'My name is Lio and I speak five languages.' He did indeed speak excellent Italian, excellent English, rudimentary French and a few phrases of Spanish and German. Records from his nursery school attest to the fact that he was speaking and writing far above

average and his social skills were extremely sophisticated. He charmed everyone he met and everyone marvelled that he was only four.

He was as athletic as he was intelligent. Last winter shortly after his fourth birthday he learned to ski while visiting family in Italy. He took to it so naturally and so well we imagined it would always be something that would give him pleasure. He climbed mountains with us and slept overnight in mountain refuges from the age of two. This August he learned to ride his bicycle without stabilisers and riding his bike on holiday with us was one of his (and my) greatest joys. Every night either his mother or I would put him to bed with a little song and with suggestions for the wonderful things we were going to do the next day.

Today life is very different. Bedtimes now are not the scene of pleasant expectation but of a relentless torrent of pain and tears. Lio stares blankly for minutes on end at the picture of him and his mother beside his bed. Every night he says '*Voglio Mamma.*' ('I want Mummy.') And every night I must tell this precious four year old that his mother is dead. He then asks why. That is where my spirit sinks because I have no answer for him. He tells me that he wishes I had died in the crash instead of his mother and I can only tell him that if it were possible for me to trade places with her I would in an instant. He sobs to me how beautiful she was and how no one will ever be as beautiful. When he finally does drift off, he occasionally cries out in his sleep and tosses and turns constantly in search of a more comfortable position for his now deformed leg.

He wakes almost always before 5.00 a.m. moaning in pain because his knee has become swollen in the night. I dose him with paracetamol and ibuprofen to try to settle him a bit longer, but it seldom works. As I lift him from the bed and carry him downstairs to his wheelchair, he shrieks in such pain that my right ear now has a constant ringing in it. Where our days together were once filled with fun and adventure, they are now an exhausting struggle with the very normal and mundane things of life: holding a spoon without hand tremors, going to the loo without causing too much pain to his unbending knee and trying to get him to concentrate for more than a few seconds on the simplest of tasks.

Where Lio was once destined for a truly great and exceptional life I now think a 'normal' and 'average' existence would be a tremendous accomplishment for him. He may never walk again; he may never hold a real job or feel a sense of accomplishment in the adult world that was his birthright; he may never ride a bike again; he may never do a crossword, or speak French again, or have a wife and a family of his own, or do all of the things that I once took for granted in his future. He will have to have several tremendously intricate and dangerous operations on his leg. Currently the consultant is proposing an operation to stunt the growth in his *good* leg to keep it growing in pace with his bad leg (already shortened two centimetres because of the accident). And as his speech falters and his train of thought gets constantly interrupted, his cognitive future is nothing but a giant question mark.

The loss of Sasha is not just devastating to me and to our son. Indeed the whole of our intellectual community has lost a person of exceptional talent and potential. Sasha was one of the most accomplished of her generation of Renaissance scholars, with publications too numerous to list here. She pioneered new areas of research, was a staple on the international conference scene and was recognised all over the world for her innovative approaches to literature. But she was not just an academic; before she died she had nearly finished her first publishable children's book. She is missed by all who knew and all who read her.

My own professional life is all but finished as well. A year ago I started a new position as senior lecturer at the University of Sussex. I was revamping its digital media curriculum and adding new graduate courses. My own radio projects had been on stations in a dozen countries and my own writing was very well known. I had just won a prestigious Arts and Humanities Research Council grant to write a book in 2007. Now instead of researching for my book I spend what little time I have researching paediatric orthopaedic surgeons and acquired brain injury rehabilitation treatments. Lio is completely dependent on me and I may never be able to return to my old work and my own projects again. Before I was at the top of my game; now I am an anonymous carer of a handicapped child. I cannot see the day when I will be able to enjoy the things I once enjoyed: the pride in my own work, the travel, the pleasure in seeing Lio excel and the company of someone nearly as wonderful as my wife.

Yet I would be dishonest if I said the two months of Lio's hospitalisation were without joy. Holding him as he gradually came out of a coma after two weeks, seeing him smile again for the first time, watching him eat again for the first time, hearing him speak again for the first time and witnessing how his tremendous struggle to recover moved both hardened nurses and seen-it-all-before doctors to tears has filled me with a happiness that is impossible to describe. But perhaps the most touching moment of all for me happened ten days ago when Lio said out of the blue, 'I expect the driver of the lorry is a bit sad too.' I was left utterly speechless. It is my prayer that Lio never loses this angelic empathy and that his recovery continues in both mind and body.

Yours faithfully,

Martin Spinelli

For whatever reason, my statement was read out in open court at the sentencing hearing. I was not prepared for this. Paul, our police liaison, however, thought that it was quite an achievement, as victim statements are seldom read in open court. But I wrote what I wrote for the judge, and more so for the police officers who were working hard to get a conviction that might help our civil case. They asked me, they said it would help, so I did it and I did it as openly and as honestly as I possibly could. There were, of course, journalists in the court and they printed much of my victim statement in the next day's papers. *The Telegraph* ran the biggest story: half a page, with an enormous photo of Sasha and Lio. Apparently they had also called to speak to me at home, but my mother wanted to protect me so she fielded the call. What she said didn't really bother me, but I do regret what she didn't say. She didn't mention that we were planning on establishing a memorial scholarship in Sasha's name at the University of Kent, something to ensure her memory would live on. I would have liked a mention of that in the story.

When my family read the story in *The Telegraph*, they were shocked. They were shocked that I had not told them so many of the things I had been feeling and grappling with. They also knew I wasn't expecting the victim statement to appear in a national newspaper and were worried how I would react, so they hid the paper from me and didn't say anything about it. A day after the story came out someone mentioned reading it in the paper and I was puzzled. I asked Nigel and Penny and, once they realised I knew, they showed me the copy that they had been saving. Apparently, they also wanted to protect me, from what exactly I can't quite say.

Yet, when I first saw it, I was mortified. I was hurt and felt slightly exploited somehow. But these feelings did pass and I realised clearly in that moment of having the story in one of the most widely read papers in the country that what I was experiencing had value to people, meant something to people, perhaps might even bring a sense of hope or possibility or determination or strength to people. I realised that telling stories plainly and clearly about human events and tragedies and suffering (and efforts to deal with them) had a human value. I realised that so much of the literature that I used to snipe at, literature in which people expressed their feelings, was profoundly valuable to a profound number of people – that it could reach and comfort and help in both practical and more esoteric ways. Perhaps it's even simpler than that. Perhaps stories about overcoming loss and sources of hope are simply necessary to the human psyche.

The small crisis of seeing our story in the paper was completely transforming. When you're thrown without warning into a sea of fear and anxiety and anticipation, you discover (as with so many things) that you can swim, that you have the resources to survive. It may be difficult and even painful that first time, but most people manage it quite well and some even come to like it. In the end, you can make it work for you: being put into a public situation where you are forced to articulate, and articulate in a careful and considered way, your feelings and your beliefs about a tragedy can help in your own psychological and spiritual healing. It's a kind of therapy. But also, having it as part of some printed public record that you can find on the internet months, even years, after the fact is tremendously sustaining.

In the weeks that followed I was contacted by several journalists wanting to do stories about Lio's miraculous recovery and about how we were managing after the crash. It was often very hard talking to reporters about what happened, and I would be lying if I said allowing myself to be drawn into public introspection was never difficult or embarrassing. I did tear up; I even found there were moments when I couldn't go on. But those tears were good, I cherished them even, because they brought me closer to Sasha, they brought me closer to what we had and they allowed our life together to be a part of me again.

On Sunday, 12 November, my departed father's birthday, I went to hear mass at Westminster Cathedral in London. It happened to be, coincidence of coincidences, the feast of Saint Lio, patron saint of choristers. Choir voices ebbed through the incense-filled air and I felt again as if I were floating among the statues over the nave. I saw myself from above in a packed cathedral without an empty seat. It was a situation strange beyond my ability to express: my father's birthday, the feast of Saint Lio, and the day Lio and I were returning home. I knelt long after the mass in front of candles I'd lit for Lio, Sasha and myself. I took this convergence of things as confirmation of how special my son was and of how lucky I'd been to have him as a child, and as an affirmation that we were on the right path.

That afternoon we all drove down to Lewes. Lio was delighted to be in his own room again and in his own bed again, surrounded by his own toys again. I tried to breathe his happiness into my own lungs. This was the first step on the long and weird road of being home without a wife and mother. Even though my brothers had dutifully packed away most of Sasha's clothes, her presence, and her absence, were inescapable. She was and she wasn't everywhere: in the brilliant white paint she'd chosen for the walls; in her excessive collection of tea and tea-making paraphernalia that had colonised half an entire kitchen cupboard; in the paintings she had done and others she had spent real money on (often without consulting me); in our enormous empty bed. Surrounded by it all, I became slightly hyper and manic, but I was determined not to let returning to our house, to Sasha's house, be traumatic or be stained with too many tears. I lit a fire in the small coal fireplace. I found the best bottle of wine in the house, a bottle of pinot noir that Sasha and I had been saving for our next anniversary, and opened it. I cooked a nice meal of chicken with balsamic vinegar and capers and we ate well.

Penny's spirits were failing a bit; her face was long and her eyes were downcast. But she held Lio close to her and managed to keep it together throughout the evening. That night, to try to start our new routine as normally as possible, I put Lio to sleep in his own bed. He wanted to wear his favourite orange-and-brown spider pjyamas. I slept in the bunk bed above 'to keep an eye on him', I told myself. But in truth I didn't want to sleep in our bed, Sasha's bed, my bed, alone. I left that bed for Nigel and Penny; my mother slept in the converted attic. As I drifted in and out of sleep that night, I felt sure that Sasha was there in that house. I knew she was with us and would continue to be there somehow. Having come this far, having crossed this hurdle of returning home, being comfortable in that house without the sound of Sasha's sweet voice, it really did seem as if anything was possible.

On Wednesday, 15 November, two months and eight days after the crash, Lio started at his brain-injury rehabilitation centre in Charleston. It was an abortive start and a terrible low point after the transcendence of Lio's leaving hospital and our weekend. I had called two days before he was meant to start, on Monday, as had been agreed, to find out what Lio's schedule for the week was going to be. When they told me that they planned to put off his start a whole week, I was so angry I couldn't see straight. After two months of constant therapy in the hospital, after having promised Lio a similar daily regime of therapy to start on that day, it felt like we were being put off.

'This is not what we were promised,' I said, kicking up a fuss on the phone to the junior administrator on the other end.

'Mr Spinelli, all I can tell you is Lio is not on the schedule this week,' the administrator attempted to calm me. 'From what I can see, the therapists simply aren't available.'

I was not about to lose the momentum of Lio's recovery. 'When I made the decision to place Lio with you, it was based on your promise that he would begin as soon as he was discharged from the hospital. If you had told me you couldn't schedule him this week, I would have put off his discharge, or placed him somewhere else. This isn't right,' I seethed.

'I'll talk to the manager and the therapists and see what we can manage,' he said.

'Thank you,' I said, not meaning it. I put down the phone and fumed while my mother looked at me with concern. I called my lawyer for some insight and support, half wondering whether I should threaten to get litigious with the rehab centre. He settled me a bit and said that he was sure they'd be able to find some space for Lio this week. He asked if I thought the upheaval of moving back up to London to put Lio in the other potential rehab centre was worth it. I said it wasn't and put the phone down again. Then I called my friend Rene. She called them bastards, and said we were being treated shabbily, but couldn't offer anything else. I put the phone down and hugged Lio for a very long time.

Later that afternoon the phone rang and they ultimately managed to squeeze Lio in for an 'evaluation morning' on Wednesday. We met the physiotherapists, the speech and language therapists, the occupational therapist and finally the paediatrician, Tracy Green. It was Tracy's sweet face I'd encountered when I had come to visit Charleston while considering which rehab centre was right for Lio. She told me about the facilities, about what they could offer him and, crucially, about his treatment beginning the Monday after he had been discharged from the hospital.

When I met her again that Wednesday, I spoke with her alone in one of the consultation rooms as my mother looked after Lio in the lobby. She hadn't picked up on my frustration when she smiled gently and started to tell me about their plans.

'We've scheduled Lio for three sessions of speech and language, two sessions of physio and two sessions of occupational therapy a week,' she said.

'That's a lot less than we've been used to in the hospital,' I interrupted.

'We don't want him exhausted by the end of the week, do we?' Her voice became ever so slightly patronising and a bit more English.

'I'm particularly concerned about his leg and his physiotherapy.' I was not going to be put off. 'He's used to getting five sessions of physio a week and that's what I and his orthopaedic surgeons are expecting he gets in rehab. Two sessions just aren't enough.'

'Our feeling is that he only needs it twice a week now rather than five, and two is what we can offer.' Tracy was digging in her heels. 'You have to realise that there are limits on what we're going to be able to do and on what he's going to be able to achieve. Let's focus on getting him into school rather than his therapy.' As if the one were not related to the other.

I tried to calm myself, but with insuppressible emotion I said, 'What you're offering us now is different from what we originally discussed. This is not what we agreed and we need more.' I was coming to pieces at this point. I needed to convince her that Lio needed more therapy, but I couldn't get the message across. Once again I found myself drowning in loss and limitation. My voice started to crack.

'*You* have to realise' – no longer able to hold back the tears – 'that Lio is all I have left in the world.'

After a long pause she said, 'I've heard it all before.' In those five words I experienced what was absolutely the cruellest and most thoughtless thing anyone has ever said to me in the course of Lio's recovery and indeed my entire life. I was split in two by the callousness of her statement. She, only a couple of years younger than me, could not have possibly heard it all before.

I wanted to jump up and shout: 'Well, excuse the fuck out of me! This has never *happened* to me before! It's not every day that you lose a wife and your only child suffers severe brain damage!'

'I've heard it all before' – that's what she said. If she had known what was going through my mind in that moment, she would have called security instantly.

If instead she'd said, 'I know you were expecting more, but this is all I can offer you at the moment and if you'd like some help finding private therapists to fill in the missing sessions I can make some recommendations.' Fine.

Or if she'd said, 'We simply don't have the resources and Lio is not nearly as badly off as most of our patients.' Fine, too.

But 'I've heard it all before'! She's lucky she didn't lose her teeth. That's a terrible thing to say, I know, but I was exhausted and desperate and fragile. For months I'd been suffering from lack of sleep, lack of independence and lack of control; every dream I'd had of my future had been completely undone, my son was now utterly dependent on me and here was this Tracy telling me she'd heard it all before.

After she said that, with rage boiling inside me at a bedside manner that would have embarrassed the Marquis de Sade, I sat up bolt straight, dried my tears, stared blankly at her face, tuned out her explanations and simply resolved to find our own therapists to supplement what they were offering. I was not about to let their staffing situation dictate my son's care. It was easy enough; so easy, in fact, that I was again a little startled at my new-found ability to sidestep bureaucratic forces that I would have acquiesced to before the crash. The sensation of loss dissolved away and I'm happy to say the physiotherapist I found was better, stronger, more committed and much more invested than the one we had at the rehab centre.

All that being said, the therapy we received in rehab was often extremely good (particularly the occupational and speech therapies). Even Tracy, when she wasn't trying to reconcile available staff hours with my son's needs, was a good and dedicated paediatrician who was only ever warm and positive with Lio personally. But while I am extremely grateful for their help and the way they've followed and supported Lio's recovery, I would be lying if I said I never missed the staff at King's College Hospital. The therapists, the nurses, the doctors down to a person all made us feel not merely 'looked after' but 'cared for'. The people there made every day of Lio's future possible, and he and I will always be grateful to them.

The following week Lio's second cousin Kevin, who is a few months older, came from New Jersey to visit with his mother (my cousin) Laura, his father Steve and his older brother Kyle. They were there really to provide a sense of continuity with our American lives and to give us a sense of the option of returning to the States. Their trip was organised and paid for by my mother and it was clear that she wanted to remind me of a potential future on the other side of the ocean – which was no bad thing.

It was, of course, wonderful to see them. But from the very first day I remember feeling somewhat heartbroken at watching Lio and Kevin play together. Even though Lio was slightly younger, he had always seemed to match Kevin in conversation and curiosity, and he could be even more sociable. But now, hearing Kevin talk with inflection and seeing his eyes dart about only drew me to how slow and monotone Lio's voice was and how lacklustre his eyes were most of the time. Lio would fumble for words while Kevin was engaging with the world and the novelty of a new place. Perhaps that was part of it, perhaps the surroundings were simply familiar to Lio and that's why he looked dull by comparison. This was something that I could tell myself at least to soothe my anxieties in the short term. While Lio's recovery had been miraculous so far, it was moments like this one that reminded me of how far we still had to go.

On 27 November, two months and twenty days after the crash, Lio went to school for the first time. It was the school his mother and I had chosen for him, the school he should have started at only four days after the crash. The idyllic Iford & Kingston Primary was a small village school, nestled in the South Downs, with views of sheep on rolling hills and chalky-white cliffs in the distance. Sasha and I had looked at every single school in Lewes. We'd spent days talking to head teachers and reading government reports on each of them. We visited classes and spoke with children and staff. Iford & Kingston was the last school we visited and we found the children there the perfect combination of happy, spirited and well behaved. The head teacher was smart, congenial and fun. And even though it meant a drive rather than a walk to school we knew the day we saw it that it would be perfect for Lio. We couldn't have known how perfect. In the days after the crash, I called the school and left a message about what had happened. I told the school staff I didn't know when or if Lio would be coming to school but that I would keep them informed. Through a host of other people (social workers, police and hospital teachers), Lio's school followed his recovery. His reception class sent him a lovely card with photos of all the children and drawings and their attempts to write their names. It held pride of place on the wall in Lio's room at the hospital and it was like a little arrow towards his future, a sign of what lay beyond in the outside world. I knew one day he would be joining those children in the photo, learning with them, playing with them, making friends with them. I imagined Lio in that photo and when I did he was smiling his old smile and his eyes were sparkling with their old sparkle.

The school was amazing in its preparations for Lio. The staff informed all the parents, they prepared all the children, they organised out of their own budget a special assistant to be with him almost every morning to help him get the most out of what was going on in class. They were brilliant. They provided more support than I could have possibly imagined. On his first day Lio hobbled on his yellow frame into the playground with all the other children, his little blue bookbag hooked on the fingers gripping his walker. He was clearly dazed, he was clearly in awe, but like me in intensive care on those first few days, there was a kind of serenity about him. There was a calmness on his slightly confused face that was beautiful to behold. He was not frightened or taken aback but seemed to revel in his special status. As I look back at the photos of him surrounded by his new friends in his shiny yellow-and-blue raincoat on that first day, it again brings tears to my eyes. Two months before, a doctor had told me that this day would never come to pass. Two months before, I didn't know whether my son would live or die. And two months before, therapists were telling me that Lio would be changed for ever. But there, on that day, Monday, 27 November 2006, my son Lio was at school. Normal, regular, mainstream comprehensive school. The joy that I felt in those simple words 'normal, regular, mainstream' was indescribable. Normal, regular, mainstream.

I stayed with him the whole of that day. It was also a completely new experience for the teachers. They were extremely keen to help but unsure how to get started, and because of this they seemed glad to have me around at the beginning. But for Lio's part, even though he started school months after his classmates, his assimilation happened with very little effort. That first morning I stood in the corner and watched him learn how to play a matching number game with a little girl named Lizzie, who would become one of his closest friends. And he did it. He did it! Slowly and unsteadily at first, but he did do it. It is hard for most parents to comprehend the near ecstasy of a moment like that: when you have the expectation of a normal first day at school, with all the usual apprehensions and excitements, then you have that expectation ripped away only for you to claw it back again. It's a remarkable feeling and I remind myself to hold on to it, that sense of profound joy and gratitude that Lio is in school and learning like lots of other children. True, his 'issues' did keep cropping up and were a nuisance. Sometimes rather than struggling to find words to communicate he would just point at things and make faces. The other children would usually just give him the thing that he was pointing at, which was usually just the right thing to do. He would fatigue very easily and often after only 15 minutes or so of sitting upright he would collapse into a heap. The teachers never made a fuss about this or pushed him, they would just guide him over to the pile of pillows in the 'listening corner' where he could lie down and rest for a bit. Neither he nor other children seemed to mind any of this; it was probably only me who really fretted over these things while hovering in the background.

Most of the other parents at drop-off and pick-up on the playground were kinder than I could have hoped. With unafraid smiles, so many of them walked right up to us and said some version of: 'You must be Lio. We've heard all about you and how amazingly you've been doing. You must come round for a play date when you feel up to it.' A few gave us a wide berth, as I might have done before, not knowing what to say, but they were the minority. I knew seeing him on that first magical day at his pleasant little school in slightly rainy England that one day the vision I conceived in the hospital of Lio at his university graduation walking up to the podium and making a speech would come to pass. I knew also that the road before us would be a long and difficult one, but we were off to a galloping start.

This is what I wrote on Lio's website about his first day of school:

> Lio passed another milestone today: his first day at proper school. He was extremely excited (although these days it doesn't take much to get him extremely excited) at putting on his school shirt and having his name written on his bookbag. He is walking with a frame, at a slow but very determined pace. He insisted on walking all the way to the car this morning and on

walking all the way out to the playground at playtime. All of the children, every one of them, were so warm and welcoming that several times I found myself unable to speak. His teacher, Mrs Dumbrell, has already proven saintly in her patience with him and her preparation of the class for him.

But even as I'm glad he's finding his way in our charming village school, I'm also struck by how incredibly hard it must be for him. Instead of tearing across the playground to climb with his new friends on the ladders and bridges, he shuffles along gingerly with a little bit of fear and apprehension in his eyes, not wanting to get knocked over. In the classroom too he is obviously 'slow', struggling to communicate, his voice shaky and off-key. He is very easily distracted and a couple of times he couldn't follow some very basic directions. In the context of other children his own age it's impossible to ignore how far he still has to go. But he is 'going' and there is a tremendous amount here which gives me hope: two months ago I would have never imagined we'd be going to school this year (even if it is only a couple of hours a couple of times a week).

Two days later Lio managed a few steps without the aid of his walker or anyone else. He walked for me in our little front room. I didn't ask him to; he just wanted to walk, he desperately wanted to try to walk. Tentative and wobbly and a bit scary and hard to watch, but he did manage a few little steps. There was a sort of sweet recompense in this. While living in England during a year's research leave from Brooklyn just before Lio's first birthday, my mother had become extremely ill and I was afraid she might die. I flew back to the States to be with her for several weeks before Christmas 2002. Sasha and Lio were coming soon after to spend the holiday season with us in New Jersey. When I met Sasha and Lio at the airport, Lio, previously only crawling, walked down the arrivals ramp into my waiting arms. I was delighted and scooped him up and whirled him around, but I was also gutted that I hadn't been there for his first steps. That was the life we had chosen: a transatlantic life of career building, but we also risked missing precious events never to be duplicated. Or so I thought. In seeing Lio walk for the first time after the accident, I got to re-live one of those unforgettable moments of his childhood that I thought I'd lost forever. I got to see him walk for the first time when before he was not walking. As I leapt with joy and held him close, it again seemed like we had somehow been given back a stolen piece of our lives.

But our little moment of triumph was made all the more poignant by another tragedy. That evening we learned that Lio's friend Jack from hospital had died from his brain tumour. Even though I knew his medical situation was very different from Lio's, I found the news of his passing more painful and frightening than I could have anticipated. It underscored in my mind how blessedly lucky I'd been in Lio. But more than that it threatened to pull me back down into the despair, confusion and uncertainty of those first hours after the crash. The news forced me to think about something that I'd been working hard to exclude from my mind, struggling to completely push out for months: that Lio could have died. That I could have lost him too. It forced this opposite future into my imagination: a life without Sasha *and* Lio. This possibility was so horrifying that to put it into words even now seems somehow dangerous: children die, and there can be little to explain it and nothing to ameliorate it. Only the tiniest of chances separated Lio's fate from Jack's: the beginning of a beautiful life versus the end of a beautiful life. What would have become of me if I had lost Lio too? Depression, dependency, collapse, suicide? What would I have become without the purpose and direction Lio gave my life? These thoughts scare me to the very core of who I am.

There was something else, too, that troubled me for a moment about Jack's death. It made me question my growing faith in the power of love and attention (and meditation) to help a child recover. It undermined my fundamental and sustaining belief, my very way of being in the world and relating to my circumstances: that in some way I could think and feel my way to a healthy son. But after a good deal of consideration I found myself mulling over Lio's own role in his recovery. Differences in medical histories aside, maybe Lio was simply different – stronger perhaps – than Jack. Lio had made it further than Jack; Lio had pulled himself back from the edge. Lio is a remarkably resilient and determined little boy. In that thought I came to understand that my own positive thinking about Lio and his recovery was not enough. I had to draw out, develop and support Lio's own nascent strength of character as well as develop his belief in his own total recovery. If I could nurture not just Lio's inner strength but also his sense of himself as strong and capable, then he really would be able to go anywhere he wanted to go in the world.

The weeks after Christmas until March 2007 were devoted to finding a solution to Lio's injured leg, a solution that Michael Kahn hadn't offered but that Daniel Warren had hinted might exist in our last meeting. Immediately before Lio's operation to remove the external fixator from his leg I'd had a few words with the anaesthetist. He was an American who had been working for the past few years at a specialist orthopaedic hospital in New York called the Hospital for Special Surgery. I told him what Dr Kahn had said about the future of Lio's leg and he, without a trace of chauvinism, said that if Lio were his child he would consider the Hospital for Special Surgery before doing anything like what we'd been advised to do by Kahn. This turns out to be a great question to ask doctors when you're trying to get clearly articulated opinions out of them (rather than just an expression of pros and cons or a range of options): 'What would you do if this were your child?'

Once we had moved back home I also emailed my friend and doctor in New York, Sam. I described the situation to him and asked if he could recommend some paediatric orthopaedic surgeons in the States. Out of our emails back and forth and through my own research I turned up three in New York that I thought it would be useful to speak to over Christmas. I wasted no time arranging appointments over the phone and on email and before long we had all three lined up.

There was a tremendous amount of activity in the period between starting school and leaving for our doctors' visits in the States. There was home therapy every day and professional therapy of one kind or another almost as often. There were doctors' appointments for both his head and leg. There were appointments with counsellors and the staff at school to decide how best to integrate and support Lio. There were lots of new friends (with lots of simple childhood curiosity) who wanted to play with Lio, regardless of his unsteady legs, bouts of confusion and the like. There was barely a moment to sleep, it seemed. All this activity was exactly what we needed: it accomplished lots that had to be done, but it also insulated us both somewhat from the inevitable intensified feelings of loss which might have made that first holiday season without Sasha more than a bit painful.

Three days before we caught our flight there was one event Lio was particularly looking forward to: his stage debut as Shepherd #3 in his reception class Nativity Play. After Mary and Joseph processed onto the stage behind Lio's friend Freddy in a donkey suit, and just before the arrival of the three glittering Kings, the shepherds came on stage right. Lio was the last of them and he teetered on with an irrepressible smile, the only resident of Bethlehem with a yellow Zimmer frame. As angels and animals piled onto the tiny stage while narrators told the story, Lio grinned and waved and winked at everyone, particularly me, in the third row. My heart beat fast. I took photo after photo of Lio hamming it up and it was almost as if he himself couldn't believe he was doing it. It was such a simple little thing, but with the memory of where we were two months ago still too fresh in my mind I couldn't help but spill a few tears. At the end of the show Steve Elliot, the head teacher, called Lio and another girl up to receive birthday stickers. Lio even gingerly ventured two steps without his walker to collect it.

While Lio was interacting better and better with all the children at school – and all of them really seemed to love him and miss him when he was away at therapy – social things that involved any physical movement remained very difficult for him. Every day when playtime rolled around, he was confused and frustrated. He would stand with his walker at the door and watch all his friends pour out into the playground. Their speed and their four-year-old jostling made him wince as they passed. He would weigh the situation up and more often than not, with eyes dropping down to the floor, go back inside the classroom and play with the Playmobil pirate ship. This hurt. I'd seen him beat such tremendous odds to get to school at all. Watching him feel excluded brought back a flood of all my own most terrible playground memories of loneliness and embarrassment. But it also shot me forward to a bleak picture of Lio's own isolated future childhood – forlorn and friendless, his youth ebbing away in front of a screen.

'Lio,' I began, as I we drove home from school one afternoon, 'I've seen you playing with the pirate ship for a few days now. Is that your favourite thing to do at playtime?'

'It's OK,' Lio said with no enthusiasm.

'Do you ever want to go and play outside?' I offered.

'Yeah, I really want to play with them all but sometimes my knee gets hurt.' There he was, working so hard to adjust, struggling with new demand after new demand, all with a recovering brain and with the constant fear of pain. On top of all that he was feeling left out and alone, as all his new friends were enjoying the full-tilt fun of their undamaged little bodies. I had to make this better for him somehow.

The next day I asked his teacher if she could encourage one or two of the other children to stay in and play with Lio and the pirates during playtimes. She was great about it and made a big deal of specially inviting children to play with Lio, which they did happily. Alex and James were his best shipmates and they spent lots of giggling playtimes pushing people overboard and following them with cannons and sharks. For minutes on end, as they sat on the grey carpet, it was possible for me to squint and not see anything the matter at all. For my part, I gently encouraged Lio to try to get involved in physical things as best he could, but I also didn't want to put any pressure on him whatsoever at this stage. I had very high hopes that the appointments with the orthopaedic surgeons scheduled for our trip back home would produce some fresh ideas about his leg and, in the end, help him play the way all little boys should.

Cognitively, he continued to make real progress. His problems were by that point quite subtle – and they were social as much as they were intellectual. His hurdles were concentration, mental fatigue, word finding, reading social situations and regaining a sense of appropriate boundaries with people. In stressful moments, he liked to pull on people's faces and was prone to self-consciously inappropriate behaviour much more so than other four and five year olds. When stressed, he might just pee on the playground, or howl nonsense, or pull his pants down and wiggle his bottom around, all of which he did while laughing wildly. The part of his brain responsible for controlling impulses and negotiating social situations just hadn't rewired itself yet and as a result we were all forced to simply deal with (or ignore) scenes like these.

This awkwardness extended to his voice as well. He really only had two registers before that Christmas: very quiet and shouting. While he didn't seem bothered at all by issues like these (and neither did his friends), and while it was even possible for me to laugh most of these scenes off, I did worry that the rest of the people in his world might not be so charitable. The week before, in a doctor's office, he was trying to demonstrate to some girls a few years older that he could speak Italian. My heart sank as they withdrew and one said to the other, 'He's a bit mad.' I hoped and prayed that he would never get discouraged. I discussed several of these behaviours with the psychiatrist at Charleston and she said that many of these problems would settle down on their own as Lio continued to recover. In any case, I was extremely grateful that he was making a genuine effort to interact in spite of everything, and that for him other people were simply fun to be around rather than a source of fear, anxiety, apprehension or opportunities to get embarrassed. This in itself was remarkable.

We also had our first multi-disciplinary review meeting at the rehab centre at Charleston before we left for the States. After the terrible start, our experiences there improved steadily – perhaps Lio's natural charm had won some of them over, or perhaps after my initial phone calls to the Primary Care Trust that controls funding to the rehab centre, and my arguments with them over what they were going to provide had subsided, they felt they could be more 'caring' and less 'professional'. Whatever it was, something had changed in our relationship. In the run-up to the meeting, they all seemed, as the hospital staff had been, emotionally invested in Lio's recovery. They even went to the trouble of getting him presents for Christmas and his birthday – they were good people. I guess it's simply difficult to learn what Lio has been through and not be moved by it somehow. But it's also difficult to get to know him and not be touched by his personality – something that seemed to have survived the crash unscathed.

Back in the States, everything proved to be much less fraught than I'd imagined it might be. The quiet, the familiar smells, the comfortable holiday kitsch, the sunnier skies, colder winter days and the great sense of space in our little corner of New Jersey undid weeks of tension. Lio loved spending lots of time with his cousin Kevin, who lived just two doors down from my mother. After only a few days, Lio was buried under a mountain of presents from people I hadn't seen in 20 years – it was worth the excess baggage charge just to see him so happy. With Lio looking so well and with us so far removed from the physical scene of the crash, it was almost possible for my mind to forget about it all and drift into thoughts of 'normal life'.

In between carollers and window-shopping at Rockefeller Center and trips to St Patrick's Cathedral, we dropped in on those three doctors. The problem with Lio's leg was a complex one: his femur had been so badly shattered in the accident that it was impossible for me to count all the pieces on the X-ray. When it had healed, it had lost roughly two centimetres in length because of the severity of the break. It had also healed badly in that his kneecap was angled out a bit and that the inner surface of the joint now had a small uneven ridge on it. But most significantly the growth plate, the band of different tissue at the end of all growing children's bones, had started to close up on the injured side of Lio's leg. This meant that his leg would probably grow crookedly. Looking through some very difficult and gory medical books on limb lengthening and straightening had convinced me that there were things that could be done. But when the first two doctors we saw delivered a 'wait and see' verdict I began to lose heart a little.

Enter doctor Roger Widmann at the Hospital for Special Surgery. Lio, who had only just been introduced to 'Mr Men' books, eventually took to calling him 'Dr Tall' because he was, well, very tall. Rather than sensing a self-consciousness of his own limits, I was immediately struck by Roger's confidence in reading the situation and in having a solution in mind. Confidence is always a tricky thing to gauge in doctors and you have to look to other aspects of their personality to figure out how you should process it. Confidence with any trace of smugness, arrogance or a tendency to repeat things rather than engage with the nuances of your questions should set off warning bells. Confidence, as it was in the case of Dr Tall, mixed with clarity, conviviality and enthusiasm to take on a project, is extremely reassuring. I told him what other doctors had said, both in England and earlier that week in New York. He described Michael Kahn's leg shortening proposal as 'somewhat old-fashioned' ('somewhat medieval' was how I had come to think of it) and similarly said that the 'wait and see' approach was a bit of a cop-out because we knew what was going to happen. We knew (or rather he knew) that Lio's leg would grow at an angle because the growth plate had already started to close. He recommended having an operation to stop the closure of the physeal bar (to stop the growth plate attaching to the bone) and to clear out bone fragments that remained unattached in Lio's knee that were blocking his range of motion. He said, in his examining rooms high above the East River, that he would do this not later than the summer, as the angular deformity that might appear by then would make it difficult for Lio to use his leg without other short-term operations to straighten it as well. If all went according to plan, the leg would grow straight and might even straighten out some of the deformity that had developed since the crash.

At least now I had a procedure on the table, a better solution for his leg than stunting the growth on the good leg and halting the deforming growth on the bad leg. I had a procedure in mind that I could now propose to other doctors in England or in Europe to save Lio the inconvenience of too much transatlantic travel, to save him being out of his lovely new school for eight weeks, disrupting the new and rewarding relationships he was developing with friends, and taking him out of his house, a house that we had only just returned to with a great deal of effort. The ideal solution would be to find someone who was prepared to do the procedure in the UK.

Everyone likes to believe that the doctors in their particular hospital are the best, are at the top of their game, know everything about their speciality and can handle anything thrown at them. It validates our own sense of who we are and the choices we've made in life: I live in a good place, in a cosmopolitan city, in a technologically advanced society and of course my doctor, the doctor I just happened to get when I came to the hospital, is going to be among the best. It's the Lake

Wobegon effect applied to medicine: 'All our doctors are above average.' Well, and this was a very hard lesson for me to learn, our doctors are not the best. That is a simple statement of fact: your doctor is not the best. In fact, the very notion of 'the best' cardiologist or 'the best' gastroenterologist or 'the best' paediatric orthopaedic surgeon now seems absurd to me.

Medicine is changing all the time. It's impossible to expect your doctor to keep up with every advance in his or her field. Doctors, especially good ones, develop a handful of particular procedures that they do lots of and do extremely well. What this means in terms of diagnosing patients is that they tend to see various problems in terms of the procedures *they do best*. They tend to apply *their* procedures to a *range* of cases. Their specialties are often culturally determined: different procedures are done more or less in different countries, depending on how the health system is organised (private systems are too quick to operate, for example, while national systems are too slow), what medical regulation is like, what the medical training is like and which ailments the local population is particularly prone to. But there is no 'best doctor'. In a world like this you have to become an amateur expert very quickly about your own health and the health of your family. The most you can hope for is to not be dazzled by the first few opinions, or tempted by pie-in-the-sky solutions, en route to the best approach for your particular issue. And unlike with Lio's brain injury, where the care was driven by urgent needs and crisis management, with his leg we seemed to have the luxury of a bit of time. Or at least that's what I thought.

A Burglary

It almost never snowed in our part of England. And no one ever got burgled in our quiet little town. But in late January of 2007 both things happened. This is how I recorded it on Lio's website:

> I'm hoping that last night's extremely rare and beautiful snowstorm will be a soft and fluffy line under the events of the past few weeks and that 2007 can begin properly and happily today. After a month of the warmest winter on record, with cherries blossoming in mid-January, this morning Lio awoke excited to find two inches of snow on the ground. We dashed off up into the Downs to enjoy the world for a few minutes before heading to therapy.
>
> After a positively lovely Christmas and New Year's in the States and Italy, returning home to the stress, the decisions, the daily regime, the oppressive sense of uncertainty and a wet, grey English winter depressed us both. On the train coming back from the airport the usually bubbly Lio drifted off into stone quiet introspection and I was unable to pull him out of it. Then, one week later, our home was burgled. It was a sloppy and rushed job; they took some wallets with cash, credit cards and IDs, a notebook (of all things) with my little memories of our time in the hospital, some drawings Lio had done, lots of phone numbers, emails and some of my jottings on brain

injury rehab, and – tragically – they stole my laptop (but not the power cable for it). That computer contained the only copies of photos of Sasha, Lio and I during our last year as a family before Sasha died, and notes and contact information on various brain and leg treatments for Lio. It was absolutely priceless to us but worth very little to the thieves (second-hand two-year-old laptops don't fetch much). I was left heartbroken and desperate.

The next morning I set to work checking all the garbage bins around Lewes and putting up flyers offering a £500 reward, no questions asked, for the safe return of my computer. Over the next several days I organised more radio, TV and newspaper interviews than I can remember. It was tremendously difficult, humiliating even, describing over and over why my laptop was so important. But in the end having the tragedy of the crash once again made into painful, public spectacle proved worth it: it got the computer returned. Four days after it was stolen, I got a call from a Lewes taxi driver. He told me that he had just been reading a story about it in the paper and he thought he had found my computer in the back of his cab. He said that someone had left it on the back seat a few days earlier. I asked him to come right over, which he did. I recognised my laptop instantly, took it inside, plugged it in and turned it on; it was indeed my computer and none of our files had been messed with (although there was some wireless software added onto it). I thanked him over and over again and wrote him a cheque for the reward money I'd promised. He took it and drove off into the night, leaving me trembling with relief.

I called the police to let them know I got my laptop back and the next day they told me they'd picked up the taxi driver and arrested him for handling stolen property. They were troubled by the fact that he had held on to the laptop for four days before turning it in. While I'm glad the police are doing their jobs, I am a bit bothered by this turn of events. I'm really grateful to the man for getting me back my priceless photos and think he did me a huge favour. If it turns out that he's not involved with the burglary and genuinely didn't know it was stolen, then I intend to do something nice for him (the police took the reward cheque off him). For me, at least, if not for my would-be good samaritan, this chapter has a very happy ending. Not only did I get my computer back but the whole episode was also a tremendous boost to my faith in people. In spite of how distressing the theft was and how awful it was going on the media, the police and reporters were all extremely kind and sympathetic (and were all truly delighted to hear we got it back). But even more so, complete strangers not only offered care and support but also volunteered to add their own money to the reward. I was repeatedly touched and a bit humbled by it all. There are so many good people out there.

Now, like making tracks in the new snow, we are moving forward. Lio's calendar is full of dinners, parties and play dates; he really is the most sought-after boy in town. Everyone says hello to him on the street and at school, and (maybe because of all this lovely attention) he is steadily regaining his own unique social sparkle. We have our laptop back with all the wonderful photos of Christmas in the States and New Year's in Italy, where family was amazed at how well he was doing, theatrical friends put on elaborate and magical puppet shows just for him, he was the only child brave enough to sing for La Befana in the town of Sospirolo (in Italian, no less), and complete strangers said, 'He really is an exceptional boy.' In a few weeks we're visiting paediatric orthopaedic surgeons in Bristol and Germany, and by then I'm hoping we'll have enough information to make the right decision about his leg. He's integrating so well into school. And this morning, as he looked out of the bathroom window at our white garden below, he said with pure delight, *'Guarda! Mamma ci ha mandato giù la neve dal cielo!'* ('Look! Mamma has sent us down snow from the sky!')

What stuck with me from the burglary episode was the fact that the taxi driver had been arrested. I was cut up by this, as I didn't want the person who had helped me to be punished for it. He might have held on to the computer longer than he should have done, he might not have handled an item of left property according to proper procedure, but he did the right thing in getting the computer back to me. The police held him and questioned him for the better part of a day.

More than a month later I got a letter from the police saying that formal charges against the taxi driver had been dropped. I was relieved. I called up the police and asked to talk to the detective who had interviewed him. I spoke at length with a sharp-sounding woman who seemed fairly certain that the driver had been telling the truth and had innocently found the computer in the back of his cab. I then asked her if she could give me his phone number because I wanted to see that he got the reward I had offered. She said she couldn't and reminded me what other police officers had told me the day after the burglary: that offering a reward for the return of stolen property is in itself against the law. It's against the law to offer a reward to get your stolen stuff back! The rationale is that if rewards were allowed, the whole country would be engulfed in chaos, as everyone held everyone else's things for ransom. Fortunately, after the burglary the police said they would turn a blind eye because of what was on my computer. The detective I spoke with on the phone also softened in the end and said that she would contact the driver and ask if he was open to me contacting him. I never heard back from her.

As fate would have it, a couple of months later our local paper did a story about a fund-raising event for the scholarship we had set up at the University of Kent in Sasha's name. On the front page of that issue of the *Sussex Express* was a story about a man who had stopped to help at the scene of a road accident and then had his own car totalled by another vehicle. I recognised the photo of him instantly as the taxi driver who had returned my computer – then as now it seemed like the universe was punishing him for wanting to do the right thing. I resolved to try to turn things around for him. I called up Steve, the writer at the paper whom I had got to know quite well over the months because he had been following Lio's story closely. I told him that I wanted to get in contact with the man on the front page to offer him his reward cheque for £500. Steve said he would take care of it. The next day I got a call from the cabbie. I told him that I wanted to give him another cheque and he arranged to come round later that day. When he arrived, I could sense he was a bit apprehensive. I thanked him again abundantly for what he had done, wrote him the cheque and told him to take it straight to the bank before doing anything else. He laughed a bit and before he left I booked a cab ride with his company for the next day.

By four months after the crash we had seen eight highly recommended specialist orthopaedic surgeons in four countries on two continents in the hope of finding the best way forward with Lio's leg and knee. These were followed by countless phone calls and emails in different languages, trying to clarify the details of what each was offering. One of the most incredible of these meetings happened in Munich, where we saw a doctor who had been recommended by a surgeon in England. At the end of his consultation, he simply threw up his hands and said plainly that he didn't know what to do, but that he knew someone who might be able to help – in Berne, Switzerland. This doctor knew that we only had limited time during our visit to the continent in search of a surgeon, so he got on the phone there and then in his office with his colleague in Berne and arranged for us to have an appointment with him the next day (a seven-hour drive away). This kind of service was amazing to me; I had never experienced anything like it either in Britain or in the States. But his kindness didn't stop there. He then left me in the hands of one of his junior doctors who not only printed out a map showing how to find the hospital but also found us a hotel, called it and made a reservation for us (my German being terrible). I was grateful for their honesty in simply saying they didn't know what to do, but I was bowled over by their compassion and willingness to help.

I must admit that at times I wondered what we were doing flying from one doctor to another given that most of them seemed flummoxed about how to get a good leg out of what Lio had. Sometimes it felt like a waste of a lot of time and even more money. But we met some wonderfully capable and interesting people. The doctor we met in Berne, for example, Teddy Slongo, was a real character. We did most of that consultation in Italian because his English wasn't terribly good and my German was much worse. His name had also come up in a consultation we'd had in England as a surgeon who did 'implausible' work in limb-lengthening. He said that he would certainly stop the crooked growth on the injured leg. But, he said, if he did what had been advised in London and operated to stunt the growth on Lio's good leg he would find himself in a Swiss court on charges of child abuse. He proposed a series of leg-lengthening surgeries for Lio at various stages of his growth. But given that these meant that Lio's leg would have to be in an elaborate frame for several months each time I needed to consider it very carefully. Did I really want Lio to have to spend such a big chunk of his childhood incapacitated in such a painful contraption?

Lio had just finished an extremely long spell of hospitalisation and medicalisation; he was integrating into school and making friends. He and I were rediscovering our old physical relationship. We loved to wrestle. We would each get down on the blue carpet at opposite ends of our small living room and beat the floor with our hands. We would growl and scowl at each other and Lio would more often than not explode into a fit of giggles. Then, CHARGE! During our first attempts he was apprehensive, but soon enough he regained a bit of confidence in his physical body and he would go at it. He would drag his super-leg behind him, but in our wrestling it moved more than at any other time. I would advance a bit and then grab him under the arms and pull him on top of me as if he had knocked me over. I would groan and we would roll around for a while and try to pin each other. I was, obviously, much more careful with him than I had been – always hyper-alert to his head and leg – but we did it, and we did it more or less as we used to. I revelled in these moments with him as much as he did and I'm sure they were playing a part in his general recovery, too. The thought of losing our wrestling and other physical fun to accommodate more months in hospital, especially after we had only just clawed those moments back, was very hard to entertain. In the end I decided to keep Slongo in reserve if we needed limb lengthening, but I wanted to try to find someone in Europe who could coax straight growth out of Lio's injured leg and spare him as much surgery as possible.

Two weeks after we got back we saw another doctor in England whom I wish we had met months earlier. His name was James Hunter and he worked at a hospital in Nottingham. He had the remarkable ability to synthesise all of the options that we had been given by all of the doctors we had seen. He explained them in relation to one another and what we should and shouldn't expect from each of them. He said that he personally could not attempt the re-activation of the straight growth that Roger Widmann had in mind back in New York and that he thought that the only surgeon in the UK who might have tried the procedure given the state of Lio's leg had just retired. But, he said, if I had found someone willing to try it, even if it meant moving to or staying in New York for a long period of time, that would be the best solution. That's what he would do if Lio were his son. He was brilliantly clear and, like our doctor in Munich, I was touched by his humility and I trusted his honesty.

I'd like to say that I decided the next day to book an operation at the Hospital for Special Surgery, but I didn't. I was unable to decide and still harboured hope of finding someone in Europe to do it. But Lio's leg soon forced my hand. After having made tremendous strides (literally) in physiotherapy in the periods before and after Christmas, we suffered a setback: overnight Lio's leg, which he had been able to extend quite well and put a good deal of weight on, became swollen, extremely painful and locked at about 25 degrees. While the pain subsided somewhat, he still couldn't straighten his leg or put much weight on it. His agony every morning made me decide to just stop considering and make a choice. Seeing your only child in serious pain clarifies thinking quite quickly. Even though Dr Tall had said there was only a 50–50 chance that the procedure would work, I was glad to have found someone who saw in that 50–50 chance the possibility of helping a little boy have a much healthier and more normal leg, rather than seeing it as a procedure that shouldn't be attempted because it might fail. I booked the surgery for the third week of April.

While we were focusing on coming to a decision about his leg, Lio continued to bound along mentally. In spite of all our traipsing around, I took heart every week from his brain's recovery and how he continued to defy expectations. He was getting on extremely well at school and had a fabulous week performing in the school's annual 'Spring Tea'. He and all his classmates were the things that go bump in the night and keep little kids awake (he was rustling curtains). We made some home treatment changes over the half-term break: earlier nights, much more reading and sound/voice practice time with just him and me, introducing a twice-daily cocktail of dietary supplements and a few other things. The result was that he had another big surge in his recovery. His voice was still a bit uneven and he still had a long way to go in concentration and attention, but we were getting there. People who hadn't seen him for a couple of weeks marvelled at his improvements.

Our next big obstacle was emotional instability, especially when he was tired. Late in the day he was prone to melting down if things didn't go exactly as he envisaged they would (like me putting a piece in a puzzle that he wanted to put in), or if one of his friends was doing something he shouldn't (like doing dives into the baby pool). But I instituted what we took to calling 'Rule #1'.

Rule #1 was simply: 'Do not panic.' And when he had a particularly frustrated moment, I was usually able to calm him by repeatedly asking him: 'What's Rule #1?' When I did this, he would most often settle quite quickly, emit a sobbing little laugh and say, *'Non farti prendere dal panico!'* ('Don't panic!') This tickled me perhaps more than it should have.

In the middle of February, five months after the crash, there was a special day of tributes for Sasha at the University of Kent when colleagues, family, friends and former students reminisced and read. The experience was as moving as it was painful, but Lio provided a sublime moment of comic relief when, encouraged by his cousin, he limped up to the front and interrupted his uncle Jeff's speech by reciting a moment from his favourite book: Mr Nonsense building his house up a tree to be nearer to the ground. While the day was difficult, it was also deeply heartening to be reminded by people we had never met (from professors to porters to ex-students) what an amazing person Sasha was.

One of her students in particular, someone who was on her Drama Survey course during Sasha's last semester at Kent, was especially moving. This bright, blonde twenty year old spoke for about ten minutes in front of a room crowded with her professors about how Sasha had upended her entire class's perception of Samuel Beckett, the writer of comic nihilism. She told us about how Sasha, in the face of her students' committed existential angst, had managed to invite them to find traces of something hopeful and life-affirming beneath Beckett's bleak jokes. This was my Sasha.

I continue to marvel at how many people Sasha touched in so many different spheres of life. The Thursday before Sasha's tribute at Kent I went to the 30th annual Lewes

Arms Dramatic Society charity adult panto. Sasha and I had acted in the panto in years past and we were always in the audience. Her most memorable role, at least for all the men in the pub, was in *Peter Pan* about six years earlier, when she had played a Wendy who finds herself wearing a tight, black leather cat suit when she enters the lost world. The current year's panto, a particularly smutty and salacious interpretation of *Babes in the Wood*, was dedicated to her and all the proceeds from the production were donated to the Sasha Roberts Scholarship Fund. It was standard Lewes Arms pantomime fare: ridiculous situations, ridiculous costumes, and lots and lots of very basic double entendre. Our friends in the cast, wanting to make sure that I didn't completely disappear into caring for Lio, jokingly made it a condition of their donating money to Sasha's scholarship that I help write one of the scenes, as I had done in years past. So I went out a few nights with Moose, my co-writer, and we managed to cobble together some really awful stuff like:

> Guy: Your two henchmen were looking at me a bit queerly so I sent them off to go and play with their halberds. *(gestures suggestively)*
>
> Sheriff: Ah, halberds in the hands of that dastardly duo. I suppose you could call them the 'Axes of Evil'!

And later on when the two babes are making fun of the French Guy and the Sheriff:

> Sharon: What do you call a Frenchman with a sheep under one arm and a goat under the other?
>
> Tracy: I don't know, what?
>
> Sharon: Bisexual.

It's precisely the kind of politically incorrect, lowbrow silliness that made Sasha laugh every year. I'm sure she was as proud of having her name on the panto as she was about her more serious memorial up in Kent.

Counting the Taxis

The trip back over to the States for Lio's leg surgery was utterly exhausting. Gatwick Airport has become nothing but a tedious labyrinth of queues and security checks in recent years. It feels like you now have to show your passport eight times before you get on the plane. I hadn't thought to sort Lio out a special wheelchair escort, so I pushed him along in the stroller while I pulled our bags behind us. Lio was frustrated and in pain much of the time. I fought quite hard to imagine that travel might once again be as easy and enjoyable as it had been in the past and I had to struggle to suppress a real desire to punch a man in front of us in line who kept carelessly bumping us with his bag. But maybe my feelings of agitation and frustration had more to do with the fact this trip was not going to be a vacation; it was going to be difficult and painful, and the stakes were extremely high. I'm sure Lio, unusually whiny, picked up on my anxiety and was feeding it back to me.

On the other side of the ocean, my mother was waiting for us with a great big smile for Lio. She had returned home several weeks earlier after having stayed with us for more than four months. She was incredibly helpful and did everything I'd asked of her. It was a real turning point in our relationship in that we began to relate to each other as two adults trying their best to make their way through the world rather than as parent and child. I would be dishonest if I said that she had never upset me during that period, that we had never slipped back into our old way of relating in which she frustrates me by telling me obvious things (and in which I upset myself by feeling I need her approval), but it was a giant step forward. Nigel and Penny had also found a little apartment in Lewes, which they used during the week to help ferry Lio to his therapy sessions at Charleston and to be with him in school. The reserves of strength that I was able to tap from my family during these months were immense and I will always be grateful for them. It was in precisely this spirit that my mother greeted us coming down the ramp from Customs at Newark Airport – with balloons and presents and praise for Lio, as if he were a soldier coming home from the wars.

Two days after we arrived we had a preliminary appointment with Roger Widmann (Dr Tall) and an appointment with his colleague, Scott Rodeo, who Lio took to calling Dr Handsome for similarly obvious reasons. Roger would do the part of the surgery involving Lio's growth plate, while Scott would work on Lio's knee. These two doctors proved to be remarkable both as surgeons and as human beings. They were generous with their time, patient with their explanations (and re-explanations) and confident that they would be able to make things better for Lio's leg.

A few days later Lio had the operation. We stayed in some guest rooms attached to the hospital the night before the surgery. We had to follow the same rules we had learned from other operations: no food or water for Lio from the midnight before the surgery. In the morning Lio, in spite of a few tears about not wanting to have another operation, seemed prepared for it. In the hospital, wearing a gown that was too big for him, he was again greeted as if everybody, *everybody*, already knew him. To some extent, his story had preceded him. I had given the doctors and their secretaries Lio's website address, and news of this boy who had recovered so miraculously and so quickly from severe brain injuries had caught people's interest. But Lio was such a naturally sweet and sympathetic boy that I'm sure lots of people were merely responding to his personality as they experienced it. They all just glowed with warmth and compassion in a way that perhaps only people who work in expensive hospitals can. Once they learned that Lio spoke Italian, it seemed like all the Italians in the building came down to say '*Ciao!*' before Lio's operation, to wish him well and to invite him to beaches back home.

After the surgery, which took about four hours, the doctors came out, found me in the waiting room and told me how well Lio had done. They had been able to remove all the blockages to his knee rotation and to completely re-open the closure that had occurred in his growth plate. Roger had filled up the gap with bone cement to make straight growth possible. As I sat looking out at the river in the waiting room, praying, meditating, seeing Lio well in my mind, I thought that all those weeks and months of traipsing around the world to find the right person and place really had paid off. Absolutely everyone in the hospital, from the technician who fitted Lio's leg brace to the secretaries in the offices and the doctors who spent loads of time with us every day just radiated a positivity that was infectious. Also aesthetically and atmospherically it was a beautiful building (as hospitals go). Lio's room was directly over the FDR Drive, with a view of the East River, Roosevelt Island and bridges over the water. When he got bored, we would play 'count the taxis' or 'guess what that boat is carrying'. But I think, in Lio's mind, the best thing about it all was getting to eat ice cream for breakfast the day after surgery, something he told his friends about for weeks afterwards.

Only hours after the operation, Lio started his physiotherapy. He had great relationships with his therapists, Amanda (in the hospital) and Katie (out of the hospital, near my mother's place, where we were staying).

They were both very good at making his sessions more play than 'exercise'. But there were aspects of his rehab that even they couldn't sugar-coat: from immediately after the operation, Lio had to be in an automatic leg-bending machine for six hours a day. The first couple of weeks in it he needed continuous attention because the settings had to be changed every few minutes, because he was slightly too small for it and his position needed to be adjusted, and because he was just in real pain. But after about three weeks it became less demanding: I would put him in the machine, play some games with him using letter blocks, try the matching pairs memory game, and another game where we invented a silly story in Italian line-by-line. When he got too bored for the games, I would usually set him up with a crappy DVD about dogs who fart and play basketball or something. I was a bit uneasy about his choice of entertainment during this phase, especially given Sasha's hard work of exposing him to documentaries and opera early in life, but I couldn't resist hearing him laugh.

When he wasn't in his leg-bending machine, he was meant to be doing a range of leg exercises three times a day. These almost always involved serious pain for him, sometimes to the point where he would hit me and scratch me and tell me that he hated me (something his pretty therapists were spared). This tore at my heart, but we'd been told often enough by doctors (and Lio understood this as well) that pain today equals a better leg tomorrow. And it wasn't all bad. The pain and exertion were tempered by daily play dates with Lio's cousin Kevin, and even in the midst of his torturous physio I was struck by how happy and buoyant Lio remained in general. As soon as anyone walked into the room, his face would split with a smile.

For better or for worse, there would be a lot more physiotherapy in our future. Both surgeons said when we saw them post-op that we needed to continue intensive physical therapy for four months after the operation. After four months, it would become considerably more difficult to get additional range of motion out of his knee but that less frequent sessions would be needed to maintain the gains he'd made. This meant that as soon as we returned to Lewes we would start up physio again with Nicola, Lio's therapist there. Lio had his best therapy relationship of all with Nicola, perhaps because he'd seen more of her, more consistently and over a longer period of time than any of the others. She read him books while she bent his leg and I'd try to do some word-finding exercises with him.

We eventually learned from Dr Tall that the operation to deal with the growth plate damage couldn't have gone better, but we would still have to wait several months to see how Lio's leg was growing – straight or crooked. I was extremely optimistic. My only regret over the whole procedure was that I had waited longer than I probably should have, looking for a solution closer to home. In the three months that we were trying to figure things out, buzzing around the UK and Europe trying to find someone who might help us with another way forward or with the same procedure on offer in New York, Lio's leg was getting more and more crooked. By the time of his operation, it was unnaturally bent out 17 degrees. If I had gone with my gut feeling instantly to have the op in New York rather than waiting, his angular deformity might have been only ten degrees or so.

Perhaps I was also trying to prove something to myself in those intervening months. Perhaps I wanted to demonstrate to myself that I would stop at nothing to find that mythical 'best' way forward with Lio's leg; that I was going to do everything within my power and skills to get a renewed leg for Lio – if that meant researching into the wee hours and becoming an impromptu travel agent, then so be it. In 15 years' time, I didn't want to have any regrets about something I could have investigated but didn't. But this little psychological insurance policy turned out to have some consequences of its own and I eventually discovered we didn't have quite the luxury of time that I'd been led to believe. Even though Roger had told me that I could have waited another few months before I really had to decide, I often blame myself for not acting sooner and for letting his leg grow awkwardly crooked. A lesson learned (again): trust your instincts. You may not be a doctor, but you know your child best. While his leg was crooked, I was told that there was the possibility that it might straighten on its own; and I console myself with the fact that I did save him from the leg-shortening that was on the cards early in England. For that I am very happy.

Even though we had only been with my mother Trudy in New Jersey for four weeks, we'd seen the weather change from snow to beautifully warm spring days. It was quite nice being back in very comfortable suburbia, and Trudy was great about letting me catch up on some much-needed sleep. I went into the city a few times, trying to deal with necessary paperwork there and getting a social recharge from some old friends. And even in those days, as our future remained an uncertainty, I remember beginning to feel more calmly happy than I had felt in a long time. Perhaps it was precisely because I wasn't able to think about the future in any concrete way. I spent almost all day almost every day with Lio, watching him improve, knowing that I was pulling him along; simply experiencing life through the eyes of my little boy was rejuvenating. Being forced into a position where I flatly could not deal with so many of the apparent 'necessities' of life that had so often nagged me in the past, being forced into a situation where previously 'pressing' decisions about a future career or radio projects simply didn't enter, was utterly liberating. My thinking used to revolve around these books and articles and esoteric broadcasting pieces – my work was simply who I was. But in those days of Lio's recuperation I didn't even notice they were gone.

Being forced to slow down and focus on my son changed my perspective, my perception of what's valuable. I gained a sense of what is truly worthwhile and important. None of my old projects were as rewarding and nothing could ever be as fulfilling as what I found myself doing in that moment, and what I continue to do. This, I think, is something few modern fathers experience. As I sat with my son, hour after sometimes painful hour, working through his stacks of speech exercises – picture cards of little stories that he had to categorise properly, or words he was meant to remember – and hour after hour of bending his leg and hour after hour of doing puzzles and threading beads to help his hands regain their dexterity, my life had become clear in a way that I could have never imagined. My life was not at all glamorous, not at all prestigious, but those desires were now not just simply unimportant, they had evaporated. They weren't there. This was a completely unexpected blessing. There was and is no place I would rather be and nothing I would rather be doing than helping Lio improve. Considering how physically attached to my computer I had been only a few months earlier this itself seems another little miracle.

There's a story that says the most photographed barn in America is the most photographed barn because it's the most photographed barn. Something similar started happening with Lio at around six months after the crash. He had, in a funny sort of way, become that most photographed barn. Lio became famous and that fame gained a momentum all of its own. It just happened: he was a beautiful, promising and charismatic little boy to whom something unspeakably terrible had happened. He was a 'natural' in many ways, and his recovery was galloping along at such an incredible pace that the media (both the medical media and the mainstream media) couldn't resist him. His website also played a part: designed as an efficient way to keep family and friends informed about his progress, it became a resource for journalists and producers. Doctors and therapists and other medical people who treated Lio passed his website address on to colleagues and other patients and before long we were receiving little messages of support, fan mail even, from people on other continents.

Then, with the theft of the computer, Lio was on television again and our story was all over the radio. From there, he was in more newspapers and in national magazines, with details of his awe-inspiring recovery. I freely admit I cultivated all this: I wanted him to develop a profile, to be a little bit famous. At the time, I was casting around for things to compensate for all his other losses, and mini-celebrity status seemed to be something within his grasp, something that would make him feel special and something that I (having worked in media for years) seemed uniquely suited to help create for him. So, after the trauma early on, we didn't miss an opportunity for Lio to get his picture in the paper.

In my moments of doubt, I sometimes worry that this amounted to exploiting him or pimping his tragedy somehow, but he does really love it. He loves looking at his website and showing it to his friends and feeling special about all the things he's done and the things that have happened to him, things that no one else he knows has experienced (thankfully). But I also put time into developing a profile for him and building his website because there were days when I found it easier to deal with the virtual Lio rather than the real one. The virtual Lio never wakes up at 5.00, never cries in pain, is never irrational, doesn't have recurring nightmares and never breaks anything. Lio's media persona never hits me, never tells me he hates me, never refuses to cooperate. Exhausted by these things, sometimes I would prefer the company of my virtual Lio to the Lio with real anger, real fear and real scars; and sometimes I would even send the real Lio off with his grandparents or a babysitter so I could spend some quality time with the virtual one.

That's brutal, you might think. But my energy was fading: too many interrupted nights and early mornings; too much patience burnt in asking Lio ten thousand times to just be a little more careful about spilling things; too many sessions where, try as I might to engage him, he would just stare at me blankly and take me back to those days in a coma. One early morning after a rough night I was carrying Lio down the stairs as usual, and Lio was poking me in the mouth, in the eyes and up the nose. He did this every morning in spite of my hundreds of calm and gentle requests for him to stop. On this particular morning, as he scratched the delicate skin inside my nose with his nail, I turned sharply and bit his finger. I bit it really, really hard, to the point where I was sure I was going to draw blood. I bit my brain-injured, motherless child. He screamed and cried. Then I cried.

I put him in his chair at the table, held him tightly and said, 'I'm sorry, I'm so, so sorry, Lio,' over and over again.

'I will never do that again, but please, you have to stop poking me in the face when I'm carrying you. OK?' He was in too much of a state to respond.

That night he and I spent about half an hour looking at his website, reading the comments and looking at the photos. He wanted me to scroll down to the very early pages, where there was a photo of him still in a coma.

He stared for a long time and then said with a trace of satisfaction, 'That was me.' In the end, the virtual Lio might have been good for both of us.

Part 4

Beauty makes our life better; it makes us feel alive. It brings us joy, or peace, however fleetingly. Hence, the absence of beauty is indeed a form of deprivation; an absence that does damage to our quality of life. We do not wish for our children – and, by extension, humanity – a life without beauty of any kind. Thus beauty is fundamental to the better life of mankind. It is our ethical responsibility to strive not only for the necessities of life – food, shelter, life itself – but for quality of life for all: for the things that make living worthwhile. It is, consequently, our ethical responsibility to strive for beauty.

– Sasha Roberts

Number 10

The first spring after the crash was filled with a series of intense events and occurrences. Perhaps the most bizarre of these was an invitation for Lio and me to come to 10 Downing Street to play football with Prime Minister Tony Blair. While Lio's leg was recovering extremely well, he was still a long way off playing footy, so I couldn't help but think that it might be a wild joke one of my friends was playing. But it wasn't. He really was invited to play football with Tony Blair.

After some thought on how to tell Lio about this, I simply sat him down and said that Tony Blair had heard about how extraordinary his recovery had been and had invited him over to play. Once I explained exactly who Tony Blair was, Lio was thrilled by the idea. The grown-up version of the story is a little more complicated. The football match was really a photo opportunity organised by King's College Hospital and the Wallace and Gromit Children's Foundation. As I understood it, the foundation, along with a significant contribution from the government, had just donated the money needed to build a new, state-of-the-art, multi-sensory rehabilitation suite in the paediatric wing at the hospital. They wanted to kick off the construction with a big press event and a football game with the Prime Minister and some of the child stars from the hospital seemed to fit the bill.

According to the organisers from the hospital, the plan was to have a handful of recently discharged super-patients play ball, with Tony Blair as the referee and with Wallace and Gromit in goals. Lio was terribly excited for days and told almost everyone he met that on Tuesday he was going to Tony Blair's house to play. They would smile the smile that you give children when they're telling wild stories, then I would intervene and let them know that Lio was telling the truth. But, as I repeatedly tried to explain that Lio had all the facts right, the whole situation became more and more surreal in my own mind.

Four weeks earlier I had received an email from one of the fund-raising people at the hospital whom I hadn't heard from for months. Whenever they'd asked me, I'd written little blurbs about how Lio was doing and since the autumn they had been using the story of Lio's recovery in various fund-raising campaigns. By this time, he had become a sort of unofficial mascot for them. The invitation seemed bizarre but appealing and at this stage in our adventure I had learned not to be surprised by anything. But I couldn't quite get my head around the idea; I had just read an article in some magazine about the lush gardens at No. 10 chocked full with birdhouses, ponds and shrubbery. Where were they going to put the goal posts? There was also something a bit cavalier about the preparation for it: there was no vetting or security protocol or warnings about what you couldn't bring with you; there were no background checks, all we needed was a photo ID. I joked with my in-laws that it was probably some elaborate immigration sting operation designed to get people like me and Lio deported (but we were both legal). I ultimately embraced it and began to play out little scenarios of our potential meeting with Tony in my mind. I imagined telling him all about Lio and what he had been through and saw Tony being visibly moved by the story. I saw myself at the end of our encounter giving him a little slip of paper with the address of Lio's website. Later that night

I imagined that the PM would turn on his computer, read more about Lio's progress and then leave us a little comment. Delusionary, you might say, but that is what ran through my mind for an instant. The thought of people reading about Lio's recovery is something that I have always found both comforting and motivating, whether it's just a friend or a head of state.

When the day arrived, we went up by train to London from Lewes. Graziella, Lio's Italian au pair, dropped us off at the station on the exact spot where Sasha had dropped me off before she drove away, leaving me with a stomach full of butterflies. We got good seats and on the journey up I got a call on my mobile from Rachel, one of the hospital fund-raisers, who just wanted reassurance that we were on our way.

We arrived at Victoria Station with an hour and a half to spare, so we headed to a café near Westminster Cathedral. As we sat at the window, I with a cappuccino and Lio with a bag of crisps, the courtyard in front of the cathedral began to fill up. A very elaborate funeral was just coming to a close, with a horse-drawn black hearse with high glass sides parked in front of the main cathedral doors. A coffin was placed inside, on it the word 'Grandson' was spelled out in white carnations. Obviously, I couldn't help but think about my own blessed good fortune with Lio. The procession left, Lio and I finished up and we headed out. I put him on my shoulders and we went across to the cathedral to light some candles. Lio knelt next to me in between the side chapels in front of a Madonna and Child saved from a much older church. As I looked down at him, I marvelled at how well he was bending his knee and let myself feel joy at the sight. But he seemed to bounce up as soon as he knelt down. Then he got behind me and started shoving my back over and over, anxious to meet his new best friend Tony Blair. It was not the most meditative of moments I've ever spent in a cathedral, so I gave in and we got moving.

After a quick Underground journey, we emerged in front of the Houses of Parliament with still almost an hour to spare. I was feeling uncomfortable and uneasy about things, uncertain about the day yet still trying to stay focused on my vision of a nice chat with the PM. I had jokingly been asking all our friends if they wanted me to ask Tony anything on their behalf. The best response came from Graziella, who said I should ask him if he had a nice, wealthy, mature (but not too old) nephew who might be looking for some Italian lessons.

With so much whirling around in my mind and with a lot of time to kill, I decided to take Lio over Westminster Bridge. We walked to the middle and just took in the scene. There were boats, the London Eye with an enormous advertisement for a new *Spider-Man* film in the centre of it and the water moving under us. Lio kept asking what would happen if he were to jump in the river. I kept telling him he would drown as I held tightly on to his torso, keeping him on the ground. He kept asking me why he would drown and I kept telling him because he couldn't swim all the way to the side of the river – he kept insisting that he could. I tuned him out for a few minutes and thought about everything, about the whole adventure from the very beginning, about Sasha and I and our history in London, about our first kiss late on a winter night while waiting for the bus along a cold stone wall in front of St James's Park, about dancing in the aisles at Ronnie Scott's Jazz Club and some woman asking Sasha if she was Cuban, about having sex up against some fencing behind a van in some car rental lot for the sheer joy of having sex outside in the city (those outings were usually her idea, but I missed them), about art galleries and the British Library and hundreds of really exquisite conversations we'd had over great and not so great meals out. We had conversations. We talked and we talked. We talked about philosophy, about literature, about languages, about intricate and abstract ideas, about art and artists, about radio and about Renaissance poetry. As I remembered our missing conversations, I began to rehearse with her in my mind what I was going to say to Tony Blair when I met him.

At that moment I felt loss, I felt profound loss; my eyes started to sting and a tear dripped down to the tip of my nose suspended perfectly over the Thames. I waited for it to fall into the water below. It was like Sasha, distilled emotion about to mingle with something like itself only infinitely bigger. My tear never dropped. I snapped myself out of my melancholy in a panic. We were on the most crowded, traffic-snarled bridge in London and Lio was no longer in my hands. I wiped my face as I spun round and round. Oh no. What had happened to him?

After a moment's terror the back of Lio's head emerged in a small crowd of tourists that had gathered in front of a very loud bagpipe player on the pavement. The moment of not seeing him was gut-wrenching but I convinced myself I was certain he'd be all right. And he was. I pulled him back to me for a moment, hugged him and gave him 50 pence to put in the piper's hat on the ground.

I heaved him up on to my shoulders again and we headed for No. 10. When we got there, we were still a bit early so we went across the road and had a sandwich under a statue of some Victorian general. Or rather I had a sandwich. After having picked out egg mayonnaise on brown bread at a shop back in Lewes, Lio was now refusing to eat it. I brushed his hair, bought some batteries for our camera and went back to No. 10, where we waited another few minutes until the fund-raising people from the hospital turned up. Rachel and her colleague Peter arrived and they looked very happy to be there. From the very first time I met them, I'd always been a bit uneasy around them, as they often seemed slightly too happy for jobs surrounded by so much pain. They loved Lio, though, and were glad to see us. Lio and I were doing some leg-bending exercises as he held the tall iron fence that cordoned off Downing Street. Peter and Rachel snapped some photos of us and introduced us to the organisers from the Wallace and Gromit Foundation. They all seemed so young to me, with such amazement in their eyes.

As the other children and families arrived, we were introduced; they were mostly organ-transplant patients. One of them was roughly Lio's age and I remember being a bit troubled seeing them together. The other boy was perky and precocious, speaking quickly and flitting around. I remembered Lio a year before, with his perfect accent in Italian, his clever little jokes, his love of playing with words and his truly impressive social skills; but when my eyes focused on the Lio in front of me, the Lio clinging to my legs awkwardly and wincing a little bit from the lingering pain of the exercises, my heart ached. I had fallen back into that familiar trap of comparing Lio to other children, comparing him without comparing his ordeals to theirs, without appreciating what he had been through, without seeing his tremendous strength in getting to where he was in that moment, his tremendous strength in simply surviving. But how would the world see him? Would they know about his past, his experiences and his secret reserves of strength? Or would he seem just a little boy not as bright and sparky as his peers?

I put those thoughts to one side and reminded myself that these other children had simply had different experiences. We were ushered inside a small guard post and our names were ticked off a list. We emptied our pockets and sent our bags through the X-ray conveyor. As we wandered up to the famous door of No. 10, we passed police with body armour and automatic rifles.

'Are those real guns?' asked Lio. 'Will they shoot people?'

'Only if someone tries to hurt the Prime Minister,' I reassured him.

'Will they shoot people to kill them? To make them dead?' This was a scenario that meant something to him. 'Or will they shoot them in the arm or the leg to make them stop?'

I didn't answer.

'I'm sure they would only shoot people in the leg because they couldn't really kill anyone. Killing is not good,' he said and I hoped he would leave it at that.

There was a permanent encampment of photographers and journalists stationed in front of the door to No. 10. You got the sense that they just stood there all day and photographed anyone who came and went. It was the kind of thing that I might have done in my life before the crash: hustled and elbowed, waiting for some story on the great and the good that I might have been able to sell for a bit of money and another line on my CV. From where I stood in that moment, though, I had a hard time identifying with them – they all seemed so tired and grey, even the young ones, and I found myself thinking about what they were doing in terms of drudgery rather than excitement. After everyone in our group was accounted for, the kids went in front of the door with their parents, then without their parents, then with a football. It was finally revealed that the ball was the only piece of gear that had made it. The car carrying all the equipment for the would-be football match had broken down on the way and as a result there was nothing to play with.

Lio was in my arms and beamed for the cameras. After a few minutes, the door of No. 10 opened and out walked Wallace and Gromit and gave the children high-fives. The smallest child, Franky, was scared of the costumed figures and didn't want to go anywhere near them. After another minute or two, the door of No. 10 opened again and someone came out. I couldn't quite make out who it was because Wallace and Gromit were in the way, but I knew that it must be Tony Blair. He stuck his head between the two costumes and said hello to Lio in my arms in that slightly silly voice grown-ups sometimes use with children.

'Right, this is it,' I thought and fumbled to remember what I had prepared on the bridge.

Presenting Lio like a basket of flowers in my arms, I said, 'This is Lio.'

Tony Blair said, 'Oh,' with a bit of puzzlement in his voice.

'Yes,' I said, 'this is Lio. He's the bravest boy in England.'

Tony was taken aback by this a bit, slightly embarrassed perhaps, and said, 'Oh,' again.

I launched into Lio's story very quickly: the crash, the coma, the fear of death, the dire prognoses and then I panicked and blurted out, 'And now he's here with you.' At that point I let out a sob. It was much more emotional than I expected it would be.

Tony said, 'He looks great, like he's made a full recovery.'

I told him that we were still in therapy, and I started to tell him about Sasha but teared up again and my voice refused to work. Tony tuned me out as graciously as possible and turned to face the cameras before moving on to another child. I turned to the cameras too and reached inside for something else to say. But it was no use; the moment had passed and my voice had abandoned me. It was not my finest hour. I felt slightly ashamed for imagining the kind of interaction I'd imagined. I felt sure Sasha would have done better and probably not have missed the opportunity to give him a good haranguing about the war.

I wandered around aimlessly in the crowd, dejected, clutching Lio and feeling like I'd failed. A few minutes after that initial botched encounter with the Prime Minister, I pulled myself together enough to ask him for a photo of us three with my camera. I found someone to take the picture and moved in next to Tony. After the snap, he asked about Lio's recovery, which I said was going unimaginably well. I then asked him about his own son also called Leo. I asked how old he was. Tony appeared to be a bit thrown for a moment and paused longer than any father should need to pause.

He finally said, 'Six . . . no, now seven.'

I thanked him and wished him well as he walked off. I thanked him not so much for the photo but for the mistake he'd made with his own son's age. In that long pause I recognised the incredibly special nature of the relationship that I now have with Lio. Few fathers and sons on the planet are as close as Lio and I. As I'd pulled him along physically and cognitively over the months, he had restored me emotionally. He was the reason I got up in the morning and the reason I pushed myself to go on. I'm sure this means there will be lots of counselling in the future for both of us, but, in that moment at least, I couldn't help but see that future as dazzlingly bright.

A few days after our visit to No. 10, we passed another poignant milestone: Father's Day. Lio made me a delicate little card at school with a blue sailboat on it. We spent the afternoon taking a walk with Graziella around the sweet village of Alfriston not far from the sea. We played in the churchyard, walked along the canals and then had a drink in an old village pub. That evening Graziella went out dancing and Lio and I had dinner on our own. Afterwards we played with his marble run. While we were building the track, he started, in an unsettling five-year-old way, calling me 'Sweetheart'. This was odd because that's what Sasha used to call me. I don't know where he'd picked it up; I think he must have just remembered Sasha using it – we had been talking about Mamma's salsa dancing as we were driving back from dropping Graziella off at her dance venue.

'Wouldn't it be nice if Mamma were still here?' he said, remembering her fondly and without tears.

'Yes,' I said. 'It would be positively wonderful.' I took his hand and led him up the stairs for bed.

Sasha, and her way of being in the world, had almost completely occupied my mind for days prior. It had only just been her birthday. She would have been 41. Rather than spending the day feeling absolutely miserable and drinking quietly and alone in some country pub, I, along with Nigel, Penny and Jeff, decided to throw a big party in Sasha's honour at the Grange in Lewes – the same place we had held our wedding reception. It was a bit of a risk, as there was another event happening in Lewes that afternoon organised by the big and important Cliffe Bonfire Society. I scheduled the party to begin after the Cliffe gathering, hoping that a few hardy friends (or maybe just some friendly drunks) would stagger from one end of town to the other to help us celebrate Sasha's life and eat and drink a bit more. It was very much a party, a celebration, rather than a memorial service. With loads of help, we decked the place out with hundreds of photos of Sasha, her paintings, her etchings, her collages, her children's book illustrations, her poetry, her academic writing, some videos of her on my laptop and a CD and headphones with some recordings of her talking about the Devil in Renaissance literature for a radio project I had done a few years earlier. It was, if I do say so, an impressive affair. We also had Sasha's favourite salsa music playing loudly all evening.

Sasha was really into her dancing and she was fantastically good at it. Many evenings she'd try out new moves for me on our living-room carpet; she would explain that she was working on a particular flourish of the hands or trying to get her feet just so after a turn. It was like a little game for her and she was meticulous about it. When she was done practising, she always had this slightly dishevelled but utterly serene look about her. It was pure pleasure to watch. Dancing was very much her thing, like radio was mine. She tried them all: rock 'n' roll, tango and ballroom, but salsa was the one that had captured her imagination. It was fun and provocative. 'Like an argument with your lover that you know is going to end well,' she once told me. I took some lessons with her before we got married and I'm proud to say I managed a flawless cha-cha-cha at our reception, but it never really took hold. Before her funeral I found Sasha's favourite salsa clothes (a short and shiny black dress with thousands of small strings of beads hanging from it that would fly up from her thighs as she spun, a black bra with red piping and velvety black shoes with serious heels), brought them to the undertaker and asked that he dress her body in them before he closed the lid.

For Sasha's party, I thought it would be a nice idea to get Miguel, the DJ at Sasha's regular Sunday night dance, to come and play music for the party. When I phoned him, he knew that Sasha hadn't been dancing for months, but he didn't know why. When I told him what had happened, there was a long and anxious silence on the end of the phone. Then he launched in and wouldn't stop, no matter what I tried to say. He just kept repeating that Sasha would tell him and everyone at salsa over and over again that she and I had the best marriage and the perfect son. Lio and me were all she ever talked about, apparently. While it touched me deeply to learn that we were her favourite

257

topic of conversation at salsa, it also struck me as a bit odd. I had always imagined her time at salsa as purely her own, away from everything else in her life, but it seems I was with her even there. She would get so tarted up to go to salsa that I could get a bit jealous, just a bit. She would never invest that much eyeliner in our evenings out. I never once thought she would get carried away on the dance floor or make an illicit hook-up, but seeing her look so glamorous as she left the house often filled me with the desire to have her there and then three steps from the front door. The thought of her dancing still makes me happy. Unfortunately, Miguel didn't make it to the party.

Lots of Lio's friends and their families did turn up, though; they tore around and danced and played. About 50 or 60 people shuffled through in all, more than I'd expected. Everyone heaped praise on Sasha and Lio and me. I soared.

'Heaven must have called her up to teach the angels how to draw,' the mother of one of Lio's school friends said to me near the pages from her children's books. I smiled and thanked her genuinely but felt a touch uncomfortable. It was a beautiful thought and an image I could accept, but there was something about articulating it that made it seem less real. Sasha would have understood exactly how I felt.

We finished all the food, left only a few pints of Harvey's (the local beer) and a few bottles of wine, all of which – I'm pleased to say – made their way home with other people. As the party broke up and the guests left, and even the friends and family who stayed late to help clear up had gone home, I found myself completely alone in that solid sixteenth-century building with stained-glass windows and dark wood panelling. I made my way to the big front room where Sasha and I had had a band playing for our wedding dance. I put my arms out as if holding Sasha ready to dance. I remembered the music; this one was a waltz, a simple waltz, the kind that Sasha had taught me how to do years before. I heard it faintly and began to lift my feet in threes. I smiled and began to twirl around slowly. But the music got faster, then faster still. My pace quickened, my circles tightened, my teeth clenched and I raced into a kind of delirium. The hospitals, the doctors, the never-ending therapies, the frustration, the fights, the Lio I worried I would never see again, the rage, the panic over my own uncertain future all came crashing down on me. I tripped and fell hard on the wooden floor. After a few seconds, with all my might, I pounded the ground with my fist. Dizzy but not worrying about falling further, I got up as quickly as I could. My hand hurt for weeks afterwards.

'So Lio, why are you calling me "Sweetheart"?' I asked him, as he and I went in the bathroom at the top of the stairs to brush our teeth.

'*Perché ti amo*' ('Because I love you'), he said simply. I really didn't know how to respond, so I just left it.

The next morning I checked my email. I had sent some recent X-rays to Dr Tall back in New York. He'd looked at them and sent a reply to me. It sat in my inbox for a few hours before I had the courage to read it. I needn't have worried, though: it was *fantastic* news. The angular deformity of Lio's leg had not only not got worse since the operation (a real fear) but had improved. Prior to the operation, the angular deformity had been 17 degrees, but in the recent X-rays it measured only 14 degrees. This meant that Lio didn't need another operation that summer and, at least for the time being, his leg was growing well. I was ecstatic. Lio was nonchalant, as if he was expecting such a great result all the time. After months of extremely intensive leg work, I now felt like I could return to focusing more on his head – there are

259

only so many hours in the day and those cognitive exercises had slipped a bit.

Our days soon settled into a steady rhythm of speech and language therapy, school, physiotherapy, music therapy, writing practice, concentration and memory practice, and regular play dates with school friends whose parents continued to be a marvellous combination of warm, generous and curious. Similarly, our weeks became a more manageable pattern of meetings with teachers, therapy with professionals and weekends up in London to spend time with Nigel, Penny and the extended family.

The doctors' appointments were fewer and farther between, the grief at the loss of Sasha settled into a constant but gentle ache and even my taste for beer returned. So, seven months after the crash, I decided that I would make the most of things and try to reconnect with the world socially. After helping Graziella translate her CV into English, I went out one evening in search of old friends in some of the local pubs. My feet took me to the Swan in Southover, Lewes, where I ran into Karen, a close friend of Sasha from London. I was happy to see her and also happy to see that she had already knocked back a few.

We chatted, she bought me my second pint and asked if I was looking after myself. As this conversation spun on, the first I'd had with a friend in months, I began to feel worried and a bit defensive.

'So,' she said. 'Have you returned to normal life yet?'

I felt a bit judged. 'You know, Karen,' I said, 'my normal life is flash cards at dawn, five kinds of exercise with Lio's leg every day, memory games, doctors' appointments, therapy appointments, phone calls to the educational authority, rubbing vitamin E into Lio's scars, emails to lawyers and, maybe once a month or so, a walk round town in the evening.'

'So you haven't gone back to work, then?' she said.

I almost spewed beer out of my nose. Was she joking? 'I *am* working,' I barked. 'Just not at what I used to, not at the university. The traditional nine-to-five thing is just not going to be in my future for a while, if ever.' I snorted a laugh, but I was getting pissed off. I couldn't tell if she was intentionally winding me up or being serious.

'You know,' she continued, 'I knew Sasha for years and years before she met you, and I'm sure she wouldn't want you wasting away on your own, just you and Lio. You should think about going back to your job – or maybe even finding someone for you – you've got to get on with things. You're too young for this to be the end of you.'

'Maybe it's the beginning,' I said to my half-full glass. She was drunk and not paying attention and I was catching up fast.

It certainly would have been easier for her if she'd been able to relate to me as she always had done, as the person she knew before the accident. It would have been much easier for her and for everyone if (as I was pressured to do in hospital) I'd just accepted change and defeat and disability and moved on or moved back into my old life. It was hard for Karen to relate to my new situation and, honestly, I didn't want her to think of me as someone radically changed. I was still the same person that she knew, the same bloke with the same mind and the same personality, now just struggling to deal with things that life had thrown at him. My situation had changed, my perspective on what's valuable had changed, but had my character changed that much as well?

'So how did your thing go with Tony?' Karen asked distractedly.

'I came to pieces a bit, but Lio was charming as ever. He—' she interrupted before I could finish.

'You know he'll never fully recover,' she blurted out.

'Shut the fuck up!' I hissed, slamming my palm down on the bar and making it sting. 'You don't know what the hell you're talking about! Just how much research have *you* done into paediatric neurology?!' I snapped. 'But forget that. If I don't believe in Lio's recovery – if he doesn't believe in his own recovery – then you're probably going to be right, it's all over. But fortunately I think differently.'

Karen, now on her back foot, started to explain: 'Easy, Martin. I was just trying to get you to prepare for the worst.' Once again Sasha's last words rang in my ears.

'I don't see much difference in preparing for the worst and inviting the worst to happen,' I countered.

'Look, I do have some insight into this myself. Three years ago my father had a tumour and the doctor told me and my sister that he was going to die,' she responded. 'I accepted it there and then, but my sister didn't. When he died a few months later, it was much easier for me to handle than it was for her.'

I faded away into my beer. Why must experiences always be made 'easier'? Why is that so important? Are we that weak, that fragile, that delicate that we have to soften every blow before it comes, even the ones that might never land? Some experiences are *necessarily* hard, *necessarily* difficult, and what's most important is not how you anticipate them or even feel about them, but what you *do with them*, what you make of them, how you go forward from them. It certainly would have been *easier* for me to retreat into the bottle when what happened happened. It would have been *easier* for me to just leave all Lio's care to doctors, therapists and the larger British medical system. It would have been *easier* for me, as it would have been easier for doctors, therapists and friends, if I hadn't clawed for every inch of Lio's recovery. But that would have been abandoning our son's future to the cynicism that Sasha warned me about. And I wasn't about to make it easier for anyone at the expense of Lio's future. Some experiences are essentially hard, but that's not to say that those same experiences can't also be valuable, wonderful even, and transform lives in unimaginably beautiful ways if you're open to possibilities.

I resurfaced and looked Karen in the face. Now she was the one staring silently at her almost empty glass.

'Doctors say what they say for their own reasons a lot of the time,' I observed. 'In those first weeks in hospital, some doctors seemed to revise Lio's "best-case scenario" upward every two days. And at every stage they were wrong. They underestimated. To look at Lio now, he seems a perfectly normal boy with a perfectly normal childhood.'

'He is amazing,' she admitted and I hoped that something I had said had finally started making an impression. 'I've also gone further than they told us to expect.' She was talking about her own history. 'I've been pretty resilient, too. My father called me "a survivor" but it was as much down to his work as it was down to anything I did.'

I had forgotten that she had had a blood disease since childhood.

'It was terrible,' she said. 'When I was a little girl, I remember kicking and screaming and trying to bite my parents when they gave me my injections. They were told I probably wouldn't live to see 20.'

'And now here you are in front of me at forty-two, three sheets to the wind,' I teased. 'Your parents weren't exactly focusing on preparing for the worst when they were treating you, were they?'

'They were doing what they had to do,' she said. 'But they still might have been preparing for the worst. I can't say.'

Now that I had regained my momentum, I wasn't going

to be put off by her uncertainty, whether she was listening or not. 'OK,' I countered. 'Why don't we take a good look at this "preparing for the worst" approach and see what it actually does both for medical types and for patients. Let's see who it serves.'

'But it's doctors' experience that—'

'First' – I waved her off with my hand, not wanting to be derailed – 'preparing for the worst lowers the stakes, it lowers the stakes for the recovery; it takes the pressure off doctors to get patients better. It says: "you can only go this far" and when you only get that far everybody is satisfied.'

'But you said that Lio's neurologist wasn't like that,' she replied.

'Yeah, but I think he's the exception that proves the rule.' I bit my tongue. She had hit a nerve and she wasn't letting up, but exploding at her wasn't going to accomplish anything. Why didn't she get it? Was I not expressing myself clearly? Through almost the whole of Lio's medical ordeal so many doctors seemed to consistently low-ball their prognoses. It's a strategy that works well for them – but less well for the patient. When they underestimate, doctors are treated like miracle workers if you exceed expectations, and like gods if you make a full recovery. I'm not even sure that this is something they do consciously because every one of them had always seemed authentically concerned for Lio and invested in his improvement. But when they play down the potential for your own or your child's healing in the short term, they don't have to really push themselves to get the patient as far as he might go. It seems they'd be less likely to struggle with a patient explore new techniques, try new things or suggest other medical professionals with other treatments. The pessimistic approach says: consider yourself lucky that things *are not worse* and only expect things to get marginally better. It's simply safer.

'You make it sound like they're almost afraid that someone will get better,' Karen chimed in again.

'No,' I said. 'But there *is* a lot of fear around. I think there is a tremendous amount of fear about giving a prognosis that's too optimistic, especially in England. If doctors do that and the person in the bed on the ward doesn't meet expectations, then the doctors look as if they've failed somehow. It must be awful to have to explain to parents why their child hasn't recovered as well or as quickly as predicted.' And then, I thought to myself, doctors come to be reviled rather than revered, they're charlatans rather than saints, because they haven't delivered what was expected. And I understand how no one likes to feel like a failure.

'With you hanging on every word that comes out of their mouths, it sounds hard for doctors to say anything at all.' Karen wasn't giving in.

The corners of my mouth curled up and I agreed but wasn't going to be sidetracked so near to home. 'There's very little real difference in telling families to be prepared for the worst and telling them to expect the worst,' I said. 'And that's poison.' When you expect the worst, thought and energy that you might direct at your child's recovery is wasted in imagining him as crippled or impaired or somehow *less than* he was before. And then momentum builds towards this crippled image that you're holding in your mind. I understood this, too.

Karen finally threw in the towel soon afterwards, but I couldn't help replaying our conversation over and over again in my mind on the walk home. When you hear underestimated or pessimistic prognoses, it's easy to see them as absolute limits for your children. Instead of imagining a future together like any other young family

265

imagines a future together, a future of fun and adventure and accomplishment, simple survival and existence become the goals.

When Lio's grandparents, infected for a short time by the negativity of some of those early malformed diagnoses, started telling Lio things like 'Maybe golf is a sport you'll be able to do' or 'Maybe you can take up rowing' or 'Maybe you can sell things on the internet when you grow up', I had to leave the room. But eventually, steeling the courage, I intervened by inviting Lio to think about his own future of possibilities without limits. I asked him where he wanted to travel to when he got better. Egypt, Turkey and Morocco were his answers; we had been talking about camels and he wanted to ride one. I asked him whom he'd like to meet in a few years. The Power Rangers and spacemen; I don't know if he meant astronauts or aliens. I asked him what he wanted to do when he grew up: underwater diver, magician and fireman, in that order. What mountains he'd like to climb: Pizzocco, near our mill. And what languages he'd like to learn: 'All of them,' he said without even thinking. With consistent (and often forced) focus on these visions, on these dreams, I like to think I was able to push out the fretful, the negative and the frightened. Because I spent more time with him in and out of hospital than anyone else I like to think my approach held those shards of a bleaker future at bay. He could do anything, he *can* do anything; he can climb mountains, he can write books, he can create art and music, he can learn all the languages he sets his mind to, he can charm anyone he meets.

We met the marker of Sasha's birthday head on with a party. But I worried that I wouldn't be able to deal with our first anniversary after the crash quite so well. I wasn't about to put on another party and I definitely didn't want to sit at home and let the day pass unnoticed, so I decided to get the hell out of the country. I wanted to do something that Sasha and I might have done together to celebrate and, somehow, to try to remember and to try to forget at the same time. I hoped to soften the inevitable pain but also wanted to recall or even recreate a bit of grown-up fun. I wanted to convince myself that joy in the outside world still existed and was still available to me, and remembering and re-living some of the happy moments of our lives together seemed like an excellent way to start. And I found, in the middle of June after the crash, that mixing pleasure and grief made for a strangely alluring cocktail.

I knew if I did it on my own I would feel the loss more than anything else, so I began to consider a travelling companion. Yet this move was not without its risks. My memories of our great marriage had sustained me for months. Those memories had probably also become more idyllic and more perfect with the passage of time. The problem was that as I came to depend on these refined memories of our storybook life, of our adventures, of our deeply shared interests, of the sheer physical joy of being with Sasha, any new fun or pleasure or adventure might threaten those memories, might threaten to weaken the fragile emotional support structure I'd so carefully built up around me. If you have fun travelling, feel joy in someone else's company and experience old delights in new ways, then the absolute perfection of your past life might reveal itself as less than perfect. Your sustaining image of a beautiful past begins to unravel in the joy of the moment. But beyond that, simply making new memories without Sasha was a frightening prospect. How could I manage to hold on to those vital reminiscences about what we had while at the same time trying to find pleasure, or at least avoid pain, and relax in the present?

Before I could talk myself out of things with my worrying and second-guessing, I invited my old friend Rene to come to France with me for my wedding anniversary. The email I sent to her now strikes me as over the top, a panic of desperation and conditionality, of pre-emptive regret in making the invitation and pleas for my asking such a crazy thing not to destroy our friendship. I had met Rene several years earlier when she had hired me to work on the sound for a film she was producing; it was a fun job. We'd had lots in common: a love of art and literature, a taste for urban life, a political awareness, a slightly troubled appreciation of the divine and a love of parody; we also now both had deep and committed long-term relationships in our not-too-distant pasts that had each ended too suddenly.

After the crash she'd shown this remarkable ability to listen to me and just sit with me and watch the tears flow – and even shed a few herself. On one occasion we were out at a particularly loud and cheap Chinese restaurant while Lio was being looked after by his grandparents and she said something so sympathetic and insightful that I thought about it for weeks afterwards. In fact, it continues to give me solace even to this day.

'You know, Martin,' Rene said. 'You and I are extremely lucky. We've each had something that very, very few people ever get to have in their lives. You and I have both known what it is to be truly in love – we've both known real love. When I think of other people I know and their relationships, they've never experienced what I experienced with my boyfriend Mark for nine years and you had with Sasha for fifteen years. And that's worth thinking about from time to time and remembering.'

She was right, of course. But, more importantly, Rene's words helped me make the transition to a new and much more positive way of grieving. Before that comment when thinking about Sasha it was easy for me to get trapped in an experience of loss. Too often I thought only about how much I had lost and how I was going to deal with that loss. All around me there was pain and absence; photos of Sasha were difficult for me to look at for more than a glance because they shot me into a panic of missing her and pain in remembering what I no longer had. Rene's pithy little comment shifted my focus; it shifted me into a positive reminiscence of what I'd had. My memories and my trinkets of the life before the crash would still certainly cause me sadness, but also – I could now hope – they might eventually give me an equal amount of joy. I can now look at photos and remember with pleasure our honeymoon in Greece, our trips to Italy, our breathtaking hikes up implausibly high mountains, our love-making in the open air, our fantastic wedding that everyone talked about for years afterwards and the simple pleasure of hearing 'I love you' every day. I could now hold those things in my mind and consider myself incredibly fortunate to have had them, to have experienced them, to have had the life that many people dream about for years and never manage to hold. We had it.

You might ask, would it have faded? I don't think so, but it certainly would have changed and grown and evolved. The more important thing is that what we had was rare and beautiful and it will remain precious to me, with Lio as a constant reminder of it. I had it. It's gone, yes. But I had it. And when I had it, it was blissful and transcendent. And when I had it, I like to think I was grateful for it – although on this score I know I fell a bit short sometimes, especially in the months before the crash. All this flowed out of Rene's comment and that comment was the reason I asked her to come with me to France.

Conversation is like a drug for me. When you're in tune with someone in a conversation, when you can make funny, ironic, playful comebacks to what they've said, or extend their thoughts with a bit of insight of your own, or take their ideas in a new direction, something intimate and unstated goes on, something magical happens. On the ferry ride over to the harbour town of Dieppe, Rene and I brainstormed ideas for her grant application to set up a database on the aesthetics of old German film – something Rene had been working on for years. It was fun and energetic and my mind hadn't been stretched like that since the last summer with Sasha and our many conversations about the social need for beauty. I remembered how I smiled with Sasha in my mind as I beamed with delight over my conversation with Rene. I talked about cinematic blank space as 'pure potentiality', a cool, if slightly pretentious and academic way to think about the dark celluloid. I was so happy I clapped like a little boy with ice cream in front of him.

I just let myself go and we talked all day. As we ambled through the medieval streets, Rene was completely at ease and relaxed. She leaned on my shoulder once to adjust her sandal and we teased each other about how terrible our French was. We even, in a totally clichéd moment of French romance, ran through a fountain in the centre of a square after a freak summer rainstorm had soaked us to the skin. We had four bottles of wine between us that day and as the hours ticked on into night I remember finding her hand (once or twice and only for a few seconds) as we walked. Things were getting complicated. The problems came simply in how badly the whole excursion made me miss Sasha. This experience was exacerbating that pain more than it was alleviating it. I hadn't actually realised how much I was missing her because my daily life was so absolutely concentrated on what I was doing with Lio. With Lio in front of me, there wasn't room for me to think about anything else, let alone get lost in self-pity. I missed the talking about art and politics and literature and philosophy, about food and wine, about abstract things like beauty and everyday things like dancing. I missed simply hanging out with her, I missed having her by my side and just having a companion to walk through old towns with. I missed the human contact – apart from the sex – the pleasure in feeling my hand on her skin or her arm in mine. I was recreating many of these feelings with Rene, but did I really want to confuse things by opening up a physical relationship?

As the evening glided along, I remember putting my arm around her and even putting my hand up to her cheek as we neared the end of the fourth bottle over dinner. It was exquisite to have that moment of physical closeness, of delicate human contact, so real and so warm. She never pulled away and there was never anything sexual in it. After collapsing in our separate rooms without so much as a kiss on the cheek, we woke late the next morning and had a croissant breakfast on a pebbly beach. Rene was a bit withdrawn and frowning, and I put my hand on her arm in a friendly gesture of concern. She said in a slightly laden way that she had to tell me something.

'Martin, this is hard,' she stuttered a bit. 'I don't really know how to interpret what's going on. I mean the hand-holding and the touching.'

I pulled my hand away instantly, 'I'm sorry, Rene.'

'No, it's nice,' she said. 'But what does it mean? Anyone watching would think we were lovers.'

'Oh,' I mumbled and paused to think. 'I miss things,' I said at last. 'I miss talking, I miss words, I miss testing my ideas with someone else who's on the same wavelength. I miss sharing my experiences with someone. And all of those things have been rolled up with physical contact for me for so long I can't seem to manage one without the other.'

'That's OK,' she reassured. 'You don't have to—'

'And obviously,' I interrupted before she could go on, 'I miss the physical side of things, too. But here's where it gets really tough – most of my attention and all of my love is focused on Lio, and that's the way it's going to be for quite a while.' I slid back on the pebbles a few inches. 'I don't want to be reckless with anyone's heart.'

'I understand completely and I'm sure you can see why I was confused,' she said without a trace of judgement. 'It's good that we talked about it. It's early days yet and I know that you've got more than your fair share of things to sort out.'

I mustered a gracious smile and nodded by way of thanking her. What I didn't tell her then was that I was still far too much in love with Sasha to even begin to consider a proper relationship with anyone else.

But, as is often the way with these things, the rest of the day became increasingly intense. We bundled up our stuff in the hotel and went to buy some food for the return ferry journey in a couple of hours. After our stop at a cheese shop, Rene had a little bike accident and opened up a serious gash on her shin right around the corner from the hotel. I got directions to the hospital from our friendly concierge and I quickly led the way on our bikes. We arrived, Rene passed out, she got ten stitches from a very handsome and flirtatious French doctor (I joked she should get his phone number), we missed the ferry and booked in on the next one that left at half past midnight.

The sun, our slight hangovers, the stitches, a bit more rich food than we were used to and the intensity of our earlier conversations made the rest of the day tumultuous. We talked of first loves and failed loves and of families and dreams. She broke down in tears at one point because her best friend was expecting a baby any day then. Rene was 40 years old, without the child that she desperately wanted and without the job she felt she needed before she should have a child. I realised in that moment, as I struggled to comfort her as any friend would, that the pain in the world was more diffuse than my own. My pain came on suddenly and with tremendous force, but I was certainly not unique in having it. There was Rene worried about making the most of her future, while I was worried about keeping alive my past.

Hours later, after a few more tears and some reconsideration of the absolute value of conversation on my part, we found ourselves in a bizarre Tex-Mex bar on the harbour with loud music and loads of 20 year olds. Some beers arrived and Rene wanted to make a toast.

'To the past's future,' she said with a cat-like smile. I struggled to process this for a moment and then lit up. Toasting the future of the past was a bit like focusing on the beauty of a perfect relationship even when it's ended; it says the past was wonderful, the past was beautiful and its dreams of the future were right and true and wonderful as well. It recognises those hopes and projections as valuable in and of themselves even if they only now exist in memory. Thinking of those hopes and dreams respects and validates the past; it reminds you that you were loved and that you had a future of almost limitless possibility. But in an odd way it also celebrates your current future: it reminds you that thinking and imagining what you want for your life is in itself a good and powerful thing. Even if what you're thinking doesn't come to pass, your thinking motivates you, moves you forward and makes you happy. As we drained our beers and ate our microwaved pizzas, we took turns sharing little nuggets of our pasts' futures and smiled light and easy smiles. I felt like we'd managed to save something somehow over that meal in that odd little waterfront bar.

Io Spio

Like most schools, Iford & Kingston Primary holds an annual Sports Day during the last week before the summer holidays. Parents are asked to help run the different events, like the egg and spoon race, the long jump, the (styrofoam) javelin throw and the obstacle course. Lio entered into the spirit of it completely, laughing, joking and having fun for the most part. I, on the other hand, found it extremely difficult because in situations like this one it's almost impossible not to compare Lio to other children his own age.

It's not just the physical comparison – which is hard enough in itself – but also the mental comparison: he wasn't able to follow simple directions like the other children, having to be reminded two or three times before each event, sometimes to the frustration of the parents in charge and the other children. Then there is the psychological comparison: he was simply more volatile than the other kids. During his first event, he came trudging to me in tears because something didn't go well. I couldn't quite work out what had upset him and suddenly got worried that he didn't want me to watch him do the events because he was embarrassed. Maybe he didn't want me to see him fall down and finish last in every race, or maybe he was concerned that I was going to leave and not watch him. I held him tightly for a minute and then, as if nothing had happened, he pushed me away and headed off for his next event.

When the dust settled, Sports Day was not all bad. I loved watching him kick the football and afterwards he loved telling me over and over again how he won the javelin throw. Yet, during this period of Lio's recovery, both he and I were happiest dealing with things on our own, just the two of us. I preferred things one-on-one because relating to him like that meant I never saw him as lacking compared to anyone else. There were so many things that he was *not* lacking: he was far more emotionally developed than his classmates, far more understanding and sympathetic, and he was even brighter and sharper some of the time than a few kids a year above him. But one-on-one I could really focus on what he was doing; I could focus on his improvements and it was easy for me to remember that he was still very much in the recovery phase of his injuries.

But, no matter how hard I tried, it was impossible to keep the world at bay. A few days after Sports Day, Lio visited his classmate Daphne after his regular physiotherapy. She was writing a birthday card to her cousin. She'd written 'Happy Birthday' neatly, with some flourishes on a card, and had drawn a very nice picture of her bedroom with a touch of perspective. There even looked to be a sweater hanging up in a closet. She handed me the card, which I took nervously. It was so good. I praised Daphne but looked sideways at Lio, who was looking sideways at me. Lio was concentrated on my response. I knew that he couldn't have produced something like that, but I also knew that before the crash, less than a year earlier, he could have done. I had a folder hidden under my bed full of his pre-school artwork to prove it.

Lio picked up on my anxiety, grabbed my arm and began yanking on it. He howled that he wanted to play outside. A year earlier he seemed ahead of most of his classmates in almost everything: he shared better, spoke better, drew better, listened better and wrote better. But there with Daphne he might have been miles ahead in terms of experience but he seemed miles behind in things that mattered more concretely. In spite of my best efforts to keep these feelings at a distance, they ate me up inside almost every day. Fortunately, seeing that I was stymied if not completely paralysed in the presence of that card, Daphne's mother shooed us all out the door into the back garden to kick a ball.

In my calmer moments, I told myself that not comparing Lio to other children meant valuing him for what he was rather than what he wasn't, for what he was doing rather than what he wasn't doing. But I couldn't help it. I even told him on a few occasions that he was not behaving as well as his notorious playmate Brandon. This, in the short term, only made Lio a bit jealous of Brandon and increased his bad behaviour, which in turn made me escalate my rhetoric. Once at the dinner table I even heard myself saying, 'Lio, you used to be so good, but look at what's happening now. You're behaving like a little baby.'

Tuning me out completely, and focusing intensely on his glass of water, he picked it up and silently poured it all over the table, watching it spill without a sound. Graziella got up and retreated into the kitchen because the scene was too much for her.

Lio's motivation to try had been damaged; he spiralled downwards and finally started saying over and over again: 'I'm a loser, I'm a loser.'

'Oh, Lio!' I said, realising that I had failed badly and was setting ridiculous standards for him. 'You are not! You beat what the doctors thought when they said you would die! You beat what they thought when they said you would never walk again or speak again! You are a great and determined kid who everyone wants to be around! You're a symbol to everyone of what being strong and brave is!

You play music better than me.' I said all this for myself to hear as much as for him.

Seeing he had lit a fuse, he turned his head straight at me and said, 'I'm a loser, just a loser,' and then began to cry.

This was excruciating. But I learned from it. When he would throw out his 'loser' line, I would realise instantly that I had seriously messed up. I would pause, reassure, give him a hug if he'd let me and then just back off. Then I would reassure myself that in spite of his tremendous progress he was still recovering from injuries that made it hard for him to self-regulate, to assess situations and respond appropriately. His recovery had gone so well that it was easy for me to forget this sometimes. This, in itself, was no bad thing.

If at home I was getting better at controlling this impulse to compare, out in the world I was still prone to it, especially when his speech would falter as he tried to communicate with other kids. The trick, the tremendously difficult trick, was in finding ways of seeing him *in situ* with his friends and classmates in the most positive light possible. This meant often looking at the road behind us rather than the road yet to be travelled; it meant comparing him to the Lio who was in a coma, comparing him to the Lio who was in a wheelchair, comparing him to the Lio who was almost killed, rather than comparing him to everyone around him. Lio's race through all this would be a very long one, but in the end, I decided, it would only be against himself. This is a lesson that I've since tried to apply to my own life. And I reminded myself when the temptation to compare him to his peers crept up on me that I need go no further than comparing his experience of the world and of life with those of his classmates. He really had seen more, felt more and stoically battled through more in his few years than all the 50 year olds I knew.

Fortunately, with the end of school and the beginning of the summer holidays opportunities to fall into the comparison trap virtually disappeared. We went out to Italy, as we had done every summer since Lio had been born. Lio excelled: he was in his element. We drove out with friends – Phillipa (a neighbour in Lewes and one of Sasha's closest mates) with two of her four kids, Jenny (ten) and Robbie (five, the same age as Lio). Lio took them to all his favourite mountains and lakes and castles. I had got each of the kids a nice little journal, with some markers and colouring pencils, and each morning they wrote and drew a little picture about their adventures the day before. And we forgot. There were days when I forgot about absolutely everything that had happened. There were days when we just enjoyed life with young children. At the end of the trip, driving through France, we stopped to visit some more friends. They took us to an adventure tree park, where you put on rock-climbing gear and head off into the branches to climb bridges and do little obstacles. Lio talked about it for months afterwards. He was a normal boy, doing normal boy things, creating memories and enjoying his summer holidays like any other.

That summer in Italy and France Lio and I spent hour upon hour, day upon day together. With the exception of the hospital, it was the most concentrated time we had ever spent in each other's company. While we were away, we had builders do some work on our house in Lewes. They converted the one large bathroom into two smaller bathrooms. When it was just Sasha, Lio and I, we used our one toilet as a 'family bathroom', but with grandparents, helpers and au pairs now in the mix, privacy and pressure on our single commode were more of an issue.

These building works meant a lot of packing, re-packing

and unpacking stuff around the house, which in turn meant facing more of Sasha's things – things I had simply left untouched since she'd died. Make-up, soap, shampoo, toothpaste and vitamins. The vitamins were especially poignant because in amongst them was a large, half-empty bottle of pre-natal supplements. Sasha and I were trying to have another child when she died. In fact, she had got pregnant in her last summer but within weeks lost the pregnancy. Those pre-natal vitamins were a reminder of what we had not done, of all our unfinished projects and plans not come to fruition.

Out in Italy I had such dreams about her. Her skin on mine, her hair tucked behind her ear, her perpetually smiling face, her lightness, her energy and her curiosity. I missed talking to her and yet when I dreamt of her I often couldn't get her to speak to me. She smiles, she kisses me, she holds me tight, she touches me, she shows me her writing, but most often she will not speak to me. I miss those moments of intellectual and emotional closeness more than the moments of physical closeness. Graziella, Lio's au pair at the time, was very sweet; but (maybe because of the language gap) she was not a great talker and didn't share most of my interests. She often preferred to sit in silence while we ate lunch together rather than venturing anything in less-than-perfect English. I would often try to start something in Italian but without much in common (other than lost loves) I found her slight lack of engagement often hard to negotiate.

Even the house itself was different: it was neater and tidier, with a real Italian's appreciation of clean, and that in itself could make me a bit sad. It was less rambunctious and noisy, with much less music. There was less laughter, less silliness, fewer completely goofy games of dressing up and improvising little scenes. Meals were more tense, with less talking about real things and more correction of everyone's grammar in English and Italian. Most evenings were now deathly silent, with Lio asleep, Graziella at her computer and me at mine tapping out our emails or Graziella studying and me researching until sleep. It was more house than home.

So I contented myself with my dreams of Sasha. I withdrew into them and prepared for them, and they were beautifully fulfilling in and of themselves. I discovered a little trick: if I thought about Sasha long and hard just before going to sleep, if I looked at photos of her or if I looked at some of the little books she made for me or letters she wrote to me, I would often then dream of her. I don't think I will ever stop dreaming of her. I would never want to, even if someone else came into my life.

It was 5 September, one year minus two days after the crash. Lio's first day at school starting on the normal date as a normal child was rapturous. He was electric with excitement as he ran to play with the other kids. We lost each other in the crowd on the playground and for a minute I worried that he would suffer a bout of separation anxiety. Then he cried out: *'Papà, Papà, sono qui!'* ('I'm here!') Maybe, just maybe, he saw some anxiety flash across *my* face and wanted to reassure *me* that everything was OK. He had woken up early that morning bristling with energy, ready to show Mrs Dumbrell the summer journal he was so proud of.

To see him get in line in the playground with all of his friends was positively surreal. If I'm honest, I was a bit too tired that morning to appreciate it fully. But I sensed it was a vitally important moment, and Lio sensed it too. He was happier than the other children, but he's always happier. Bouts of euphoria were one of his remaining issues. He would usually end the day with one, but that morning he had bounced out of bed with wild giddiness at 5.30; I'm sorry to say I was not as quick out from under the covers. As we dressed and washed, he talked about seeing his friends again and seeing his teachers. One of the things I was happiest about from my own work the previous spring was insisting on and struggling to get a Statement of Special Educational Need for Lio. This meant that he would have his own teacher with him in the classroom every morning and one afternoon each week. She would sit with him and it meant that any remaining problems with concentration could be dealt with.

While he giggled with his friends in line about his summer adventures, I couldn't help but be touched by a bit of sadness. A proper first day of school should have been without a mark, should have been unmitigated by the tiniest bad feeling, but I fell into comparing him again after a summer without it. In the context of other children, Lio acted up more, did more silly dances and squeezed people's faces. As he tried to give a sloppy kiss to Freddy, Alex looked at him in confusion. As he wiggled his bum at Lizzie, she whispered something to Deirdre, who laughed. Emma pushed him away as he tried to pull her close. Lio's brain was misfiring at all the excitement, but Duncan (who was a bit older) put his arm around Lio and succeeded in getting him to relax. Some of the other kids then picked up where Lio had left off and started doing the same bum-wiggling dances, as the teachers fought to get them in line to go into school. As they all settled, a less chaotic chatter began, but when Lio opened his mouth I couldn't help but notice that he spoke more slowly than his friends, struggled to remember details and stammered when trying to express them.

His speech still had strange cadences: he would get lost in what he was trying to say sometimes and couldn't speak when there was a lot of noise and distraction or when there were other people talking or after urgently interrupting someone with important information. At home, with just him and me, it was very easy for us to negotiate all these issues, and we had become so good at it that at times it didn't feel like anything was wrong at all. But surrounded by playmates his age, it was again impossible to avoid facing the work we'd yet to do. Later that day, however, in reading my old notes from months gone by and in looking at the first photos on Lio's website, I was struck even more profoundly by how much work we had done already and how far we'd come. I keep clinging to the words of a random paediatric intensive care nurse we'd met at the swimming pool months earlier.

'Two years,' she said. 'They've told you it will take at least two years, maybe more, right?' She was talking about recovery time for paediatric brain injury. I was encouraged and reminded myself that we still hadn't reached the halfway point in our marathon, and maybe even that was a long way off.

The question I struggled to avoid during this period, the question that haunts the sleep of all parents who find themselves in this situation, is a question invited by orthodox medicine's way of thinking about the brain: what would my child be like if the accident had never happened? What would he be doing, how would he be speaking and writing and drawing, how would he be behaving and interacting? It's a question that sees the brain as a fragile Venetian glass sculpture to be appreciated as is, and, once cracked or broken, ruined forever. I've come to see the brain as a living organic creation capable of growth, re-growth and regeneration. The power of this image of glass and the fear of absolute loss is so great it has an almost hypnotic power that, in my weaker moments, drew my imagination to it. If you're not careful, the image of broken glass can consume you.

The antidote for the panic invited by the 'What would he be like?' question proved a slow and steady dosing of myself with books about paediatric brain *development* rather than injury. The more widely I read, the more I began to understand that while trauma can certainly cause changes in brain function, so do dozens if not hundreds of other things (for the worse and the better). Trauma may be a major event but in no way is it an isolated factor. Virtually everything a child does alters his or her brain chemistry and development. Look at the foods they eat: refined sugars, the wrong fats, chemical additives – some argue even the natural sylacitates in some fruit – can affect brain chemistry and development, as does the simple amount of water they drink. Diets rich in protein, amino acids and essential fatty acids alter the landscape of the brain in different ways from diets high in carbohydrates. Look at how they're learning: curriculums with or without daily music and movement affect brain development, as does exposure to and practice in other languages. Are their home and family lives stable and loving, and are their relationships with their friends happy and fulfilling? Emotional stress, especially constant and sustained stress, can interfere with healthy neurological growth and function. Similarly, the amount of competition and collaboration children are involved in affects the way brains develop, as do parental and societal expectations for that competition and collaboration. What kinds of entertainment and leisure activities do they pursue? Lots of 'screen time' affects neurological development in different ways from lots of 'face time'. Sleep – the amount, the quality and the frequency of it – is also a crucial neurological influence. And so are a myriad of environmental factors from exposure to toxins like heavy metals and allergens to chemicals in drinking water. Simply exposing your child to new things, new experiences, new ideas, new places, new languages stimulates the development of neurological pathways. So while a trauma will have consequences, so will a host of other events, occurrences, habits and decisions in a child's life. The volume of research on this is now overwhelming.

I consoled myself with the knowledge that while I hadn't been able to do anything about the accident I was certainly in a position to decide well about all these other factors. I was also comforted by the fact that Sasha and I had from the beginning given Lio a great developmental start. Beyond being consoled, I was in fact inspired because I saw how much power and control over his development was in my hands and how well Sasha and I did with that power from the beginning: Lio ate super brain food. He had languages and music. He had peace at home and adventures abroad. He had attention and love from the most capable mother imaginable. In some strange and terrible way, he was the most well-suited boy in the world to have had this happen.

When I picked Lio up in the playground after school that day, he stumbled out beaming and presented me with his bookbag stuffed full of start-the-year notices. He was happy, if a bit haggard, as were most of the other kids. I grabbed him up out of the throng and swung him around until both our heads spun. Then I asked him to tell me three things he did at school that day. He groaned, remembering this little memory exercise from the year before.

'I played,' he said.

'What did you play?' I wasn't going to let him off the hook that easily.

'I don't know . . .' He started to laugh nervously, with a hint of frustration. 'Stuff in the playground.'

'Come on, Lio. I've got a flapjack in the car with your name on it.' I'm ashamed to admit how often I resorted to bribery and how well it worked. 'If you can tell me those three things before we get to the car, I'll give it to you straight away.'

'Does it really have my name on it?' he asked. One corner of my mouth curled up in a perplexed half-grin. I couldn't tell if he was stalling for time or if he really had got lost in the language.

Just over a year after the crash, I wrote this entry on Lio's website:

> Every day is another step forward with Lio. The little milestones are too numerous to list since our last update. But one in particular that gives us both tremendous pleasure is Lio's riding his bike again without stabilisers. This is something he had just learned to do before the accident and now he's up and at it again, ready to show you or at least tell you about it at the drop of a hat.
>
> We started some months ago with a large tricycle as part of his physiotherapy. We've been doing physiotherapy every day, at home or with a therapist, and (as his knee-bending was improving and as his balance was returning) getting back on the bike was the obvious thing to do. A couple of weeks ago we visited his orthopaedic doctors in New York, and according to them all our work has had a remarkable pay-off. Lio's range of motion in his leg is much more than they had expected and (more importantly in terms of long-range issues) his 'super leg' is growing and the growth is straight. The angular deformity hasn't got any worse and, at least in the short term, another operation seems unnecessary. Watching Lio show off his leg tricks in front of the doctors was something I will never forget.
>
> Some milestones throughout this past year made

me giddy with anticipation – like leaving the hospital and Lio's first day at proper school. For others, I had to really work to make them positive, or to figure out a way to try to avoid them – like Sasha's birthday and our wedding anniversary. The one-year anniversary of the accident was going to be very difficult for me. Fortunately, the next week Lio had those doctors' appointments in New York, so I arranged to fly out on that day. Part of me really did just want to flee, to be so occupied with the stress of international airport security as to be distracted from the memories of a year ago – every detail of which is still running through my mind like a constant video loop. I'll be able to face things more squarely next year when we'll be even further along with Lio.

But the memories had a way of finding me even in the insanity that is Gatwick Airport. As I was about to turn off my phone while we were waiting in the plane for the last of the passengers to board, I saw that I had a message. Normally I would have just ignored it, but for some reason I didn't this time and grabbed one of Lio's markers to scribble down a phone number on the edge of a page in his open colouring book. It was a reporter from the *Argus*, the daily Brighton paper. He had noticed the date as well and wanted to write a follow-up story about Lio one year on. Lio was happily colouring dinosaurs on his tray table as our plane was being held at the gate, so I called him back. He was extremely nice, funny even at times; we chatted for a bit and eventually things came pouring back. I think I held it together well enough and he ended up writing a very nice and sympathetic piece about Sasha's passing and Lio's stunning recovery from near death to the healthy, happy little boy that he is today.

When we got back from the States, my answering

machine was full and the emails were piling up. Several other reporters had seen the story in the *Argus* and wanted to do a variety of pieces commemorating Sasha and celebrating Lio. Over the next few days we were on BBC TV and radio and were interviewed and photographed for a story in the magazine *Woman's Own*. Every year the magazine nominates about a dozen children as 'the bravest child of the year'. They wanted to include Lio on this year's list. Lio really relishes the attention – he's more at home now in front of cameras than the doctors and the therapists he's often posing with. Part of me hates having to drag everything up again, having to get a bit choked up with another journalist just when I feel I've got a lid on things. But Lio really loves it and in the end the pain that I have to go through ebbs away, I dry a tear and I'm left feeling a little bit good. As I'm forced to bring up these emotions about Sasha and about our life together, I not only remember them but also I re-live them and I revel in them. I have known real love and know it now with Lio.

I see so much of Sasha in Lio: his *joie de vivre*, his enthusiasm, his startling determination and tenacity, his slightly maddening tendency to wake up before 6.00 every morning ready to do his best work of the day. Mornings are usually great for him; we usually get in some drawing or some speech and language practice before breakfast. In these moments, it is genuinely possible to forget the nightmare of a year ago and to think that he doesn't have very far left to go. It's only when I see him in the context of his peers that I realise where we have to focus our attention now.

These issues are subtle: he continues to have concentration problems, he is easily bored and distracted and stays on task about half as well as others. One of his neurologists is proposing Ritalin but I haven't yet done my homework on it (I don't know much about it beyond its general bad press for being over-prescribed). His drawing still isn't as sophisticated as it was before the accident. He hasn't quite regained the social skills that were his hallmark before as well. His voice is still raspy, especially when he gets excited, and he still lacks an understanding/control of appropriate volume (although this is much much better than it was five months ago). His speech is generally slower and much more deliberate than his peers. But we've been working on this every day with his 'homework': we play hours and hours of '*Io spio*' ('I spy'), which is really good for getting him to focus on one object for a couple of minutes and gets him to describe it in various ways. Even better is 'The Odd One Out'; it's when he's struggling to articulate the odd one between a cricket ball, a cricket bat and an apple pie that I get the best thinking and speaking out of him. Sometimes he really surprises me with his creativity.

But what remains the most troubling thing for me are his bouts of euphoria (which usually come in the evenings) where he just laughs wildly and runs around doing crazy dances and repeating the same words. It's impossible to talk him down when he gets this way and I wouldn't mind so much except that when he's like this he loses all sense of danger and risk, throwing himself in the deep end of the pool when he knows he can't swim and climbing up the outside of stair railings, etc. Still, I would much rather have him like this than with bouts of impenetrable depression. And I'm confident that we will tame these demons as well, even if we have to clothe them and feed them and make them our own.

But most importantly, as all of the news coverage has noted and as all our friends (especially those who only see us infrequently) keep saying, his change and development and recovery have been nothing short of miraculous. As his speech and language therapist told me only a couple of days ago, if you didn't know his story, to look at Lio on the playground with his friends you would barely notice a problem. I am extremely grateful for this and feel sure that one day this whole tragic episode will only be a distant memory for him.

The evening after his first day of the new school year I marked Lio's height on the wall in the living room as I had done before: 3 feet 7½ inches. I was astounded to see how big he was and how much he had grown. There is a touch of sadness in this, watching him evolve before my eyes. But even though my joys might have been higher and my insecurities deeper because of Lio's particular situation, I told myself that this pang of melancholy had to be a common experience. You're not able to fully enjoy a stage of childhood before your kids are through it. Or perhaps you're only coming to appreciate (rather than tolerate) an age when they leave you in the dust with your flash cards and your nursery rhymes.

But Lio wasn't the only one making progress. As he was starting his second year at his little village school with the same sweet teacher, I remember having this gripping fear that he wouldn't be able to keep up with his friends. All parents want their children to excel, to be good at things, and even (the tendency to compare is hard to shake) to be good at things relative to their classmates. Even the most enlightened parents want their children to feel fulfilled in what they do and have a sense of accomplishment. While Lio's accomplishments were coming (faster than anyone expected), they were also peppered with frustration. At times he would get tremendously anxious at not being able to do things that he wanted to do or even to communicate what he wanted to communicate to the point of yelling, kicking and screaming. When I mentioned this to his doctors, even the one I trusted above all of them, his neurologist McCormick, I was encouraged to start considering a pharmaceutical solution.

This frightened me because Lio was an amazingly joyful boy with the most gorgeous personality. Lio would invent stories with his toys about a bus driver who kept parking his bus outside a castle and who kept getting told off by a grumpy king – and would giggle over and over as he repeated the scene; he would kick a ball off the wall beneath our kitchen window and it would bounce into the flowerbed behind him again and again and he would giggle; he would climb trees too high for him to climb down and he would laugh rather than cry until I came to help; in school when anyone did the slightest silly thing you often couldn't get him to stop laughing. He was very happy. But this happiness itself was becoming a bit of a problem. Specifically, his giddiness meant that it was hard for him to stay focused on anything for more than a few minutes. While some parents of Lio's classmates lamented the fact that they could only get through four pages of a book with their children without them getting distracted, I kept quiet about how grateful I was when Lio managed to get through just one page.

His perpetual happiness caused me to worry that he might miss educational opportunities being offered to him in the moment. I was afraid that if he fell behind now because of a lack of concentration (on top of all the school he had missed because of surgery and doctors' appointments), he might find himself always struggling to catch up and to keep up. What made matters worse was that these thoughts often drifted to the lack of Sasha in his life. She was so exceptional in so many areas: writing, music, dancing, painting, drawing and elegant grown-up thinking. She could have offered him so much more than me alone. Every parent's goal, their simple dream, is for their child to have a better life than they have had, to do more and see more than they themselves have done and seen, to have more opportunities than they have had, and perhaps simply (and not necessarily tied to the others) to be happier than them. For the first four and three-quarter years of his life, Lio had ticked all these boxes. He had more stamps in his passport than most 60 year olds; he was the nicest boy in nursery and certainly the most empathetic among his classmates; he was so proud of his languages. My only worry before the crash was that one day his Italian might be better than mine.

One year after the crash my energy was spent more prosaically on getting him to sit still for a few minutes to focus on the simple book or drawing in front of him. I wasn't really concerned to push his mind and his imagination in new and interesting ways as we had done before. I still wanted to teach him new languages, new ways of drawing, new ways of seeing, new ways of being in the world, but before we could even entertain those things there was this tremendous struggle just to get him to sit down or to stand still.

I was scared of the long-term effects of psychotropic drugs. The reading I'd started to pick up had led me to believe that they could be quite addictive; in the US, Ritalin is classified as a Schedule II drug along with cocaine and morphine. I had also gleaned that it was only ever a temporary solution to problems with concentration and attention: it may help you concentrate in the moment but it does nothing to improve your concentration overall once you're off the drug, the problems return). I'd also come across some alarming studies that warned of everything from brain shrinkage to the drug's ultimate uselessness in helping with real-world things like educational level and career development. But worse, I began to worry that it might snuff out what was left of the spark in Lio's eyes, that it might curb his imagination, his ability to make connections between things, to live a creative life. It might slow down the fidgetiness of his body so that he might read better, for example, but at the same time it might restrict what he might be able to do with what he was reading.

In the long run, I was far more interested in his *thinking* than in his rote learning. I knew from one of my own fields (media and sociology) that there are studies and there are studies, and that you can find or *create* a study to argue just about any point you like; the trick is knowing which are the studies worth paying attention to. I, with my novice but steadily developing understanding of paediatric brains, was having a hard time separating the research wheat from the chaff. The professionals I spoke to were not much help in sorting things out, with about half of them saying drugs would bring some benefits for Lio and the other half saying that we shouldn't use them.

So before we started popping Ritalin or anything else, I committed myself to trying as many alternatives as possible. I had long and extremely productive conversations with Lio's occupational therapist at Charleston and scoured the internet for days and days based on her recommendations. In the autumn of 2007, I emailed a woman in California who made weighted vests for children with attention and sensory problems. Apparently, said Lio's occupational therapist, weighted vests provide just the right kind of stimulus to children who find the urge to bounce and fidget irresistible. I ordered the vest and another pressure vest made of the same neoprene material as wetsuits. We tried them and Lio much preferred the pressure vest, although it is difficult to say if it did anything for him because he would pull it off after a few minutes at school and they wouldn't put it back on him.

Hours and hours in books and on the internet also led me to lots of vitamins and nutrients. As twice-daily supplements, Lio was taking: marine phytoplankton because it contains the right kinds of fatty acids and proteins for brain development; blue-green algae to get rid of any heavy metals in his body and to provide chlorophyll and a range of naturally occurring B-vitamins to help the brain; Omega 3 oil, an essential component of brain cell growth and maintenance; flaxseed lecithin, which contains choline, which is an essential neurotransmitter; and ginkgo biloba, shown to increase blood flow to the brain. He was also taking glucosamine with chondroitin for his knee. As I discovered each one of these through my own research and through conversations with doctors, therapists and practitioners, I had gradually introduced them into his diet and by the start of his second year at school he had been taking some of them for several months. While I was occasionally told by the more sceptical that there was 'no hard clinical evidence' that some of these things worked, I'm not someone who now sniffs at anecdotal evidence. I'm convinced, and I'm not alone, that these supplements have played a significant part in Lio's recovery over the long run. Yet in spite of all these efforts, and in spite of the progress that everyone was observing, he remained unable to sit still to the extent that his classmates could.

But while I was worrying about his hyperactivity I also began to worry that I might be pushing him too hard. Did I really want him to feel the pressure to perform I had sometimes felt as a child? Having been through so much already didn't it make sense to comfort and protect him first and above all? I wanted him to progress and develop and to accomplish things; indeed it was my bright vision of his dynamic future that had pulled us through those most demanding days a year earlier. But now, in my flashes of second-guessing and reconsideration, I wondered who that vision was serving most. Perhaps the worry about his hyperactivity (like so many others in my life) was silly. Perhaps it was unnecessary. But I like to think that even if I might have held that worry too tightly in my mind I wasn't guided by it on a daily basis. I was praising him profusely every day. At every bedtime, I would tell him precisely what he had done well that day, and only the things he had done well. I played with him for hours every day and gave him plenty of time to move around and just feel his body in motion. And we really were doing everything possible to make his recovery happen: every morning, often from very early, we were downstairs playing his speech and language therapy games and doing some physio. And even though I couldn't get rid of the fear about his hyperactivity, and the fear about him not operating as well as he might, I was not yet convinced that he should be put on drugs.

Other parents consoled me by telling me that all children develop at their own pace and that I shouldn't fret. It's not that I didn't believe this, it's just that I couldn't get my memories of how exceptional Lio seemed before the crash out of my head. I wish I had been clever enough to consider exactly what I meant by 'exceptional' when I was twisting myself up with anxiety over how he was doing in school. Before the crash he might have been exceptional, but he was exceptional in a very ordinary, mundane and ultimately uninteresting way: he was a very bright, clever and curious child. In truth there are millions of very bright, clever and curious children – at least one in every classroom. One year after the crash he was exceptional in a much more *exceptional* way: at his tender age he had survived a near-death experience, he had defied elite medical opinions about his best-case recovery only three months after the crash, his resilience had got him invited to meet the Prime Minister, his tenacity and strength of character had grown tremendously in the face of the loss of his mother, his recovery from terrible injuries had got him on national television and on the cover of magazines with huge circulations and he had a website he could show his friends documenting it all. He was tremendously strong, and well known for being strong. He was now *really exceptional*. I had to believe that this new confidence with people and in front of people, coupled with this lack of the usual childhood social fears, would serve him well both now and in the future. When we went to restaurants and Lio got tired of waiting for his food, he would hop up, find the waitress (or even go into the kitchen) and ask when it was coming – something very few five year olds do. When I looked ahead with a positive spin on this trait, I saw it dissolving the second-guessing and the embarrassment that had so paralysed me as a young adult.

There were no easy answers to be had about medication, and my thinking was confused and often contradictory. When I tried to apply the greatest lesson from the weeks in the immediate aftermath of the crash – to trust my instincts – I found myself unexpectedly being drawn to Ritalin. It might just help him learn, and even get him to a point where he's aware of, and can self-regulate, the impulses that interfere with his learning. Simply making a decision one way or the other would end my own anxiety. On the other hand, it's not something that would make him happier – it would be impossible to make him happier. But is the euphoria of his recovering brain authentic happiness? Perhaps 'happiness' itself should be put aside in favour of other things, such as long-term independence, a pride in his work and a sense of fulfilment in what he does. Yet are these really a better standard than happiness? Should these concerns, concerns obviously a part of our culture's focus on 'work', really be our goals? Even now I struggle with these things and even now I still haven't decided about the Ritalin.

As I was beginning to grapple with these issues over pharmaceuticals, we had Lio's one-year review at Charleston. While obviously I was grateful for his progress and the fact that he seemed a normal and happy boy day in and day out on the playground, it remained extremely important to me that he continue to get the professional help necessary for him to keep heading towards that full recovery that had focused my mind for so long. I worried that this meeting might be where those in charge decided to cut off some of that help.

Tracy, his paediatrician at Charleston, contributed to these fears as the meeting began to unfold. Almost every time I opened my mouth with a concern about Lio she would chime in with some version of 'That's not abnormal for children his age.' His issues might be subtle, but they were not 'normal'. It's not normal for Lio to speak as slowly as he does or to have problems remembering where he lives or to have a raspy voice. Their agenda was pretty clear, and in the end I decided that it was fine; Lio's care was always best and his advances were always greater when I was the one undertaking or organising his treatment.

All in all, I am glad the meeting passed as it did. The less time Lio had to spend at the rehab centre, the better we'd both feel. It would have done him no good to identify with the other children there, children with extremely serious disabilities, longer than absolutely necessary. And there was certainly a logic in what the staff at Charleston were saying. I had watched the language of some of the therapists change over the past year, evolving from 'he won't fully recover' to 'if he recovers' and finally at this point to 'when he recovers'. Even Tracy seemed to have shifted her terms from 'accept his limitations and move on' to 'he's ok, let's get him out of here and move on'.

As with the other problematic characters on this journey, Tracy also proved to be a very decent person. Despite my earlier encounter with her, she was a good human being; tired, overworked and stressed certainly, but essentially a good human being. On many occasions I saw her light up with authentic pleasure at seeing how well Lio was doing. And I know that cruel encounter some ten months earlier will always taint the way I think about her. Relationships with doctors are not like relationships with lawyers or mechanics or reporters. They are strange, emotionally charged affairs, almost like romantic relationships. But unlike real affairs of the heart these are arranged marriages, arranged by fate, chance and the randomness of what hospital you end up in. They can be intense and intensely difficult. The disposition of the doctor-partner you find yourself with is unlikely to be completely compatible with your own. Plus, there was the simple fact that she was a woman, a late-30-something professional woman, slight with long blonde hair, and English. I couldn't avoid projecting Sasha on to her and feeling Tracy came up short.

40 Years

On their 40th birthdays, some of my friends had fantastic costume parties arranged by their partners, with bands and dancers and expensive booze lasting until the small hours of the morning. Unbeknownst to me my friends in Lewes had been organising a birthday party for me at the Lewes Arms. I had no idea about it and even actively tried to find out if someone had organised something by fishing for information from Graziella several weeks before. With a well-intentioned lie, she said she didn't know of anyone planning anything; so I decided there and then to take matters into my own hands. I was not going to let the day pass without notice and nothing seemed more pathetic to me then than planning your own 40th birthday party. I also wasn't sure I really wanted a party. Escape and tranquillity have always been my preference to large bashes. Sasha and I had flown to Rome and stayed in a nice little bed & breakfast in the mountains outside the city for her 40th birthday. I remember sumptuous meals and exquisite wine and gorging ourselves on wild berries in a little village surrounded by medieval walls.

My 40th was going to be different. I decided that I wanted to hear evensong at either Canterbury Cathedral or King's College Chapel in Cambridge. In the end, because I liked Cambridge more than Canterbury, I decided that I would go to King's. It was just going to be Graziella, Lio and me, but then when I was talking about it with Nigel and Penny they seemed keen to come along as well. Nigel had gone to school there and he'd wanted to show it to Lio for a long time. Lio loved asking Nigel about Cambridge. In particular he really liked hearing Nigel's story about getting jilted by his girlfriend, getting drunk on a punt, falling into the river and waking up the next day to find that someone had found and kindly returned his soggy underwear to his doormat.

We went up to London to Nigel and Penny's on the Saturday evening before my birthday and had a nice dinner with the whole family. We drank prosecco and ate cake. The next morning I went downstairs after staying in bed until quarter past nine and said in a loud voice with arms raised to everyone in the kitchen, 'I'm 40! I'm 40!' Then we trundled up to Cambridge and had a very sweet time punting on the river Cam. We stopped for a picnic lunch on the riverbank, with a view of King's College and its chapel, popped some bubbly and the sun shone wonderfully on us. Lio was in very good form. He was not too agitated and he was speaking better than I'd heard him speak since the crash. He only played up a little bit on getting back into the punt, preferring instead to do tricks on the fence that kept the cows out of the river. He was desperate to put his feet in and splash around, but that wasn't going to happen, not least because the Cam was deep and crowded with punts that afternoon.

Lio needed a little bit of encouragement/dragging through the town as we wandered through the colleges before evensong. When we arrived at the chapel, we got perfect seats right next to the choir box surrounded by stunning, ancient wood-and-marble carvings. Lio fell asleep almost instantly, with his head on my lap. This was a tiny bit uncomfortable and meant that I couldn't engage with it all as I would have liked, having to remain seated throughout. But in the end it was beautiful having my hand on the head of my child, imagining the new

299

connections forming in his brain, praying for his full recovery amidst the statues and the transcendent sounds of the choir in that beautiful Renaissance church. I was able to follow one hymn quite clearly. It involved, serendipitously, finding comfort in the mountains. I stared at the sun pouring through the stained glass in front of me, illuminating an ocean of saints and princes. I felt something of the feeling that I felt when Sasha and I had visited that same chapel three years earlier with a much smaller Lio. We were there for evensong as well and I remembered us, again with Lio asleep on her lap, drinking in the beauty of the sounds and the surroundings. I felt very close to her.

I had thought perhaps that day, my 40th birthday, would be the last day that I wore my wedding ring on my finger. I wasn't prodded so much by the gentle pressure from friends, family and psychiatrists to 'move on' with my life as I was by simple curiosity – I was just starting to wonder infrequently how it would feel to take it off. But in the end I decided to keep it on until Christmas. I liked the way it felt on my hand and it also made me feel close to her on a constant basis. Sasha did so much for me. She, in many ways, made me who I was; she opened up my tastes and my ideas, my experiences and my hopes, and after many years of being together our intuitions overlapped and there were times when we genuinely knew what the other was thinking. I couldn't help but feel as we sat in the chapel that Sasha was proud of me for what I had done with Lio, especially in those early mornings when he was so perky, just like his mother. It happened almost every morning well before 6.00: I – half asleep and half wanting to be asleep – was warm under the covers. My door would fly open and there would be Lio with a book or a drawing or a toy or a pencil and almost always with a big smile.

'Come on, *Papà*,' he would say and pull at my arm.

Sometimes I would give in, other times I would pull him into bed with me and we would read a bit as I tried to ease myself into the day. Then we'd head downstairs to do some word or maths exercises in his diary. Once or twice he would even turn on the computer before he woke me and try his hand at typing a bit – then he'd come charging into my room dying to show me what he'd done.

After evensong we lit candles and walked out into the last of the beautiful October sunshine. We had some drinks in a bar and then our feet took us back through King's College to the old stone bridges over the Cam. I hoisted Lio up on the wall of one of them and held him tight with his feet hovering above the water as we watched falling leaves and the punts slipping by. It was gorgeous. In the end I would not have had my 40th birthday any other way, but maybe the next year I'd let my friends throw me that party.

Throughout most of these months, and I know this sounds crazy, I would not have given up my grief for anything. And as my grief evolved and changed I grew more and more attached to it. When I tripped into sadness, I would also trip into a deep closeness with Sasha. The depth of that sadness was a reminder of what we had, a reminder of how real it was and how beautiful it was, and from that sadness (if I was lucky) I'd pass into gratitude and even joy in the knowledge that we had something special and rare and transcendent.

These bittersweet currents of grief could catch up with me at the most unlikely times, in the most prosaic places. I even found myself swimming in them when I finally had to do my US taxes for 2006. This was going to be a real test for me and for my relationship with grief. With each receipt, with each credit card statement showing evenings out together and flights to our favourite places, a wave of memories crashed over me. Her crisp and distinctive signature on dozens of slips of paper still spoke to me, flooding my mind with pictures of our past. As I looked at that signature, I imagined her hand, the hand that held the pen between middle and ring finger like a child would hold a crayon that was just a bit too big. I imagined that hand on my cheek.

Sasha used to hide little love notes for me, in my toolboxes or in the pages of books I was working with. Who knows, I may yet find another one or two stashed somewhere some day. She has a way of finding me still, of speaking to me still, of touching me still. As I was doing what needed to be done administratively in my life – like lawsuits, taxes and Sasha's estate – I would often stumble across a bit of her writing and I would get lost in the perfect, almost calligraphic beauty of her letters. Even the tops of paint cans stored under the stairs on which she wrote 'small bedroom' or 'external woodwork' can be simultaneously excruciating and glorious. And there I'm stuck in a kind of happy-painful reverie for minutes on end.

It's impossible amidst all of this mental drifting into the past to avoid a good deal of second-guessing, of playing the 'What if' game. When I saw the receipt for the plane ticket to Massachusetts for a job interview, a job I got offered but which I turned down because they weren't going to be able to offer Sasha a good position, I immediately launched into 'What if . . .' What if I'd just told Sasha it was time for a change and we were going to move to Massachusetts, that houses in England were too small and everything was too expensive, that we'd get more holiday time in Massachusetts and our jobs would be less stressful? What if I'd told her she wouldn't have to work a normal full-time job but could have pursued her children's writing and illustrating?

What if I'd just said, 'Dammit, we're moving to Massachusetts!'? Sasha would be alive and happy, Lio would not have been so terribly hurt and suffered so much, and I would not be forced to find comfort in my sadness. What if I'd been happy with less, what if I hadn't gone on those speaking engagements and not cultivated my career over tax-deductible dinners and lunches? What if I'd stayed home with Lio and not gone to that conference (now the most meaningful conference in my life)? Lio would be completely healthy and happy, and Sasha, perhaps having decided to spend the day with us rather than travelling to work, would be alive, pregnant and halfway through her next great book. 'What if' is an addictive little game on which you can burn a lot of time. 'What if' only ever looks backwards.

Fourteen months after the crash, I still couldn't listen to the radio. I used to eat, drink and sleep radio. I used to love British radio more than the radio in all the countries I'd ever visited. I had made radio for 20 years, good and interesting and significant radio. Before the age of 40, I had my own radio archive at a major research university collecting all of the material I had ever produced. I loved radio more than anything outside my family and now I couldn't bear to listen to it. Radio had also been woven into our lives together. Sasha used to listen to *The Archers* every day and I used to tease her mercilessly about it. We used to listen to early evening comedy programmes together and laugh ourselves hoarse. We used to argue over fantastic documentaries about art and politics and economics. We used to make fun of the whingeing and moaning on consumer affairs programmes. And we used to let ourselves get lost for hours in the long, creative dramas on Radio 3 – postmodern settings of ancient Greek tragedies; surreal stories about hallucinating psychopaths shooting at cars on isolated stretches of highway in the American south-west; and intense and ambitious first-person-singular narrations featuring actors like Johnny Depp or Sigourney Weaver. After the crash that old love of radio had turned into revulsion, yet I couldn't help but miss it.

I wasn't able to listen not so much because radio reminded me of time spent with Sasha – I liked being reminded of that – but because speech radio, particularly the BBC, contains two things that threatened my emotional well-being at that time. First, I couldn't bear hearing things on the news that involved death, car accidents and brain injuries (sadly, death and accidents are staples of radio news, even on the BBC). Second, and even more difficult, was the relentless and scathing criticism and negativity that are the hallmarks of so much BBC journalism. It's certainly true and I would be the first to admit that it's the tenacity and the brutal empiricism of BBC news that makes it so great, important and culturally valuable. If the US had anything like the BBC, its political discourse wouldn't be so stunted and shallow, and its administrations wouldn't be so inept and corrupt. But I simply couldn't subject myself to such cynical bludgeoning for more than a few seconds before it started to poison my own outlook.

Its criticism simply ran counter to the state of mind that I was trying so hard to maintain. As it exposed the dark underbelly of institutions, alternative medicine, investment plans, religious sects and people in general, it also attacked my abstract faith in humanity, my faith in people to help and support, and the very role of hope itself that was so vital in my work with Lio. I had to switch off. This made me uneasy, not least of all because I really used to look down my nose at people who didn't keep abreast of events in the world and whose lack of awareness was often accompanied by very naive political opinions. But I couldn't spare the emotional energy required to get involved and, inevitably, to get angry at the injustices and the corruption of the world. Beyond that, I simply no longer shared the beliefs and the assumptions of radio news, beliefs that the world is fundamentally cruel and unjust, that disaster is imminent and that people are almost always exclusively self-interested. The world is not just or unjust; it's simply there and things simply happen and you relate to them as best you can, you make sense of them as best you can. I didn't want to have to remind myself of that every time I turned on the radio.

Yet radio was in my blood. So I decided to start testing myself with small doses of FM music. But there too, as soon as the top-of-the-hour news came on, I almost always had to switch off. I simply didn't have the strength to worry about how my pension fund might collapse, about how new vehicle registration laws might mean more tax on our car or about how proposed immigration changes might create problems for me in a few years. My concerns were far too immediate and my vision focused too intensely on what I needed to be doing *today* to allow myself to get drawn into worrying that the sky was once again falling tomorrow. Yet I couldn't resist testing myself a bit further.

I turned on Radio 4 as I sat down alone one afternoon for a lunch of reheated stir-fry. My beloved Radio 4 was the best thing about the BBC: all-speech radio, with comedy in the evenings, short but clever drama in the afternoons, intelligent interview programmes in the mornings and wonderfully precise news and current affairs throughout the day. But on that day my experimental re-introduction to it lasted less than a minute. It was simply unbelievable: the first time I had actively turned on speech radio in over a year and I happened to tune in to the

305

beginning of a radio play about a woman raising a child with brain damage. The play was being billed as 'unsentimental', which seemed characteristically English and consequently made me nervous instantly. As I heard the play introduced, I forced myself to listen as long as I could. But as soon as I heard the phrase 'child with brain damage' my hand shot back to the power button all by itself. It was off before the first actor had spoken the first word.

After about ten minutes of sitting in silence I thought maybe I'd just imagined it. Then after 12 minutes, I thought perhaps it was a sign of some kind; maybe, on this one rare occasion when I had the courage to put on the radio, I was meant to listen to this programme. So I turned it on again. It was decidedly not sentimental; in fact, it was trying desperately hard to avoid any trace of sentiment at all costs. A woman was listening to a doctor tell her about her daughter's brain damage and fading in and out of listening to the doctor and imagining having sex with him. It was trying very hard to be 'literary' and that startled me because in many of my own radio projects I had also exerted myself in the same way. I realised in that instant how much my own approach to writing and radio had changed: before the crash, the 'subject' of the programme and any desire to communicate clearly took a back seat to my interest in playing impressionistically with language and sound. But this very same approach in the radio play before my ears bothered me, hurt me even, because I could not get away from what the programme *was about*. The subject, a child with a brain injury, was inescapably real to me. The pain and confusion that I knew first-hand was here being used as grist for the artistic mill; and even though I knew it wasn't about me, the story made me feel exploited somehow.

I realise now that I need not have been offended, that

this was simply not the radio play that I would have written about my own experiences. But also I realised in that moment that my own literary tastes had clearly evolved since the crash: I still like experiment and innovation, but now I think that they are best when they're dependent on real human sentiment and the desire to tell a meaningful story.

Fourteen months after the crash, Lio had a visit from Jonathan, a high-flying neuropsychologist, organised by our lawyers. He saw us at home, stayed with Lio for about three hours and did extensive neuropsychological and developmental testing on him. Our conversation afterwards was long and serious. I was really impressed with him, with his knowledge and his ability to communicate it, but most of all with his open-ended and uncategorical impression of Lio's future development (this is something he seemed to share with Lio's neurologist McCormick). His testing showed that since his hospitalisation Lio had a tremendous improvement in 'block design' (constructing shapes with coloured plastic blocks represented in drawings) and 'picture concepts' (matching pairs, finding the odd one out, etc.). But his receptive vocabulary (understanding the meaning of words he's hearing), his expressive vocabulary (communicating using his own words) and his general language skills were still weak and somewhat stagnant. Lio's verbal IQ, the neuropsychologist told me a bit reluctantly, was 82; but it was mostly very encouraging news otherwise. He went on to reassure me even on the verbal front, saying that there were dozens of different tests for verbal IQ and that Lio would score higher on some and lower on others, but the most important thing to keep in mind was that he was still on a general upward trajectory.

But then the neuropsychologist dropped a bombshell, something that scared the hell out of me.

'I know Lio's been working systematically in both English and Italian, but speaking mostly Italian,' his voice slightly higher and softer than it had been before. 'I think you should consider focusing on just one set of grammar, just on English.'

I sat bolt upright and lightning flashed across my eyes. 'But his speaking Italian is part of who he is. He thinks of himself as "the boy who speaks Italian".'

'At this stage of Lio's development, concentrating on the structure of just one grammar might help reduce the risk of a general speech and language deficit in the long term.' He continued as if he hadn't heard my plea. 'Look,' he said, 'I've just finished editing a book about paediatric neuropsychology and one of the chapters was on language acquisition, bilingualism and brain injury. I'll send you a copy, if you like.'

'Yes,' I said, my heart turning to ice. 'I'd like to read it.' I don't remember if I was lying or not.

Over the next couple of weeks I had some extremely useful conversations with several more neurologists and psychologists – conversations I wish I'd had nine months earlier but hadn't been able to organise because of the pressures of the moment. I mentioned the bilingual issue to all of them and the loose consensus seemed to be that we should concentrate in a formal way on English for a variety of reasons: its grammar is simpler, it's more 'word rich' and its phonetics are extremely irregular. The thinking was that concentrating the formal language learning on English would be easier for Lio both structurally and conceptually, and (because we would be memorising phonetically irregular words as 'facts') focusing on English now might reduce the risk of Lio having problems with abstract language thinking and dyslexia in the future. Also, at around Lio's age, language tends to 'lateralise' to one side of the brain. This lateralisation is a good thing and helps with more abstract linguistic thinking as children grow. Lio's injuries might impede that lateralisation (if it hadn't already happened), which meant that we were at an especially important time for stable, structured and consistent language input (especially vocabulary building), which meant English.

Fine, I thought. But I was not about to abandon the Italian completely. Sasha's first words to Lio were in Italian – and I'm sure her last words to him were in Italian too. She had worked so hard to give him the gift of another language: she studied lists and list of words, she practised new tenses on the train and in the toilet, and she drilled herself with new phrases nearly every day. This was simply not going to be something that would hold Lio back developmentally. The one intellectual trait that Lio rightly claims as his own was not going to be the thing that might harm him intellectually in the future. The one thing that Lio did better than anyone else in his school, speak another language, was not going to be the thing that might keep him out of university. Sasha imagined Lio as a bilingual child with a passport to a different culture and she would have never been blocked by what we were facing. It was simply up to me to figure out a way to preserve that legacy. All I had to do was to learn as much as possible about bilingual language development in paediatric brain injury recovery and find the right path through it. My instincts certainly told me that it was possible; beyond 'possible', my instincts told me that two languages had to be good for Lio in the long run. I just had to figure out how.

Nearly all of my decisions up to this point in Lio's cognitive recovery had come relatively quickly, but this one stymied me. I'd got used to making decisions more instinctively and everyone, even some doctors whose advice I'd chosen to ignore early on, congratulated me on good choices and great outcomes. Decisions about methods for helping him with his early brain recovery, about how his rehab should be undertaken outside the hospital, about when to send him to school (for how many hours and where), about when to take holidays and when to see doctors: all of these decisions came without the tiniest bit of second-guessing. But this one, the decision to abandon the dream of a child who could speak more than one language fluently, this one proved extremely hard.

Italian wasn't just his first language, it was 'our language', our secret code, the language of good food and holiday adventures, the language of fun in the mountains, and dragons and knights and wizards and castles. It would have broken what was left of my heart to watch that wither and die. I was stuck, paralysed with doubt and confusion. Not wanting to let this cripple me as much less important decisions had often done before the crash, and not wanting to let too much time pass, I forced panic out of my mind, ordered some more books on bilingual children, reassured myself that we had lots of Italian in the air and decided to start the week with some English word flash cards. We would continue speaking in Italian casually but not worry about its grammar. Then we would simply start studying English grammar as part of our normal morning routine and I would mostly speak it with him.

The strategy I adopted in the end, and one the medical people were happy with, was to 'work' systematically at English (study it, concentrate on learning words, get the agreements right, etc.) while continuing with some Italian as a sort of 'play language' casually integrated into everyday life. This seemed a good solution, especially given that we had his au pair who spoke only Italian to him; in fact, in the end it seemed like a more traditional way of raising a bilingual child, with one grown-up speaking one language and the other grown-up speaking the other.

*

Only about a week after we had adopted our modified approach to language I came to a realisation about my own life while driving to the rehab centre at Charleston. Everything I was doing revolved around Lio's recovery and I didn't want anything to distract me from that. I had been on leave from my job at the University of Sussex and I was simply terrorised about what would happen with Lio if I had to return to that job.

My internal voice kept repeating (more than necessary): 'I can't go back to my job . . . I don't need to go back to my job . . . I can't go back to my job . . . I don't need to go back to my job . . . ' I was using this little mantra to convince myself that I didn't need it *financially*, that I didn't need the money because of Sasha's life insurance and pension and because of the pending court cases. And, in truth, I didn't need the job provided we lived a more modest life. My great realisation, however, was that I didn't need it *emotionally* or *psychologically* either.

Despite what friends and colleagues were saying, that it might be good for me to return to work, I had reached a point where I really didn't need a formal job to remind me of who I was. It was no longer necessary to my identity as a person: it wasn't essential to my being, and I wasn't at all sad about that. It was not *a loss* like some of the other losses I had faced the previous year. I had, before that realisation in the car, been clinging to the thought of my job as something I needed *for me* somehow. I was Martin Spinelli, 'senior lecturer in the Department of Media and Film at the University of Sussex, media critic, scholar and radio producer dealing with a terrible thing that had happened'. I came to the conclusion on that day that I was Martin Spinelli, 'father dedicated completely to seeing his son fully recover'. If writing and radio and lecturing entered my life from time to time, they would certainly be welcome. But nothing was going to distract my focus from

Lio. We would survive financially and I would completely embrace my new role without apology. This simple realisation was extremely liberating, calming even, and after it came to me I felt extremely relaxed and happy.

My peaceful state of mind was unsettled a bit as I recognised the turning into Charleston. As our relationship with Charleston had evolved, I had become grateful for their help and support, but I could never completely shake the spectres of how they'd messed us around with Lio's start date, of the early limits on his therapies and of the more frightening limits they once saw for Lio's future. It, however, remained a useful place for information and ideas. On that day, I was to meet one Dr William Watchel, the director of a paediatric brain injury rehabilitation clinic outside New York, one of the largest in the US. He was making a tour of various brain-injury rehab facilities in the UK, exchanging knowledge with colleagues and talking with families. A handful of parents had been invited to speak with him. The first ten minutes of our exchange proved some of the most difficult for me in six months.

The mother of one of the children at Charleston, a child with far more severe problems than Lio, began the session in a desperate, almost accusatory, tone.

She said simply, 'Look, I've spoken to the neurologists, I've seen the scans and I know that recovery is not an option.'

I couldn't follow the rest of what she was saying because that phrase 'recovery is not an option' got stuck in my ears. I found those words so devastatingly difficult to hear; in fact, they were the most disturbing to enter my head since those initial prognoses in intensive care. Here was a woman who had given up hope. Here was a woman who simply did not believe in the very possibility that had sustained me for more than a year. It was as if she was not asking a question so much as simply wanting to express her pain, and I could empathise. But as much as I wanted to comfort and support her, I was completely and totally hamstrung because I heard those words in relation to Lio.

'Recovery is not an option.' I squirmed.

I couldn't get them out of my head and desperately wanted to jump up and leave the room. I wanted to run for the door and not breathe the same air that those words hung in. I wanted to tell her, and even to shake her while I was doing it, that if you allow hope to be so completely blotted out by someone else's interpretations of the scans, you doom your child to a life of pain and limitation. If you approach the situation with the resolve that your son will never recover, then, simply put, he will never recover. I know her situation was very different from mine, but there is always the possibility of improvement, no matter how small. I gradually forced myself to tune back into the discussion.

Despite the bad start, our conversation about paediatric brains, their working and how they grow and react was more hopeful, emotional and philosophical than any I'd had previously. During our chat Will revealed that he was not just a brain-injury professional but also a parent like us. Bizarrely, his own teenage daughter had sustained a brain injury several years after Will had been made director of his neuro-rehab clinic. This was tremendously reassuring and made everything he said instantly more interesting and valuable to me – here was someone seeing things from both sides of the rehabilitation relationship. Speaking as doctor *and as father*, he said something then that I keep with me to this day. He said that during his daughter's recovery he 'often traded science for hope'. Coming from someone of his standing and experience and given what I was used to hearing, this was like a shot of espresso. I was exhilarated. While I had reservations about some of the other things he said that afternoon, I held on tightly to that little pearl. I repeated it to myself over and over because it resonated with so much of my approach during the previous 15 months, an approach that had yielded results that no one could argue with.

That gem of insight helped me stay proactive about Lio's recovery. After the thrashing of the first mother's comments, it elevated me and reminded me to stay focused on what I could productively be doing rather than on things that had already happened, things past and out of my control. If you see possibilities and opportunities instead of obstacles and limitations, not only will the recovery progress better but you and your child will also feel better about the process. I had absolutely no desire to be critical of this woman and how she was dealing with her tragedy – I have only a vague idea of what she must have been going through. But her attitude simply seemed unproductive. While I asked questions about how I might get Lio to concentrate better, she wanted to know why her son was able to move at all given the nature of his injuries. While her question was directed towards a limitation, mine was directed towards a goal. I wanted her to change her approach for her own sake and for the sake of her son. Perhaps I should have said something to her about it. If anyone was in a position to do something like that, it was certainly me. I did venture it slightly, in truth more for my own psychological well-being than for hers, but she became almost competitive about the extent of her son's issues, so I didn't pursue it. Will, to his tremendous credit, redirected her question and told her to start from the movements she was observing in her son and to try to expand and develop those. He wanted her to see practical possibilities and potential in those movements. It was because he did this, and did this so quickly and effortlessly, that I didn't leave the room.

Dear Mr Vandermeulen

Dear Mr Vandermeulen,

My son Lio has begun his second year at school. He's got more and more play dates, his music therapy has morphed into piano lessons (which he loves) and he's already looking forward to his class's Christmas play and the big birthday party I promised him. After much surgery, his leg is growing straight and we're enjoying lots of little outings in the autumn colours.

Lio is happier all the time, yet, while he fills me with joy every day, something is bothering me, causing me to lose sleep, distracting me more and more. It's you. I'm feeling this growing, almost uncontrollable urge to contact you. As I had in my mind that you might be getting out of prison in a month or two, I decided to write you this letter.

I'm not sure what it is exactly that I need to communicate. It's not blame. I'm really not angry with you in spite of the fact that your crash killed Sasha and so badly hurt Lio. A terrible thing happened to my family, but I think a terrible thing happened to you as well. In many ways I think your situation is worse than ours, in that I imagine you'll feel responsible for this for the rest of your life, at least I think I would if I were in your shoes.

I know you didn't mean to do it. I know you didn't want to drive into the back of Sasha and Lio because you thought it might be interesting or you thought you might gain something by it. I know you didn't intend to harm anyone – but that somehow makes it worse, makes it harder for me and for you. You may have decided not to take the driving breaks you were supposed to, you may have decided to drive longer than was legal, you may have decided to fiddle with something in your cab that distracted you just before the accident, but you didn't decide to maim or kill.

It's a year after the crash and I can't stop thinking about you. You, in prison, must be feeling the loss of your family just like me. You must lose sleep at night just like me, maybe even with the same nightmares of crunching metal and shattering glass. I'll bet you must wonder about Lio's prospects and recovery, just like I wonder about Lio's prospects and recovery. I imagine that you must hope and pray for Lio and I to do well, just like I'm doing. And I'm sure you must want to move on from this whole sad business in exactly the same way that I want to move on from it. Yet here we remain, both trapped in the same thoughts, fears and hopes.

Maybe I'm just projecting. Is this weird kinship that I feel with you misplaced? That question, I realise now, is why I'm feeling so compelled to write you. I want to know clearly and precisely what you're thinking now. I need this much more than I need to know what exactly happened in the accident. Even more than my need to tell you that I bear you no ill will, I need to know how you're processing it all. Do you ever think this way about me? Are you wondering how I'm making sense of things too? It would help me immensely to know if you feel a connection with me. It would help to be certain that there really is this strange kind of bond between us fashioned out of sadness and grief and regret but real and present nonetheless.

Sometimes I wonder if I'm just looking for emotional scabs to pick – at least when you're feeling pain you're feeling something. I've decided that I'd really like to visit you in prison (if you'd agree to it), even if it hurts – perhaps precisely because I know it would hurt. I want to sit down with you in the prison visiting room, separated by wire-mesh glass and speaking on phones, just like you see in movies. As fate has had it, you have become an extremely important person in my life and I'd like to get to know you. I've come up with lots of flighty reasons why I want to do this, but in the end I just want to look you in the eye and close this chapter of my life. I think somehow that meeting you might help me let go of things. But when I'm at my most desperate and most agitated these days, I even imagine becoming friends with you, learning about your kids, and maybe even seeing you socially when you get out of prison. We share something that very few people share.

When I last spoke with the police months ago, I got the idea that you might be released soon and I didn't want to miss the opportunity. A week ago I called our victim liaison officer and asked her about getting you this letter. We spoke again two days later and she told me that you had been repatriated back to Belgium five months ago. She apologised, said there was nothing that she could do, and said that if you ever came back to Britain you'd have to register with the Probation Service.

So here I am, with this growing, desperate need to contact you all the more, but stuck hanging in midair, writing a letter that will never be sent.

Sincerely,

Martin Spinelli

Tackling Giants

Sometimes Sasha would accuse me, rightly, of being judgemental. Worse, sometimes she felt judged by me and that she wasn't measuring up to standards I had in my mind. But she could be judgemental as well, especially around food (now I blame her for my uneconomical tastes). When we were together, I admit, this tendency was compounded and we could judge others very unsympathetically; perhaps this was just a natural side effect of being professional academics. We could look down our noses at far right-wing politicians but even more so at their supporters. We dismissed most popular literature as trash, and made a distinction between 'movies' and 'films' (we watched 'films' at home while other people went to the multiplex to watch the latest blockbuster). We knew this was all a bit precious, but still we joked that if a film didn't have subtitles it probably wasn't worth watching. We drank wine more than beer, and decent wine too. We had, for a while, a little notebook in which we wrote our own reviews of nearly every bottle we had smuggled back from France and Italy. 'Common' experiences, like 'common' meals, were things we actively avoided when possible. We were well educated, we had seen a lot of the world, we had strong values and opinions, we knew what we liked and we usually didn't care what other people thought about it.

After the crash this discernment, this attitude, this prejudice simply disappeared. It wasn't that I recognised my old ways as wrong or that I suddenly became myself a critic of 'elitism', but my old outlook simply evaporated. I just wasn't thinking in those terms any more. Initially I was numb to experience; everything was the same, everything looked the same, tasted the same, felt the same, from greasy full English breakfasts to stir-fried Thai vegetables. Then, gradually, an appreciation of things was rekindled, an appreciation of both the full English and the stir-fry.

I was given an opportunity to test out this new, more open approach to the world later that autumn after receiving another implausible invitation, this time from Dr Handsome – the surgeon in New York who had reconstructed Lio's knee. After being thoroughly pleased with Lio's knee during our last regular visit with him in New York, he made us a proposal. It turned out he was also the official orthopaedic surgeon to the New York Giants football team, a team that I had gone to see with my father when I was a bit older than Lio. He said that, if we liked and if we were available, he would try to get us tickets to see the Giants square off against the Miami Dolphins when they played at Wembley Stadium in London in November. Lio was really excited. I was tickled by this and felt sure it was going to happen. Without fail, I got an email a few weeks later from Dr Handsome saying that he had told the owner of the Giants about Lio and that he was happy to give us tickets and even bring us down onto the field for the start of the game. When I told Lio, he exploded with glee.

We came back early from our regular visit with relatives in Italy during Lio's half-term break to make it to the game. Our flight from Italy had been late, I was confused about whether we were meant to be at the stadium at 7.00 or at 5.30, there was horrendous traffic going out to Wembley and we didn't really know where we were going.

319

When we got there, Lio was bristling, Graziella wanted me to ask some football players for their phone numbers and I was flashing back to my father taking me and my brothers to Giants games at the Meadowlands when we were kids. It was surreal to be completing the circle with Lio on the other side of the ocean. This time, though, it was very easy just to smile and happily let go to fate.

We eventually found the enormous statue of Bobby Moore in front of the stadium, where we met our contact Allison. She and her colleagues ushered us down through a labyrinth of security personnel, fluorescent bracelets and key-carded doors until we emerged onto the field. Lio was not at all as anxious as I expected him to be surrounded by tens of thousands of cheering people. When Allison led us to Dr Handsome by the Giants' benches, Lio beamed at him straight away. He introduced us to the Giants' owner, John Mara, and to some enormous football players. I had told Lio that he was going to see some very big guys, but I don't think he'd really understood.

He kept asking them, 'How did you get so big?'

'Eating vegetables' was the usual response, which neither Lio nor I took seriously. They were all, every single one of them, from the owner and the players and the Giants' media people to the other doctors and the police officers working security, marvellously kind to us. As soon as they saw Lio on my shoulders, they would shout, 'Hey big guy!' or something over the roar of the crowd; it was as if they knew somehow to treat Lio like a little hero. Maybe they were told about us ahead of time (some of them certainly) or maybe it was just Lio radiating his natural charm, but they all seemed to go out of their way to make Lio (and me) feel special.

As the energy built up before the game, Lio was a bit startled to see the players smashing their fists down on each other's shoulder pads to get psyched up, and he covered his ears when the fireworks started going off for the pre-game show.

But he soon lost interest in the hand-shaking and the winks from the cheerleaders and started asking me, 'Will there be tackling?' Someone at school must have told him about 'tackling' because he now seemed fixated on it. Just in time for the opening kick-off I hoisted him on my shoulders again and he was treated to a resounding *crack* of a tackle about ten yards in front of him on the field. We watched about ten minutes of the first quarter from the sidelines and, after a long and serpentine trek through the bowels of Wembley, made our way up to our seats. I bought us some chicken nuggets, a cheeseburger and some chips and we took our places. The Giants were dominating the game, moving the ball every time they had it and taking it away when they didn't. I tried to give Lio a crash course in American football: how you score points, how many downs you get, which players are meant to do what. I wanted him to recognise some of my favourite plays from high school. But he wasn't interested in the detail, he was into the simple head-bashing and would rise up out of his seat every time the crowd cheered.

Just before the half-time kick-off – and, for better or worse, this is Lio's abiding memory of the game – one of the referees (at least someone dressed like a referee) took off all his clothes and streaked onto the field. I was quite surprised at how long he managed to evade the police – he pulled off some impressive dance moves for about a minute and a half. Of course this was impossible to contextualise for Lio, who now thinks that every football game has a streaker before the start of the second half.

It was there, in our end-zone seats, surrounded by dozens of quite drunk people (almost all of them Americans living in London) that I started really re-thinking, and even coming to appreciate, a good deal of the mass culture I used to reject. There is tremendous spectacle, there are loud noises, there is excitement, there is danger, there is fast food and there is alcohol – there were a couple of drunken 20 year olds right next to us who turned to give Lio high-fives every time the Giants did anything. People, people who didn't know us, who couldn't have known us, were smiling at us and asking us if we were Giants fans and where we lived and where we'd come from that day. The girl in front of us had flown over from New Jersey that morning to be at the game; her father, connected to the Giants somehow, had got her and her friends tickets. I didn't know how to respond, how to deal with all this; I was a fish out of water. After having played football myself in high school, in graduate school, I'd really come to dislike it and what I saw as the jingoism that surrounded it. Back then, it seemed to play to our lowest emotions and to bring out the worst in us rather than the best.

But sitting in the stands, on not uncomfortable plastic seats, covered from the rain that was falling on the field, surrounded by these happy drunks, I had fun, I had serious fun. It was the women who struck me the most. Too long had I been surrounded by the self-consciously frumpy women of academe, with their shabby clothes and their mechanical rejection of most concepts of physical beauty. I had heard too many lectures (sermons almost) about the objectification and commodification of the body and had been trained to detect political incorrectness a mile off. But there in the stadium I didn't even notice as these old ideas and ways of seeing the world evaporated in the excitement and chaos of the game. I was charmed by these women with large diamonds on very yellow-gold rings, hair gelled to staggering proportions, hooting while punching the air with their fists high enough so that their NFL jerseys rode up over their lower-back tattoos. They were in the moment and they were really enjoying themselves. They were having pure, physical, material fun. Could I honestly have ignored this for 15 years? As they struggled to engage me in conversation about what was happening on the field, I was attracted to them – and even though I felt completely out of my element, uptight even, I tried as best I could to give back as good as I got.

Lio loved it. We both loved every minute of it until the beginning of the fourth quarter, when Lio collapsed from tiredness on my lap. He had been up from early in the morning, flown, driven, then hiked around the stadium. He had been heaved and hoisted, dragged and carried, yelled at and cheered. I didn't blame him. We found the exit. I hefted him, slightly limp, onto my shoulders again and we headed to the train station in the rain.

Fifteen months after the crash, one year since Lio had been introduced to his friends at school as the little boy pulling himself back from the brink, things were settling into a rhythm for him socially at school – a consistent, if not altogether perfect, rhythm. After the initial fascination with Lio as a tragicomic oddball had faded, I was struck by how his classmates could look at him. These four, five and six year olds would sometimes squint and tighten when he approached, not knowing what to expect. Two weeks before his birthday party, as he was proudly handing out the party invitations on which he'd carefully penned the names of all his friends, a few of them withdrew slightly, wondering what Lio was going to do – grab their faces, hug them, try to lick them or give them a big kiss. It was sad to witness. Yet Lio was unfazed. He beamed with pride and happiness at being able to invite all his buddies to his party. As with most things, motivation and perspective are more than half the game. And while he might have been a bit too excited when handing out his invitations, he was happy, and I decided to let him go on being happy.

Lio's unbridled enthusiasm got a real outing a few weeks after the football game. My mother had booked us a family vacation on the Disney cruise in the Caribbean. I must admit I was a bit apprehensive. This was to be Lio's first real dose of the Mouse (beyond some films that he had seen on planes) and I wasn't sure how he'd respond to the hardcore kiddie drug that is Mickey & Co. I was also a bit unsure how I'd manage it. But as I was still riding the wave of our day at Wembley, I let myself be reassured.

On board Lio was ecstatic the entire time, hobbling around the ship after Captain Jack, doing morning exercises with Goofy, shaking Mickey's hand, going to kite-making workshops, watching song-and-dance shows every night, doing treasure hunts on our island stopovers and swimming in a Mickey-shaped pool. He was a whirlwind. But it wasn't all parties: we were both proud of the fact that he was one of the few kids on the ship who wasn't drinking Coke with breakfast. Every day we kept up with his speech and language exercises (usually followed by an afternoon snooze to recharge) and he even insisted on bringing his violin with us so that he could show grandmom and his cousin Jordan what he had been practising. Also, his leg was playing up a bit. Because of the angular deformity of his femur and the off-centre alignment of his knee, he kept tripping in the Mickey flip-flops that he really wanted to wear. This meant I had to carry him on my shoulders for most of the time on our shore excursions (he was getting heavy). On our stop at Disney's own island, we rented bikes – biking being one of Lio's favourite things before the crash – because it meant he could propel himself on his own, where he wanted, as fast as he liked. Unfortunately, it wasn't long before he was going too fast and careened into another girl on a bike.

She wailed on the ground, blood coming out of her knee and big toe, shouting, 'It was his fault! It was his fault!' while pointing at my Lio. Lio looked confused and a bit panicky, but I decided to see to the girl before I consoled him. Because little incidents like this seemed to follow us around, I had learned to carry all sorts of first-aid paraphernalia. From out of my backpack I pulled bandages and tape and gauze and scissors and patched up the girl as best I could. She was still crying when her father showed up. He didn't look at us but just put his daughter on his handlebars and rode her back to the medical hut.

When I turned back to Lio, he was a bit pale. 'I didn't mean to,' he said. 'Really.'

'I know,' I said and hugged him. He and I drove on in search of some quieter beaches. We made sandcastles and then headed back to the ship. In spite of a few mishaps, like the bike accident, we had a really entertaining time. Lio's most cherished adventure of the vacation was succeeding in completing the treasure hunt on the Disney island, where he was rewarded with two silvery pirate coins – something not all the other kids could boast. In the end, we came back suntanned and content (if not rested) and with me only slightly worse for wear from all the free booze on board.

Back in physiotherapy, though, it took several weeks for his leg to get back to bending as much as it did before we went away. I was finding it simply exhausting (well-nigh impossible) keeping up with the home programmes for both his leg and his speech and language. Out of urgency and necessity, for months his leg work took most of our concentrated energy. But since the summer we'd been working more and more on his language and I was hearing the pay-off – he was speaking better and thinking better. But something slightly disconcerting cropped up: the more English that he spoke with me, the more he would insist that I spoke Italian with him. He could get really animated when I spoke English and this, I suspected, was because Italian was exclusively our family language before the accident. But as he was learning more and more English in school, studying it with me and speaking it more fluently with his friends, his English was now better than his Italian. Nevertheless it was an odd scene in public when he would yell at me in English to speak to him in Italian.

We planned to go out to Italy for Christmas, Lio's birthday and New Year's and Italian would embrace us again. While we were going to be out there, I wanted to try to organise a stone for Sasha. Penny, Nigel and I had spent a couple of days during our last visit trying to find a stonemason, but we hadn't had much luck and we also needed to get the right bit of rock.

We were remembering Sasha in England as well. The scholarship fund we had set up in her name at the University of Kent at Canterbury had grown tremendously since it began. I was then and continue to be simply astounded at the generosity of people. This was generosity not just from our old friends and family but also from the international academic community to which Sasha was so important, and from the broader community of Lewes. The time and the energy people invested in raising money (more events and fund-raisers than I could count) had been simply staggering. The Lewes Arms, the Lewes Constitutional Club, Harvey's Brewery, and our friends and colleagues just got on with it and generated thousands of pounds for the scholarship. It was such a success that we were able to make the first annual award less than a year before we started fund-raising. It went, curiously, to a German graduate student named Sacsha Klement who was researching Renaissance poetry. In the report on the regional BBC TV news about the first award, I remember his difficulty at not wanting to seem too happy about receiving a scholarship that had only come about because of our Sasha's death. As he tied himself in conditional rhetorical knots, I grinned to myself and was grateful that I now had fewer of those problems.

But the most important event before things broke up for Christmas was certainly Lio's birthday party. This was to be his first birthday party with all of his school friends; he was positively ecstatic and it was almost the only thing he talked about. He had some very precise ideas of what he wanted and was eager to get involved. The party was going to be more than a birthday; it was going to be a celebration of how stupendously well he was doing and of how far he'd come that past year. But more than that, I found basking in his reflected joy was also wonderfully good for chasing away my own lingering worries about bilingualism, psychotropic drugs and knee-bending.

We held it at the Grange, where we had held Sasha's party the previous spring. All his friends came, and with them another mountain of presents. They played 'pass the parcel' and 'pin the tail on the donkey' and then bashed away at the snowman piñata that Lio and Penny had made from scratch out of balloons and papier mâché and stuffed with chocolate coins and little toys. Lio was the centre of attention and won with tremendous pride the snowball (paper ball) toss game. His single difficult moment was when he only managed to collect one of the paper snowflakes in the last game, snowflakes he had worked so hard to cut out in the week leading up to the party. I was also in fine form, dressed in red with a Santa hat. I had organised everything with great care and it all went off without a hitch. Back at home, Lio smiled as he heaped all his loot up onto his top bunk and collapsed to sleep without a sound.

*

While Lio made me happy on a daily basis in a way I couldn't have imagined before, more than a year after the crash I was still emotionally stuck in many ways. Even as the second round of holidays approached and passed, I found the thought of taking off my wedding ring remained too difficult. I simply liked it. I liked how it felt; its snug little weight was comforting physically as well as psychologically. It was more than simply a reminder of Sasha; it was a lovely material object that felt good on my finger. I spun it round when I was anxious, and when I was talking to doctors or therapists or counsellors my other fingers would always fly to it.

I had only ever taken it off once in my life, for an MRI I'd had seven years earlier. Sasha never took hers off. Once she made a circle with her thumb and ring-finger and passed the ring from one to the other, but when she saw that this made me slightly uneasy she told me she wouldn't do it again. I didn't have to ask her; she just saw it in my face. I loved her. And that's why I couldn't take the ring off. It also had a very practical function: it kept me out of entanglements with women that I'd rather not be involved with. I sometimes thought about other relationships with other people, and sometimes I even wished I didn't have my ring on so that I might not feel self-conscious in those situations. But this only ever happened for fleeting moments and only when I was feeling the lack of grown-up conversation and physical contact very badly.

I had promised myself that I would take my ring off that second Christmas after the crash. But I didn't manage it. It was just so reassuring to feel it on my finger, and it felt especially right to have it on when I was near Sasha's ashes as well. We spent that Christmas out at the mill. Some months earlier I had smuggled her ashes out there from their place underneath my bed in England because I knew she would want them to be in Italy. Even before I had brought her ashes out to the mill, it was a place inextricably connected to Sasha in my mind. But now more than ever I felt her presence in the old walls, in the trees and in the air palpably and absolutely every time we visited after the crash.

On one of the last days of that Christmas holiday I decided to walk down to the river that runs alongside the mill house. The sun had just set and there was a light snow falling. The river was mostly frozen over, yet small patches of it were still exposed and they burbled in the perfect mountain quiet. My mind came inevitably to the moments that Sasha and I had spent along that beautiful little river. The dam-building to make pools, the swimming, the jokes, the lounging about, the reading, the sunbathing, the sex. I started talking aloud to her there and then, thanking her for all her work with Lio and thanking her for the incredible year we'd had with Lio's recovery. I thanked her for her last gift to me: time with Lio, the space and the freedom to enjoy his childhood and the sense of purpose in working towards his well-being and bright future. Her life insurance, her small pension and my savings from the sale of my Brooklyn apartment meant that Lio and I could be together without me having to worry too much about working in the traditional way for the time being. I promised her that I would make the most of that incredibly painful opportunity. I told her that I loved her and that I missed her terribly. My thoughts and my feelings became very intense and I was soon swept away by a torrent of memory and melancholy.

Then, on the other side of the river Ardo, just beyond the little pool where we had bathed during our last summer together, I saw a light shine for a couple of seconds. It was a very bright light. Then I saw it a second time. I was startled by it at first. I wanted to think it was Sasha somehow saying something back to me. I shouted 'I want you!' at it. I moved closer and I convinced myself that it was a torch held by someone else on the other side of the river – but who could it have been in such an isolated spot at dusk on a winter's night? The river isn't wide at that point and I was maybe 30 paces away from where I saw it. I stood still and watched and waited. I threw a little stone at it and thought I saw it being thrown back into the river but didn't hear it. I didn't hear anyone or anything, no movement whatsoever. It was completely silent but for the soft bubbling of the river beneath the ice. I shouted 'I miss you!' again at it, thinking now that it must be another person, but there was nothing, not even a laugh at some poor fool shouting in the twilight.

Why I didn't risk the ice and go across the river I can't say. It would have been easy to cross there – shallow and mostly frozen over with lots of rocks. I regret turning my back on that spot on the riverbank and going back inside to get Lio ready for dinner. But I also took away a measure of contentment because now I can feel certain that it was Sasha rather than someone or something else. I know also that I will feel her presence again on the banks of that little river. And I do. I feel her presence intensely every time Lio and I visit the mill in the Dolomites. I decided my ring could stay, maybe until we buried her ashes, maybe forever. What could replace the life I had with Sasha? Why would I want to take off a reminder of what I had? I had lost a tremendous amount, yes, but I had my memories and I had that sensation of Sasha in my heart still. Why would I give those things up or do anything to make them harder to feel?

As with my ring, I also found myself at an impasse with Sasha's ashes. The polished oak box holding the ashes sat on a side table in our living room at the mill and Penny had made a habit of adorning it with flowers, while Lio and I lit candles in front of it. It had become, in spite of Penny's stated aim to the contrary, a little shrine to Sasha. And it was beautiful. But there was a problem. I was finding it difficult to do anything other than look at it. I was finding myself stuck in closed cycles of love and longing and memory. In the presence of my Sasha's ashes, then a year and a half after she had passed, I was constantly re-living and re-playing the moments of our life together in my mind. Constantly. At times, this was the most transcendent and rewarding thing – that sense of loss caused memories to come flooding back and those memories were good and happy and sustaining. But there were days when I found it very difficult to get out of bed, when I could be so trapped in those thoughts that I could do nothing but stare out of my bedroom window in Lewes at the side of the pebble-dash house across the road. So I came to think that perhaps finding a permanent resting place for Sasha's ashes might help me shift myself out of these comforting but difficult and seemingly endless circles.

In truth there were also less noble reasons for me wanting to put Sasha's ashes in the ground. It had been an extremely long time since I'd had a sustained, grown-up, significant relationship with a woman. Sasha will always be a part of my life, perhaps always the most important part after Lio. The old mill, our tiny paradise by the river, will also always be a part of my life and of Lio's life. And as I found myself grasping for the material-world things that Sasha could no longer give me, the thought of finding a partner and possibly bringing her out to that house while Sasha's ashes were so central didn't seem fair to any of us, not least of all Penny. Never in my life did I imagine that I'd have to consider such things.

Both Penny and Nigel were very good about my wanting to bury the ashes. Sasha's brother Jeff seemed even more keen to have the symbolic weight of her ashes taken off our shoulders. We had initially planned to bury Sasha's ashes at the mill that winter, after Christmas, but in the weeks before none of us really felt ready and we just, without any formal discussion, decided independently but simultaneously that it would be better if we buried them in the spring. Penny had broken down in tears once in front of them and I just knew that she was not yet in a position to see them go into the ground.

That spring came and went on our holiday out in Italy, and while we didn't bury Sasha's ashes and I didn't take off my ring, we did however get a bit further in organising a stone for Sasha's grave. We had in mind a very particular kind of rock that came from the Zoldo Valley, a valley that Sasha loved. Above Zoldo rises Monte Pelmo, one of the most beautiful and majestic of the Dolomites and one of Sasha's proudest moments as a mountain climber. The rock of Pelmo is this ethereal pink-orange marble and villages below are dotted with statues and fountains and monuments made from this same precious stone, stone that sculptors have coveted for centuries.

One rainy spring day, we drove and drove around Zoldo looking for some clue as to where this stone came from. In the late afternoon we found a little village with a marble fountain fashioned in an abstract female form. I read the community noticeboard and its map while across the street Nigel and Penny went into a little shop to ask some questions. We both learned more or less simultaneously that there was a small quarry up at a place called Cornigian, where the stone for all the valley's fountains came from. Nigel got directions from the shop clerk and off we went as the early evening clouds began to clear. We found the remote and tiny quarry, surveyed the boulders, decided we had found the right place, made a spiral of pink stones on the ground and headed for the bar nearby. I explained to the barista what we were after and she gave me the name and phone number of the man we needed to call about getting marble from the quarry. It was a beautiful and uplifting experience and we all (even Lio) felt like we had taken some big steps in the right direction. We would bury Sasha's ashes that summer when we were all out in Italy together.

A Beacon

The first time it happened I was paralysed by guilt and a sense of betrayal. Since our intense and not wholly comfortable trip to Dieppe, Rene and I had drifted in and out of each other's lives. Sometimes when Lio and I were up in London visiting Nigel and Penny I would go and have a drink with her, sometimes we would meet along the South Bank or in Brighton to see some art and once or twice we went for a walk on the South Downs outside Lewes. In looking back, it now seems so obvious – of course we were going to end up falling into bed together.

Rene had invited me out to a birthday party for one of her film-maker friends in the upstairs room of a pub in a pleasant corner of London. After about 15 minutes, we excused ourselves downstairs to the bar to get some drinks. We sat in a dim corner on some wooden benches and I placed our glasses on the table.

After about 30 seconds of uncomfortable silence, she said in too serious tones, 'I'm sorry, but I can't resist.' She slid her hand around my neck and pulled me to her. She couldn't resist kissing me, with strength and intensity. My heart pounded in confusion, my guard was slipping, I was overcome by desperation. When the kiss broke, I pretended nothing had happened, although I couldn't pretend I hadn't wanted it.

I was lost, gasping for air and stammering for words. 'Nice party,' I said, hoping to sound ironic.

334

'This is ridiculous,' she said plainly, as she clutched me again. 'Let's get you home.'

'That's a good idea,' I breathed and tried not to grin. I was aching and terrified. I knew exactly where this was going but tried to convince myself that I wasn't sure if I really wanted it. When we got to her place, she cut us slices of cheesecake that she had made that afternoon – cheesecake just like we'd ordered in Dieppe.

I woke up in the dark hours of the morning. I wanted to get back to Nigel and Penny's before Lio got up. Rene got up too and smiled gently as I fumbled nervously to get dressed. Without looking her in the eye, I started to speak because I felt I had to say something. Tension knotted my stomach.

'You know, Rene,' I said, 'that was really good in so many ways, but I really worry about getting too involved now because of Lio. And, like I said in France, I don't want to be reckless—'

With kindness in her eyes, she held up her hand and let her smile grow. 'Martin, I'm a grown up. I know where your energy needs to be right now. I'll be sure and tell you before I develop any expectations.' I didn't know if I believed her but wanted one last bit of closeness nonetheless – I kissed her unsteadily and closed the door behind me. As I ran to the car desperate to get to Lio I couldn't stop the rising storm of guilt in my mind and I couldn't shake the feeling that I had lost something that night. What it was, I couldn't say.

All that next day I was overcome with emotion. I couldn't help but feel that I had cheated on Sasha – a foolish thought, as she'd have been the first to tell me. I'd had a fantastic, sustaining and exclusive physical relationship with Sasha for 15 years that disappeared in a heartbeat. It was excruciating and I missed it terribly. But when it did happen for the first time after the crash, the pain, the difficulty and the self-loathing now seemed worse than the missing of it.

While these feelings did subside a few days later, I found myself absolutely crippled by fear, fear that I might have got Rene pregnant (this was a totally crazy idea because we had used protection). Irrational as it might have been, I lost sleep over it for weeks afterwards. I was completely preoccupied and every single thought in my head, every single dream that I had was about becoming a parent again. This was strangling me. I absolutely did not want it.

The one thing that I had with Lio, the one thing that I could offer him more than anything else, was time. I spent hours with him every day not just doing physiotherapy and speech and language therapy but also simply playing and having fun: we made birdhouses and collection boxes for Sasha's scholarship; we went sledding in the mountains; we visited friends in castles; we rode our bikes to the weekend market; I was teaching him how to juggle; we built Lego after Lego after Lego; we made up elaborate and hysterical stories about gatecrashing dinosaurs and princesses who tried in vain to get them to behave; we laughed and laughed; and his brain got better. Time was a present that I could give him constantly and without worry. I had just enough money to keep Lio and me afloat, not in a luxurious way but modestly and contentedly. The thought of having another child terrified me because it threatened that situation. The fear consumed me. For nearly two weeks, I missed meetings, I couldn't focus on Lio's rehab programme, I forgot legal work that needed to be done, I lost track of my research on paediatric brain-injury rehabilitation, I let contacts with doctors go cold. And all of these distractions brought with them another avalanche of guilt: the simple fact that my little tryst had happened was compromising Lio's recovery. At least that's how it felt in the moment.

In life, Sasha was always there to calm me through times of crisis (real and imagined), to reassure me that everything was going to work out well or to tell me that I was worrying for no good reason. But even after her death I found she could comfort me; in subtle, ethereal and uncanny ways she helped me again and again. I remember how gracefully she encountered most bumps in the road and I remembered how good she was at avoiding the worry trap. She made the best of things for herself and for us; I tried to emulate her. When I dreamt of her, she almost always seemed to be protecting and preserving something she had made or left for Lio and me: a book, a house in the trees, a snowman, a sandcastle. She would look out for us.

In the end, Sasha gave me exactly the sign I asked her for. I felt sure I had seen signs from her over the preceding months. More than a year earlier during our first days back home after our stay in the hospital I was particularly nervous. I looked at the future and saw everything taken away; even my positivity had deserted me. One evening I found myself walking down one of the steep little lanes in town, a street that Sasha and I had strolled down a thousand times before. On that particular late-autumn night I looked up to the sky and I said, 'Show me that you're there. Show me that you hear me. Show me something.' And, in less than a minute, I saw a shooting star. I made a very simple wish.

Now, as I walked down that same steep lane, I remembered that earlier shooting star. I thought about being in love and being in love with Sasha, and I thought about how real love has the power to sustain you even in the absence of your lover – something I'd learned over years of a long-distance relationship. But now I was losing my grip on these memories and as I walked tears of fear over the potential loss of my time with Lio began to well up. I paused in the same spot that I had seen the shooting star the previous year. I saw another star fall from the sky. It had happened again – without my asking, just like that. But in my exhausted state this was not enough. I wanted more, I wanted something clearer and unmistakable. I wanted something absolutely unequivocal.

I asked for blood. I thought to myself that if I saw some blood that night I would know everything would be all right. Completely crazy, I know, but that's what I had in my mind. I walked up over the High Street in Lewes, up through the castle barbican and down the other side in the direction of the Lewes Arms. But, not having been out for ages, there was no one there that I recognised, so I had a pint and went to the next pub in the hope of finding someone to talk to. Down through the barbican again and past the Grange Gardens, I headed into the Swan. Maybe there I would find someone to snap me out of my insanity. I went in and looked around the large front room. There was no one I knew. But just as I turned to go I saw our old friend Karen coming out of the Ladies. I hadn't seen Karen in months; in fact, I hadn't seen her since she upset me with her remark about Lio's recovery. I gave her a big hug and a kiss on the cheek. When I withdrew, she asked me how I was doing and I faked a pleasant enough reply. As we started toward her table, I asked Karen what she had on her cheek. A small red drop was forming about an inch below her eye. Now, it was a cold winter evening, and Karen's skin is quite thin on her face, and my beard was short and rough, but even so this had never happened before.

'What?' she said. 'Oh, it's nothing.' As I continued to insist, she touched her cheek, examined her fingers and said, 'Ah, damn your stubble! You should shave that stuff off.' I smiled a very broad smile, stepped towards the table and didn't need to fake anything for the rest of the evening.

*

In the middle of the second February after the crash, I decided to go to our local church late one morning and light some candles for Lio and for Sasha. It happened to be Ash Wednesday and, even though I didn't need much of a reminder that to dust we all return, I decided to stay for the service. It was extremely peaceful and I spent much of the time contemplating the beautiful white-gold ring on my finger. I decided there and then that for Lent, which I'd often let pass unobserved, I was going to organise myself into my work. I would no longer content myself with scattershot reading around paediatric brain development, I was going to be very systematic about it and set aside time for it every day and also set aside time most days to write things that I had simply been aching to write (like this book). But in order to do this I was going to have to deal with some distractions; I was going to have to sort out some memories that clutched at me continuously. They were lovely and I needed them and I'll always have them, but I also needed to not have them pull me away from things that required doing on quite such a consistent basis.

I came back home, went to my room and looked squarely at Sasha's pinboard, which was propped up against the wall on the top of my desk. I'd put it there as soon as we had returned home from hospital. There were all the things that she liked to look at while she worked: photos of Lio with his friend Theo from nursery school at the University of Kent, photos of Lio dressed as Joseph for the Christmas pageant at Jigsaw Day Nursery in Lewes, postcards of mountains that we had climbed, some of Lio's artwork, a photo of her at 39 looking 19 on roller blades outside her parents' house in London and a brochure from Hadrian's Villa near Rome that we visited on her 40th birthday, just her and me. It was wonderfully easy to get lost in these images for minutes on end when I should have been doing something else.

So, slowly and gently and lovingly, I took everything off her board. I put some of the things in a folder that I put in her box of souvenirs in my bedroom. I put some of the postcards of our mountains on my pinboard, along with a draft of a poem that she was working on for one of her illustrated children's books; and I put a little love note that she wrote me for no particular reason in the corner of her self-portrait, which hangs at the side of my bed. In reality, I guess I just moved things around rather than definitively organising them away. But I've integrated them into my space, they are now my memories more than they are hers and at least my line of sight is clear while I'm working. With this, I shifted myself slightly out of the inertia of missing her.

The word 'miracle' used to make me a bit uncomfortable. It seemed too easy, too uncritical, too simplistic – especially for an academic – and it often made me wonder what I was being sold. Worse was when someone used it whom I really didn't respect intellectually and my impulse was to refute it immediately. While the word can still put me off, and while I think it's much fairer to simply provide the unvarnished details and let whoever is listening think about things in whatever way works for them, I do believe what happened with Lio was a real miracle. And more than a few doctors now use that term without hesitation when talking about him. In the wake of the crash, I have become much more relaxed and charitable when I hear people use that word and words like it. This, I think, is a good thing.

My new-found ease was tested that second winter after the crash. I had spent several months investigating various alternative ways to keep Lio off Ritalin. When I met William Watchel, the American doctor who came to visit the rehab centre at Charleston, the first thing I asked him was if he knew of any other approach that might be worth trying before we went down the route of psychostimulant drugs. He said one of his patients, a nine-year-old girl called Charlotte who had suffered a brain injury worse than Lio's, was getting very good results with a combination of osteopathic, vitamin and electrical field treatments. But, he added cautiously, he was not in a position to recommend them. He was happy, however, to put me in touch with his patient's mother.

Through emails over the course of a couple of months and finally on the phone, she told me about an osteopath in a coastal town in southern New Jersey that they'd been seeing. She said that this osteopath Beth, along with her mentor Stephen, had coaxed tremendous progress out of her daughter where everyone else had failed. I was curious. And even though the mother sounded a little too exuberant (a little too evangelical), what she said about Beth and Stephen's potential was exactly what I was hoping to hear. The more I probed her daughter's story of near death and incapacitation, the more her incredible recovery seemed to resonate with our own. Her talk of energy belts and putting vitamins in her daughter's sock at night in order for the right vibrations to pass into her body would have sent me running – if not laughing – two years earlier. But I had learned through everything we'd seen on our journey to keep an open mind and to do my own homework. A couple of hours of our time and $180 seemed a relatively small price to pay to explore a way forward that didn't involve serious drugs. There seemed no harm in investigating.

So while we were back in the New York area for follow-up doctors' appointments, Lio and I also went to see Beth in her slightly run-down office building tucked in between a suburban strip mall and a supermarket. She seemed bright and cheery and confident enough and after a few minutes I didn't really mind the door falling off its hinges and the peeling yellow paint. She touched Lio at different points on his body and then had me hold his arms and legs and hands and feet while she touched other places. She shone a special light into Lio's chest and took various pulses. While she was doing this, she talked about the 'Qi' in Chinese medicine and how energy flows into the body from the right and out through the left. She explained that she was looking for points in Lio's body where these energy flows might be impeded. This wasn't completely new to me, as both Sasha and I had had acupuncture treatments when we were trying to get pregnant.

'The lights are a bit strange, but so far so good,' I thought. 'Let's just wait and see what she comes up with.'

But when she called Stephen in Florida and he 'scored' Lio, I began to get a headache and I felt as if sand were slipping out from under my feet. He told Beth over the phone (without seeing Lio and with very little information given to him by Beth) his impressions of Lio's condition, what supplements he needed and how many sessions he should have with a special electrical field belt around his leg and his arm. While I was slightly taken aback at how he seemed to know the particulars of some of Lio's issues, and how he proposed most of the supplements I had been giving Lio already, I struggled to keep the deep doubt at bay. I began to lose faith, not just in what Beth and Stephen were offering but in the whole of Lio's recovery as well. It was also too much for my mother, who was knitting beside Lio as he sat contentedly watching a video with the energy belt around his left elbow.

She whispered to me when no one else was in earshot, 'How can someone diagnose over the phone like that?'

As Beth once again shone lights into Lio's chest and abdomen, I had to leave and get a bit of air and find some painkillers for my worsening head. I was tired; I had been doctoring and thinking about doctoring for months to the exclusion of almost everything else, and I felt like I was coming to the end of my strength.

It was as if our own miracle was undermined somehow by the 'impossibility' of Beth's methods. Why? Because Beth's office was a bit shabby compared to the offices of the New York specialists that we were familiar with? Because I saw Charlotte's mother as slightly vulnerable to quackery and by implication I was vulnerable to it as well (whether this was quackery or not)? It was as if this situation reduced me and the mother of the other child to the same level (yet both with the same incredibly good results) and my over-developed ego was uncomfortable with that. I felt like I had slipped back a bit into those judgemental ways I had left behind, and the comparative ones I was struggling to leave behind. The failing was my own then. It was not a failing with the process or with the path I had chosen to take for Lio or with our work along that path. It was a failing to be a bit more charitable with humanity. My power of positive thinking was matched by the power of positive thinking of Charlotte's mother and somehow that weakened my belief in its absolute value because I imagined myself a more clever person than her. I had faced the demon science with my own critical eyes and told it to go to hell, and it obeyed. I couldn't imagine her facing it down in the same way. I saw her more shooing it out of the door like a bad dog, but apparently it listened to her as well. Their story is as valuable as ours, and there are thousands of other stories like it out there. The trick is in finding a way to appreciate them that makes sense to you.

At the end of Lio's treatment with Beth she gave us a very specific list of supplements. I told her that Lio was already taking most of what she was recommending.

'Good,' she said, a bit surprised. 'But you want to make sure you're taking this particular brand because most of the easy-to-find supplements just aren't absorbed by the body very well.' She handed me a photocopied sheet with her recommendations highlighted. I thanked her, rubbed my temples and was glad to get out of her office. It had been a long and intense day and it was about to get longer. After doctors' appointments in the morning in one part of the state, then the visit with Beth in the afternoon in another part, we were scheduled to see the neurologist and neuropsychologist Will had also recommended to me another 100 miles away that evening. This neurologist and neuropsychologist had done hours and hours of tests with Lio over the previous days. At this meeting, they were to go over their findings with me. As we started the two-hour drive, I tried to clear my mind and prepare the questions I wanted to ask them both. I gripped the wheel tightly and began ticking things off:

'Drugs: Methylphenidate? Amantadine? Atomoxetine? Anything at all?'

'Papà,' Lio said from the back seat.

'EEG results and repeat.'

'Papà,' came Lio's little voice again.

'Lio, honey,' said my mother, 'Daddy's trying to concentrate.'

'The value of IQ scores as an indicator of real-world functioning, as an indicator of anything.'

'Papà.'

'Lio! What!' I yelled and touched the brakes sharply.

'If it's nice, can I play with Kevin tomorrow in the woods? I like playing with Kevin.'

I saw him smile tranquilly in the rear-view mirror, untroubled by anything. I tried to smile back as I put a hand on my forehead to ease the pain. 'Of course,' I said apologetically. 'Anything you want tomorrow. Tomorrow is your day.'

344

'Thanks, *Papà*,' he scratched his ear and closed his eyes. I am so lucky in his disposition.

I met the neurologist and the neuropsychologist in their separate office rooms each barricaded behind a mountain of data they'd collected earlier that week by studying Lio's brain waves, testing his concentration and reflexes with computer games, building Lego, psychometric testing with flash card after flash card after flash card, and even just asking him to stand still with his finger on the table as long as he could. They had also 'scored' Lio on a range of things, with 99 being the best percentile for his age and 1 being the worst:

Auditory Attention: 5
Inhibition Control: 5
Statue (standing still): <1
Speeded Naming: 16
Word Generation: 24
Phonological Processing: 63
Comprehension of Instructions: 37
Motor Response for Speed: 91
Motor Response for Speed and Accuracy: 8
Block Construction: 98
Design Copying: 98
Self-efficacy (trying hard): 99

After $2,700 worth of scientific analysis, I wanted to know if they thought Lio should be put on Ritalin or something like it. One said yes and the other said no.

Days later, in processing and re-processing that day of appointments in my mind, I found myself thinking mainly about Charlotte's mother. When we had met in Beth's office, she had this serene confidence about her that I hadn't picked up on over the phone. She had managed to hold on to that profound sense of clarity that I recognised so deeply in myself during those first months after the crash. It was something that wasn't communicated in the pleasantries we exchanged when we met, but when I shook her hand she seemed to float slightly before my eyes. I admired her. She and I both had an absolute conviction to make our children's recovery happen, a conviction that was so total and driving that it guided almost everything we did. We were working feverishly to figure out what needed to be done for our kids, and each of us knew with utter certainty that we were the only ones who could do it and do it right. And we didn't second-guess.

In the end, what we had in common outshone any academic differences and almost all of my earlier anxiety faded away. I discovered I could identify with her – there was a bond (almost, it strikes me, like the bond I was looking for with the lorry driver). We were both completely committed to doing the best for our children, to leaving no stone unturned in looking for a way forward; we believed it was possible when others had told us it wasn't and we had the results to prove our faith was not misplaced. When she looked at her daughter, she didn't see crutches or vision problems; she didn't even see a small girl who should have died but survived. She saw a beautiful, engaging little human being with an intrinsic value, the same intrinsic value that should be seen in all children. And when I looked at Lio I saw it too, as I might never have seen it before the crash.

On his last day at school that year I picked Lio up in the playground surrounded by the riotous buzz of kids too ready for the summer holiday. He was no more exuberant than the other children, he was no more silly or impulsive, and if he did struggle a bit to communicate his end-of-the-year goodbyes to his friends it was probably only because he was caught up in the excitement of things. In fact, when the other parents asked him what he was going to do over the summer, he said without falter, 'We're going to Italy. It's so cool there. We have friends and there are castles and big mountains.' Lio always 'presents well', no matter what the numbers say.

And when I said, 'OK Lio, time to go,' and tried to shepherd him in the direction of the car he stopped and turned to me. With a touch of pride on his face, he gave me a wicked grin and dashed off in the opposite direction towards his friends on the monkey bars. He flew off, bouncing slightly unevenly on his super-leg, but he did *run*, he actually *tore away* and impishly, maddeningly, evaded my grasp like any other slightly wild, slightly naughty six year old. His eyes were sparkling.

It was a beautiful day in late July, one year and ten months after the crash. The sun shone on the whole family: Chris, Tyler, Jeff, Margherita, Trudy, Nigel, Penny, Lio and me. The mountains were out and there were tiny wisps of cloud playing about them like toddlers around the skirts of their mothers. I had spent all of the previous day digging a hole about ten feet from the tree we had planted for Sasha, a beautiful maple that we had taken as a sapling from my mother's backyard in New Jersey after Lio was born, nurtured in London and now re-planted in Italy. I'd started early in the morning with a shovel and a pickaxe, digging into some of the rockiest ground in Europe. I had wanted to dig the traditional six feet deep but by lunchtime I had decided that however far I had got by the end of the day would be deep enough: Sasha would not have been amused if I gave myself a heart attack while digging her grave. Jeff, Nigel, Trudy, Penny and even Lio helped me dig some, too. In the late morning, Nigel found a long steel bar that made getting the rocks out much easier. I say 'rocks' but some of them were really boulders that were never going to be shifted. This caused the hole to serpentine downward almost like a spiral staircase and provided places for us to sit while we filled buckets with earth and stone. By around 6.00 in the evening, my hands had bloody blisters even through my leather gloves, the hole was about four feet deep and a solid mass of rock made it impossible to go any further. This would be enough. We all went out for dinner at a nice little pizzeria with a playground out the back. The kids played, we ordered pizza and pasta, and I cried a bit with the proprietor Simonetta, who had also lost her young husband the previous year.

In the morning, I collected flowers from all over the land, flowers that Sasha had planted, wild flowers, flowers that I had once unknowingly cut down with the lawn mower, prompting her to yell at me. Lio collected flowers as well. We made a soft and colourful little bed of them on the bottom of the grave. In the days leading up to this one, everyone had thought of what they wanted to put down in the earth with Sasha's ashes. Jeff put in the score and the lyrics of a song he had written for her. Tyler had drawn a picture: a happy, impressively detailed and touching scene of him, Lio and Sasha having a picnic on a plaid blanket, with Sasha holding both their hands – exactly like she had done once with them in Kent. Nigel, Penny and I had written Sasha letters. I had collected the jewellery Sasha had been wearing during the crash that included the still-bent rings and the necklace of moonstone. My mother put in the little prayer card she gave me when I went to interview for a place at graduate school at the University of Sussex, the place where I met Sasha. Lio wrote a letter to his mother which said, 'Dear Mamma, Thank you for taking care of me. Love Lio,' on which he drew a picture of himself and Sasha hugging and then Sasha up above the clouds.

While we were preparing the grave, I put on some very simple, very beautiful, very sad English folk music that Sasha would have loved. When the song that had moved Lio and I to tears on many occasions, the ethereal 'Canaan's Land', had finished, I switched off the music and brought out the small, polished oak box that contained Sasha's ashes. As I walked it up to the grave, I looked at Monte Pizzocco, a mountain that Sasha and I had climbed, a mountain that would look down on her remains forever. I was struck by the beauty of what we were doing. We worked in silence for the most part, everyone intuitively aware of one another's needs, visions and intentions during the ceremony. I placed the box on the bed of flowers surrounded by sheet music, letters, art and the love of her family. Lio came down into the grave and put one last drawing he had done on top of the ashes, a page of meticulous hearts that he had laboured over earlier that day for nearly half an hour. It was the longest I'd ever seen him sit still and I'm sure it was his way of trying to prolong what we were doing. Penny, who had not been able to paint since the crash but who had been trying to find a creative outlet in sculpture, had prepared forty tiny white moons out of fired clay, one for each of Sasha's forty years. Sasha had died on a full moon. She gave us each a handful and we gently dropped most of them around Sasha's ashes. We hid the rest in the little nooks and crannies around the old mill house where they would peek out at us for years to come.

We took handfuls of soil, crumbled them up into small bits between our fingers and dropped them into the grave. Handful by little handful we worked this way for nearly an hour and the box and all our tributes to her gradually disappeared under a shower of earth. I then hefted the largest of the stones that we had removed during the digging back into the hole to cover and protect Sasha's ashes. I wanted to make sure that they would never ever be disturbed. Then we started shovelling in the rest of the earth. I put on some of Sasha's favourite salsa music, and, hand in hand with Lio, we danced salsa steps on her grave to pack down the earth. Sasha had been teaching him some salsa moves for about a year prior to the crash and this was the first time he had done them since. I imagined him dancing with his mother and marvelled at how much he remembered and how good he was at following the beat. I'm sure Sasha smiled. The pink stone we had organised for her marker was in the hands of an ancient and restless local sculptor who was known throughout the region. He was going to carve a mountain, chisel in some of Sasha's words on beauty and love, and deliver us the stone later that year.

Lio had wanted us to make a beacon on top of the grave to burn in the night. These are thickish pine logs about five feet long that are stood upright in the earth. Using a chainsaw, you cut a cross down the centre of the log until you're a few inches from the ground. You pour some oil down the middle, light them and they burn impressively for hours and hours. After we had added the topsoil, I prepared the beacon and we went out for lunch and a walk at a friendly little cow stable in the nearby mountains, a stable Sasha and I had frequented for years. We drank and ate and walked and drank some more while our children played with the children of the family that run the place. The Dolomites all around us were clear and bright and caressed us. I felt the presence of Sasha so profoundly up there.

We returned home and had dinner. When the sun went down, Lio lit the beacon. It burned tall and splendidly like a point of connection between the earth and the sky, between Sasha's ashes and the stars above. Groggy and tired, Lio wanted to stay near the beacon all night long.

'*Papà*,' he said, 'can you tell me again the story about how I went up that really high, really dangerous mountain in Mamma's tummy?'

It was one of his favourite stories, probably because I embellished and dramatised it so much. I told him the slightly abbreviated version of me and Sasha climbing a cliff for six hours with coloured cords and clips and steel cables attached to the mountain; about us losing the trail halfway up and having to consult maps and dictionaries while dangling perilously, and – his favourite part – Sasha feeling him move in her womb properly for the first time when we reached the top. His gentle, contented face glowed in the firelight.

'Do you remember how we used to tease her for always being late all the time?' he said. I grinned and remembered.

We stayed out there and the reminiscing continued for hours until the children could no longer keep their eyes open. We formed a circle and walked around her grave and the beacon a few times, our last act in a day of ceremonies we had created and improvised ourselves, a day that had been transcendent. It was our final goodbye to Sasha and it could not have been more perfect. More than a day and a half would pass before the last red embers of Lio's beacon finally went cold, another little anomaly in itself. That night, nearly two years after the crash, in the light of the fire on Sasha's grave, I took off my ring.

Lio's drawing of him and Sasha done two years after the crash.